Young America

Young America

Childhood in 19th-Century Art and Culture

Claire Perry

Yale University Press *New Haven & London*

in association with the

Iris & B. Gerald Cantor Center for Visual Arts *Stanford University*

This book is published on the occasion of the exhibition *American ABC*

Iris & B. Gerald Cantor Center for Visual Arts, Stanford University (February 1–May 7, 2006)
Smithsonian American Art Museum, Washington, D.C. (July 4–September 17, 2006)
Portland Museum of Art, Portland, Maine (November 1, 2006–January 7, 2007)

Designed by Carol S. Cates
Set in Adobe Caslon type by Amy Storm
Printed in Singapore by CS Graphics

Library of Congress Cataloging-in-Publication Data
Perry, Claire.
Young America : childhood in nineteenth-century art and culture / Claire Perry.
            p.   cm.
Published on the occasion of the exhibition *American ABC*, held at the Iris & B. Gerald Cantor Center for
Visual Arts, Stanford University, Feb. 1–May 7, 2006; Smithsonian American Art Museum, Washington,
D.C., July 4–Sept. 17, 2006; Portland Museum of Art, Portland, Maine, Nov. 1, 2006–Jan. 7, 2007.
Includes bibliographical references and index.
ISBN 0-300-10620-3 (cloth : alk. paper)
ISBN 0-937031-27-5 (pbk : alk. paper)
1. Children in art—Exhibitions. 2. Childhood in art—Exhibitions. 3. Art, American—19th century—
Exhibitions. 4. Children—United States—Social conditions—19th century—Exhibitions. I. Iris & B.
Gerald Cantor Center for Visual Arts at Stanford University. II. Smithsonian American Art Museum. III.
Portland Museum of Art. IV. Title.
N7640.P47   2006
704.9'425'0747468—dc22
2005015119

A catalogue record for this book is available from the British Library.

The paper in this book meets the guidelines for permanence and durability of the Committee on
Production Guidelines for Book Longevity of the Council on Library Resources.

10 9 8 7 6 5 4 3 2 1

FRONTISPIECE: Thomas LeClear, *Interior with Portraits*, c. 1865 (detail of fig. 8).
Oil on canvas, 25 7/8 x 40 1/2 in. Smithsonian American Art Museum, Washington, D.C.
Museum purchase made possible by the Pauline Edwards Bequest.

JACKET ILLUSTRATIONS: (front) William Bartoll, *Boy with Dog*, c. 1840. Greenfield Village and
Henry Ford Museum, Dearborn, Michigan. (back) Unidentified photographer, *Playmates*, c. 1899.
Library of Congress, Prints and Photographs Division, Washington, D.C.

For GGG and in memory of GFG II

◆　◆　◆

Contents

Director's Foreword

When the Cantor Arts Center's curator of American art, Dr. Claire Perry, first presented her idea for an exhibition of nineteenth-century portrayals of children, the response of our curators was enthusiastic, as it was clear that the subject and the proposed works of art and other artifacts would make a compelling exhibition and a rich contribution to American art history. It also seemed most appropriate that the Cantor Arts Center at Stanford University should initiate this project, as the founding of the university and museum in the late nineteenth century reflected the ideological legacy investigated here. In their aspirations, both institutions were guided by the vision of childhood that emerged in nineteenth-century America, the subject of the exhibition, titled *American ABC*, and this book that accompanies it.

The American conception of childhood and its strategic relation to the health of the democratic republic first emerged in the decades following the revolution of 1776. Nineteenth-century citizens continued the Founding Fathers' deliberations on schooling, discipline, and the moral character of youth, and their debates persist into our own time. Youth has always occupied a central position as the icon of America's future. The Founding Fathers believed that the survival of the republic depended on the creation of an informed citizenry ready to assume the duties of self-government. As the United States passed through its own turbulent youth, the nurture and education of young Americans became a matter of critical importance as a means to ensure the longevity of the republic.

During the course of the nineteenth century, the United States evolved from a young republic just embarked on a great democratic "experiment" into a mature nation claiming a prominent place in world affairs. As Americans in this period struggled with the transformation brought by settlement of the west, the Civil War, new technologies, rapid urbanization, and immigration, they worked to create a sense of communal identity to bind together the nation's disparate peoples. The theme of childhood, supported by images of children in paintings, prints, photographs, and advertisements, played a pivotal role during the nineteenth century in defining the character of the American people and setting forth a set of shared values and expectations for the future.

The exhibition and the book encompass six themes that address the most important concerns of nineteenth-century Americans relating to the education of the nation's youth. "The Country Boy" discusses the agrarian ideals that underlay the earliest vision of

American democracy; "Daughters of Liberty" examines the roles assigned to the nation's future wives and mothers. "Children of Bondage" and "Ragamuffin" deal with the issues of slavery, urbanization, and immigration, while the circumstances of Native American children are the subject of the chapter titled "The Papoose." "The New Scholar" considers nineteenth-century attitudes toward children's education and the idea that a system of public schools could unify the nation. Pictures of hardy country boys, industrious school-children, and neatly dressed little girls confirmed that the newest generation was developing as it should. At the same time, insulated by the innocence and optimism inherent in the subject of childhood, images of slave children, street urchins, and toddlers on Indian reservations grappled with the most contentious issues of the day. Pictures of childhood produced during the nineteenth century were accompanied by a vast literature relating to the subject.

Child-rearing manuals advised parents on everything from teething to warts, and novels with children in leading roles, such as *Huckleberry Finn* and *Uncle Tom's Cabin*, became nationwide best-sellers. Children's textbooks—ABC books, primers, histories, and geographies—also emerged as important tools used to initiate young Americans in the practices of democracy and to promote the overarching ideal of a wise and educated citizenry. Though the United States is no longer a young nation—its government is now one of the oldest in the world—the sense of American identity mapped out in nineteenth-century images of children still works to shape our national dreams and expectations.

It is a great honor and pleasure to once again be a partner with the Smithsonian American Art Museum, which will present *American ABC* as part of the reopening exhibitions of the newly restored and renovated building in Washington, D.C. Our particular thanks go to the Smithsonian's Board of Trustees, Director Elizabeth Broun, and the museum's talented staff. We are also delighted that the exhibition will be seen at the Portland Museum of Art in Portland, Maine, and thank the trustees, Director Daniel O'Leary, and staff there as well.

Claire Perry has been purposeful in selecting works for *American ABC* that clearly illuminate its grand themes. We are very grateful to the many lenders who understood the importance of the exhibition and its particular focus, and who have generously lent the beautiful works of art that are key to the realization of her vision. This exhibition would not have been possible without their selfless collaboration.

The skilled and creative staff at the Cantor Arts Center has done a great deal to assist Dr. Perry in the completion of this project. Chief curator Bernard Barryte and curatorial assistant Jeanie Lawrence have helped with all aspects of the exhibition and publication. Registrar Katie Clifford has ably managed all of the registrarial complexities of this large project, and exhibition coordinator Sarah Miller has ensured that budgets and production schedules have been adhered to throughout. Associate director Mona Duggan and the center's development and external relations staff have also provided essential support. Kudos are also in order for the contribution of the preparation staff and others who have made manifest this splendid presentation at Stanford.

I also would like to thank Patricia Fidler and her colleagues at Yale University Press for their excellent work in producing this catalogue that accompanies the exhibition.

Claire Perry's vision has been embraced by many, and I am especially grateful to Carmen C. Christensen, Helen and Peter Bing, and the members of the Iris & B. Gerald Cantor Center for Visual Arts at Stanford University for the generous support that made this exhibition possible.

Thomas K. Seligman
John & Jill Freidenrich Director
Iris & B. Gerald Cantor Center for Visual Arts

Acknowledgments

This book and the exhibition it accompanies represent the kindness and support of many people. There are dozens of museum directors, curators, archivists, librarians, and registrars across the country to whom I owe a debt of gratitude. Bernard Barryte helped to guide and oversee every aspect of the publication and exhibition with unfailing grace and good humor. Tom Seligman, Sarah Miller, Alicja Egbert, Katie Clifford, Cari Kogler, Ray Madarang, and Mona Duggan each brought a special talent to the project, working magic with loan forms, registration, funding, scheduling, and design. Jeanie Lawrence—a true genie—fended off a thousand disasters and made everything come right in the end. And, Peaches, where can I begin?

My darling sons—Beau, Byron, Somerset, Sebastian, and Winslow—got me thinking about childhood in the first place and what it all means. My husband, Noel, inspired me every day just by being who he is—one of the finest men I'll ever know.

Introduction

Americans of the nineteenth century were keenly aware of their role as heirs of the Founding Fathers and guardians of a new nation "of the people, by the people, and for the people." The Declaration of Independence had affirmed the separation of the United States from the oppressions of the Old World and promised a destiny of unparalleled future glory. Still, American democracy was a new and untried system, and many believed the freedoms it provided also carried the seeds of its undoing. The revolutionary generation believed the survival and growth of the new republic hinged on the creation of a virtuous citizenry ready to assume the responsibilities of self-government. It was only when Washington, Jefferson, and the other titans of 1776 began to succumb to disease and old age, however, that the nurture and education of children—the future guardians of the nation's fragile democracy—took on extraordinary importance in American society. By the early decades of the nineteenth century, citizens found themselves without living patriarchs and, in the anxiety and ebullience of their new independence, began to consider in earnest the significance of the upcoming generation. Educators, ministers, newspaper editors, politicians, business leaders, and parents began to engage in heated debates about the special requirements of children growing up in a democratic society and the kind of training their unique circumstances entailed. Ultimately, afflicted by a chronic uneasiness about the health of their government, Americans set forth an entirely new range of definitions and expectations for the youngest republicans on whom the nation's future was thought to depend.

In their attitudes toward children and their approach to developing young minds, Americans of the nineteenth century were radically different from the early colonists. The Puritan devout had believed that children were the heirs, not of a glorious history, but of Adam and Eve's original sin and expulsion from the Garden of Eden. As the embodiments of this ancient evil, children were thought to be naturally depraved, requiring the use of harsh physical and psychological punishments to curb their wayward behavior. Parents were expected to invest a significant amount of time in training their children to be obedient. When gentle admonishments and sessions of prayer proved inadequate, religious and political authorities exhorted parents to adopt more vigorous tactics. These included humiliation, withholding of food, beatings, and vivid descriptions of the physical torments of everlasting roasting. "Better whipt, than damned," declared Cotton Mather, the respected Puritan clergyman and author.[1]

With the waning of Calvinist ideology during the eighteenth century and the social changes wrought by the American Revolution in 1776, there was a fundamental shift in the

American attitude toward children and their role in the family and society. The liberal theories of the continental philosophers John Locke and Jean-Jacques Rousseau, which had helped to spark the colonists' uprising against British rule, also encouraged a reevaluation of earlier beliefs about child nurture and education. Locke and Rousseau maintained that children were inherently innocent and malleable and, like adults, were unique individuals with a rightful claim to happiness and independence. Both Locke and Rousseau described the child's mind as a tabula rasa ready to take on the imprint of the environment in which it developed. The essential purity of youth placed the burden for preventing—or, at least, minimizing—the effects of worldly contamination squarely on the shoulders of adults. For Americans hoping to safeguard the noble legacy of the revolution, the responsibilities inherent in the new ways of thinking about childhood were weighty indeed.

During the nineteenth century, pictures of children embodied the intersection between changed ideas about childhood and citizens' urgent desire to ensure that the Union would endure. Appearing in increasing numbers after 1820, paintings with child-related themes were viewed and bought by the landowning gentry, well-to-do merchants with aspirations for refinement, and middle-class visitors who toured galleries as part of a circuit of polite activities (figs. 1–3). They were also discussed in cultural journals by critics who described their subject matter and technique as well as audiences' reactions to them. In turn, paintings of children were frequently published as prints and made available to a much larger audience.

Part of a broad cultural network of novels, sermons, medical tracts, songs, and social protocols through which the young nation defined itself and its future goals, images of children tended to fall into thematic categories defined by gender, geography, and economic status. These categories, including the country boy, the urban urchin, and the American girl, pictured different segments of the American populace and apportioned to each a certain place in the social hierarchy, facilitating the sorting out of social relationships that was one of the primary concerns of nineteenth-century Americans. For the middle class and the newly wealthy, images of children encouraged the idea of a shared history and an attractive array of economic opportunities. For recent immigrants, Native Americans, blacks, and others of marginal status, childhood imagery pictured very different opportunities, often involving menial labor or connections with the tourist trade.

Though most portrayals of children emanated from the northeastern United States, these images had broad appeal across the nation. Audiences with varying class and regional alignments enjoyed Currier and Ives prints of roly-poly toddlers and playful farm boys. As advances in printing technology increased the availability of publications for and about children, Americans also eagerly bought ABC books and primers published by Noah Webster and William McGuffey, and child-care manuals by recognized authorities including Jacob Abott, Lydia M. Child, and Catharine Beecher. This community of shared interests centering on the child, in turn, transcended the partisan, regional, and economic barriers that had impeded the growth of a sense of national identity. During the middle decades of the century, the culture of childhood became an important part of the processes through

FIG. 1   (above left) Platt Powell Ryder, *The Illustrated Newspaper*, 1868. Oil on canvas, 16⁷/₈ x 13¹³/₁₆ in. The Brooklyn Museum, New York. Bequest of Caroline H. Polhemus.

FIG. 2   (above right) Eastman Johnson, *Boyhood of Lincoln*, 1868. Oil on canvas, 46 x 37 in. The University of Michigan Museum of Art, Ann Arbor. Bequest of Henry C. Lewis.

FIG. 3   (left) William Harnett, *Attention, Company!* 1878. Oil on canvas, 36 x 28 in. Amon Carter Museum, Fort Worth, Texas.

which the political union of states that existed before the Civil War became the singular United States—a nation with an increasingly centralized government that defined itself by the motto "E Pluribus Unum."

Portrayals of American children reveal the slow and halting evolution of the American national identity over the course of the century. Before 1820, pictures of American children were heavily dependent on British prototypes. Though contemporary authors described American children as representatives of a radically new order, new ideas had not yet been translated into a democratic iconography. The American child took on distinct attributes during the Jacksonian era, when centers of political and economic power, as well as the loyalties connected to them, were constantly shifting. In this tumultuous period, the stabilizing network of old revolutionary elites was swept away, replaced by a changing array of politicians and parvenu merchants and financiers who jockeyed for positions of power. The new social mobility seemed to offer unprecedented freedom and opportunity for those on the lower rungs of society, but many Americans were afraid that the immature republic would not survive the radical egalitarianism of the age. In 1840, the prominent Protestant minister Herman Humphrey voiced the fears of many in his book *Domestic Education*. "It has been said a thousand times, that the practicability of maintaining a highly republican form of government has been *tried* and *settled* in the United States, however it may have failed everywhere else," he wrote. "I wish it were so: but I am afraid the question is settled, so far *only* as we have gone. What the future may disclose, who can tell? It is yet a grand desideratum, whether we have wisdom and virtue and intelligence enough to sustain our blessed institutions. The danger is, that our liberties will degenerate into licentiousness, and that the growing laxity of family government in this country will hasten on the fearful crisis."[2]

During this period of widespread apprehension about impending anarchy, paintings, prints, and photographs of the nation's children provided the citizenry with a sense of an underlying and "natural" order of American society. Many of these representations showed idealized American children in rural settings, confirming that the agrarian class Thomas Jefferson had called the bedrock of the nation was renewing itself in the country's abundant open spaces. Other portrayals openly confronted the most contentious issues of the day —urban poverty, racial inequality, immigration, industrialization—and reduced them to reassuringly lilliputian proportions. For Americans urgently searching for signs of the republic's well-being, pictures of the nation's children demonstrated that the United States was in robust health, and diagnosed a vast range of social problems as symptoms of benign "growing pains" (figs. 4–8).

An emerging body of child-related literature reinforced the optimism about the future that was inherent in pictures of children. At mid-century, as economic panics and arguments over slavery made the adult body politic increasingly ungovernable, child-care manuals, ABC books, primers, and children's storybooks represented the careful government of future citizens. Child-care manuals delved into every aspect of child nurture, from correct posture, thumbsucking, and head lice to corporal punishment and pets. Schoolbooks and storybooks generally focused on moral improvement and self-restraint as an integral part of republican education. Catherine Maria Sedgwick, one of the nation's leading women of letters, wrote: "That the safety of the republic depends on the virtue of the people is a truth that cannot be too assiduously taught; and that it is the business of the young, as well as of the old, to help on the cause of goodness, cannot be too strongly impressed."[3] As American audiences considered cheering images of the nation's youth, tracts with specific instructions

FIG. 4   Lilly Martin Spencer, *This Little Pig Went to Market*, 1857. Oil on composition board with arched top, 16 x 12 in. Ohio Historical Society, Columbus.

FIG. 5   John Mix Stanley, *Eleanora C. Ross*, 1844. Oil on canvas, 39 3/4 x 31 1/2 in. Gilcrease Museum of Art, Tulsa, Oklahoma.

for shaping young minds, and writings that described common education as the key to national harmony, the youngest generation became the icon of America's grand destiny.

A few words about my methods and intent in constructing this book are in order here. Although I review pictures of American childhood from a wide range of sources, this study is not intended to be a comprehensive examination of the topic. The selection of images I discuss represents the childhood types most familiar to national audiences and for which I could find examples in a wide range of media and texts. I excluded images of the urban elite, pioneer children, pictures of children with literary themes, and other genres worthy of discussion elsewhere. The chapters of this book center on six childhood types: the country boy, the American girl, the African-American child, the urban waif, the Native American child, and the child in school. For each category I follow different currents that lead to a fuller understanding of the images' participation in American life. I trace the origins of the subject in paintings and schoolbooks from the early part of the century and connect the works to their political, economic, and social environment through the end of the century. My focus is topical and thematic rather than chronological, however, and I give minimal attention to the early years of the nineteenth century, when American artists and the American publishing industry were most dependent on European prototypes. The book concentrates on the years between 1830 and 1900, when the most important childhood types first emerged and when they were most active in defining and influencing American viewers.

Each chapter links a childhood type with the ideas and concerns that engaged nineteenth-century citizens. The first chapter traces the connection between images of the country boy, the idea of Yankee ingenuity, and the dynamic relationship between Jefferson's agrarian vision and the mechanization of American industry. The second chapter, "Daughters of Liberty," examines pictures of girlhood in the context of women's shifting role in the expanding American marketplace. The images of African-American youth in Chapter 3 are related to debates over slavery and abolitionism and events surrounding the Civil War. The fourth chapter interweaves portrayals of city waifs with ideas about

FIG. 6   Thomas Eakins, *Study for "Negro Boy Dancing": The Boy*, 1877. Oil on canvas, 24 1/4 x 12 3/16 in. National Gallery of Art, Washington, D.C. Collection of Mr. and Mrs. Paul Mellon.

FIG. 7   Eastman Johnson, *The Pets*, 1856. Oil on masonite panel, 25 x 28 3/4 in. The Corcoran
Gallery of Art, Washington, D.C. Gift of William Wilson Corcoran.

the rise of the metropolis and the consequences of rising immigration. Pictures of Native
American children are the focus of the fifth chapter, which attempts to follow the process
through which the nation's first people became reservation residents. Linking these disparate subjects is the overarching theme of children's education, which is also the topic of
the last chapter. Schooling and schoolbooks serve as a unifying narrative in this book,
just as they did for Americans throughout the nineteenth century.

The question remains: Which children and whose culture are represented here?
Americans of the nineteenth century were deeply rooted in local affiliations and ethnic
connections, and one of the principal themes of this book is the vast range of cultures
encompassed by the larger union of the United States. Nevertheless, because of their dominant role in the nation's business, politics, and culture, the middle class and elites of the
northeast, especially New England, were virtually the exclusive source of the imagery and
texts that shaped the nineteenth-century American perception of childhood. A relatively
few northeastern artists, printmakers, educators, reformers, and clergymen succeeded in
defining how American children should look and in setting moral and educational standards
for youths across the nation. The process always involved resistance and contradiction, of

FIG. 8   Thomas LeClear, *Interior with Portraits*, c. 1865. Oil on canvas, 25⁷/₈ x 40¹/₂ in. Smithsonian American Art Museum, Washington, D.C. Museum purchase made possible by the Pauline Edwards Bequest.

course, and one of the most rewarding parts of this work has been the discovery of rich layers of ambiguity, innuendo, and unintended humor that subverted "official" meanings.

A peculiar aspect of dealing with images and texts relating to American children is the virtual silence of the children themselves. Although contemporary accounts describe American children as formidably outspoken and assertive, they had almost no voice in the texts or visual representations that exerted public influence. We have only minimal evidence of children's participation in the process through which an edifice of definitions was built up around them. Diaries and school writing books are some of the few sources of children's opinions, along with certain photographs where, through boredom or recalcitrance, children managed to have some influence on the final product. The silence of nineteenth-century American children imbues their portrayals with an aura of mystery and leaves to us the work of piecing together from pictures and stories at least the context of their experience.

Chapter 1

THE COUNTRY BOY

What then is the American, this new man?

HECTOR ST. JOHN DE CRÈVECOEUR, *Letters from an American Farmer*, 1782

In a speech given on the Fourth of July in 1876, the prominent minister Henry Ward Beecher invited his fellow citizens to take stock of themselves and the accomplishments of the century that had passed since the American Revolution. "What has been the history of a hundred years in regard to the people of America? Are they as virtuous as they were 100 years ago?" he asked. "Are they as manly as they were 100 years ago? . . . What our fathers were we know . . . but what are we, their sons? Have we shrunk?"[1] Infused with the self-congratulatory rhetoric that was expected for Independence Day celebrations, Beecher's oration was also sprinkled with hints of doubt about the meaning of progress. It alluded to the many challenges confronting his middle-class audience—immigration, industrialization, the boom and bust economy, and shifts in the role of the family. Pondering the achievements of the titans of a century earlier, Beecher wondered whether Americans had "shrunk" in comparison to their revolutionary fathers.

Throughout the nineteenth century, Americans were preoccupied by the question Beecher posed to his listeners: "What are we today?" Part of this underlying uncertainty had to do with the immaturity of social and economic institutions in the United States when compared with the venerable establishments of the Old World. Furthermore, in addition to being a young nation, the population of the United States was also youthful; in 1830, one-third of its people were less than ten years old, and the median age was sixteen. The desire to define the American character—one of the central concerns of the age— was a manifestation of the nation's society of young people. With an adolescent's absorption with personal identity and independence from patriarchal authority, Young America asserted its character through novels about frontier adventures, newspaper caricatures of political leaders, patriotic ballads, and paintings of the citizens of the republic. These productions established a set of national types that played a pivotal role in the definition

OPPOSITE: Detail of fig. 15.

FIG. 9   Eastman Johnson, *The Barefoot Boy*, 1860. Oil on board, 12³/₄ x 9¹/₂ in.
Courtesy of Gerald Peters Gallery, Santa Fe, New Mexico.

of Americanness. One of the most significant American types to develop in the art of the
nineteenth century was the country boy, a figure intimately connected to ideas about the
youth of the nation and the untrammeled nature of the American continent (fig. 9). Over
the course of the century, the image of the country boy was refined in a range of media
disseminated to a wide public, including paintings exhibited in New York galleries, magazines with national circulation, and advertisements marketing an assortment of products.
The country boy came to represent the solidarity of the national community as well as
its freedom, not only from the cultural domination of the Old World, but also from the
benevolent control of the revolutionary patriarchs.

The image of the country boy in art and popular imagery emerged from ideas about
the distinct character of the American child that figured prominently in public discourse
during the first half of the century. The widely read accounts of foreign visitors who came
to assess the government and people of the young republic helped to introduce the idea

that American children were a separate breed. Many of the observers who wrote about American children—Harriet Martineau, Alexis de Tocqueville, Charles Dickens, and Michel Chevalier—described the nation's young people as a barometer of democracy, and the behavior they observed inspired a range of different forecasts. Some considered American children to be independent-minded, honest, and charming creatures who demonstrated the nation's fundamental well-being. Others maintained that "democratic sucklings" were impertinent and unruly rascals who had applied the Declaration of Independence to themselves.

In his 1839 travelogue, the British author Frank Marryat recounted for his readers what he described as a typical exchange between a willful young democrat and his mother:

> *Imagine a child of three years old in England behaving thus:-*
> *"Johnny, my dear, come here," says his mamma.*
> *"I won't," cried Johnny.*
> *"You must, my love, you are all wet, and you'll catch cold."*
> *"I won't," replies Johnny.*
> *"Come, my sweet, and I've something for you."*
> *"I won't."*
> *"I tell you, come in directly sir—do you hear?"*
> *"I won't," replies the urchin, taking to his heels.*
> *"A sturdy republican, sir," says his father to me, smiling at the boy's resolute disobedience.*[2]

Descriptions of American children in travel accounts were accompanied by new kinds of visual portrayals that emerged in the first decades of the nineteenth century. In contrast to eighteenth-century depictions of well-dressed and well-mannered American youngsters in the bosom of family life, these later images showed independent children empowered by the democratic distribution of authority. Two paintings by John Lewis Krimmel embody the egalitarian changes that transformed American society in the first half of the century and their effect on the perception and portrayal of children (figs. 10–11). In a painting from 1814 titled *Country Wedding*, a country boy takes his place as a member of the republican folk that made up the American body politic. The work includes a familiar retinue of rustic types: the pious pastor, the neighborhood gossip, the country bride, and the well-to-do merchant. Showing the independence of spirit that was becoming an emblem of American childhood, the country boy conveys his exasperation with the solemn nuptial ceremony taking place behind him and his preference for outdoor recreations with a gesture toward the outdoors. Only the restraining arm of a female companion prevents him from quitting the premises.

In another painting executed in 1814, Krimmel expanded on the theme of the boisterous country boy. *Blind Man's Buff* portrays a group of children playing an indoor game with the rambunctiousness that Marryat described as typically American. The girls in the group jostle and spin, while the boys add an element of mischief to the scene. One young ruffian

FIG. 10   John Lewis Krimmel, *Country Wedding: Bishop White Officiating*, 1814. Oil on canvas, 16³/₄ x 22¹/₂ in. Courtesy of The Pennsylvania Academy of the Fine Arts, Philadelphia. Gift of Paul Beck, Jr.

FIG. 11   John Lewis Krimmel, *Blind Man's Buff*, 1814. Oil on canvas, 16⁵/₈ x 22¹/₁₆ in. Terra Foundation for the Arts, Chicago. Daniel J. Terra Collection. Photograph courtesy of Terra Foundation for the Arts.

slips a stool in the path of the blindfolded player to make her stumble, a trick he may have played already on the boy who lies crying on the floor. The two adults present are unperturbed by the melee, as if anarchy was the usual state of affairs in the American household.

While Krimmel represented the country boy as an incidental member of the rural community, the figure began to receive special attention as an individual subject in art during the 1820s. In this period, the United States experienced a radical reshuffling of established authority that resulted from the broadening of voting rights to include those who did not own property.[3] With the deaths of John Adams and Thomas Jefferson in 1826, there was also a national sense of bidding adieu to the last of the Founding Fathers—and an end to the preeminence of the revolutionary elite. Political leaders talked of new freedoms while citizens expressed a new vehemence in their rejection of traditional hierarchies. The election of the populist candidate Andrew Jackson to the presidency in 1828 embodied the ascent to power of the newly enfranchised "common man," a growing portion of the population that included mechanics, shopkeepers, factory workers, artisans, and small farmers who owned little or no property. Jackson remained loyal to the laborers and wage earners who had elected him and to the principle of majority rule. "The people are the government, administering it by their agents," he declared. "They are the Government, the sovereign power."[4]

The artist Henry Inman produced an early version of the country boy type in a painting

titled *The Young Fisherman* that was executed in 1829 or 1830—just as Andrew Jackson took office (fig. 12). The portrayal was inspired by European "fancy" pictures, works by artists like Reynolds and Gainsborough of attractively rustic subjects in quaint settings that were widely popular in England, France, and Italy. Though the painting looked to esteemed academic precedents, the informality of Inman's young fisherman expressed the rough egalitarian spirit of the Jacksonian era. The little angler's rolled-up trousers and open shirt identify him as a child of the common folk, one who is free to wander alone in the idyllic New World wilderness. His contented autonomy evokes ideas about the precocious independence of the American child that were discussed by Alexis de Tocqueville

FIG. 12   Henry Inman, *The Young Fisherman*, c. 1829–1830. Oil on wood, 13 1/3 x 9 5/8 in. The Metropolitan Museum of Art, New York. Gift of Samuel P. Avery, 1895.

FIG. 13   William Sidney Mount, *School Boys Quarreling*, 1830. Oil on canvas, 20 x 24³/₄ in. Long Island Museum of American Art, History, and Carriages, Stony Brook, New York. Museum purchase, 1984.

and other authors. "As soon as the young American approaches manhood, the ties of filial obedience are relaxed day by day; master of his thoughts, he is soon master of his conduct," Tocqueville explained. "In America there is, strictly speaking, no adolescence: at the close of boyhood the man appears and begins to trace his own path."[5] An eastern publisher considered Inman's picture of a young republican tracing his own path to the fishing hole an image worthy of distribution to a broad American public, and the work appeared as an engraving in *The Atlantic Souvenir* in 1830.

While *The Young Fisherman* focused on the celebrated liberty of the American child, other works took up the unruly behavior that Krimmel introduced in his scenes of rural life and astonished foreign observers. *School Boys Quarreling*, painted by William Sidney Mount in 1830, refashioned the playful insubordinations of the youngsters in *Blind Man's Buff* into the threat of a real brawl in a group of older boys (fig. 13). As two toughs square off and prepare to fight, one classmate urges them on while another rolls up his sleeves to join the melee. A black child carrying a basket, perhaps a slave on an errand for the worried neighbor who peers out from her doorstep, grins in anticipation of the impending fight.

Though the boys are still of school age, their muscular physiques and angry expressions imbue the scene with a sense of real menace.

Mount's depiction of irascible American youths linked them to the crude rabble that many believed had taken over the White House. The scene of young republicans duking it out recalled the disaster of Jackson's inaugural celebration—where roving waves of democrats smashed glassware, jumped through White House windows, trampled flowerbeds, and caroused around tubs of whiskey on the White House lawn. It also echoed current political battles raging over tariffs, states' rights, and banking, as well as prevalent anxieties that the new liberties of the Jacksonian era would allow decent citizens to be overwhelmed by the "mire." It seemed to many Americans that rebellion against law and tradition was widespread, raising to new levels of urgency the question of whether Americans would be able to rule themselves. Still, the schoolboy subject of Mount's painting confined it to the realm of childhood antics, far removed from arenas of bitter political struggle. When the painting was exhibited at the National Academy of Design in 1831, a critic for the *New York Mirror* called it "a humorous delineation and eminently successful."[6]

It was perhaps because the country boy type was associated with unrestrained behavior that images in American schoolbooks clung to earlier, more polite models of boyhood. The ruffle-collared scholars who appear in the pages of the widely used McGuffey's readers wore outfits that had been popular for middle-class and elite boys in the early years of the century. These clothes embodied the traditions of children's deference to authority, as well as the author's aim to inspire pupils with a "love of what is right and useful."[7] Boys in McGuffey's books were almost always pictured in rural settings, but they displayed few of the attributes that characterized the country type. An illustration for a lesson in the *Eclectic First Reader* of 1836 shows a group of boys frolicking on a hillside—walking on stilts, flying a kite, rolling hoops—but bare feet and torn breeches are conspicuously absent from the picture's visual lexicon (fig. 14). The skip-roping dandy in the foreground sets a standard for juvenile elegance radically different from the disheveled country boy aesthetic. His starched collar, short jacket, and pointed shoes made up an outfit that tasteful magazines such as *Godey's Lady's Book* presented to readers as appropriate attire for the well-to-do. The text beneath the image acknowledged boys' youthful love of activity, but it directed readers to carry out their recreations with decorum. "Boys love to run and play. . . . Good boys do not play in a rude way, but they take care not to hurt anyone," admonished Lesson XI. "When boys are at play they must be kind, and not feel cross. . . . You must not play with boys that speak bad words or tell lies."[8]

The disjunction between the well-mannered rural lads who inhabited the pages of McGuffey's readers and the carefree, independent country boys in paintings and popular imagery reflected nineteenth-century debates over the best way to manage children. On one hand, many clergymen and educators—inspired by Protestant doctrine that emphasized the value of self-denial and hard work—advocated the imposition of parental authority

ECLECTIC FIRST READER.   23

LESSON XI.

Boys at Play.

Can you fly a kite? See how the boy flies his kite. He holds the string tight, and the wind blows it up in the sky.

Now it is high in the air,

FIG. 14   "Boys at Play," from *The Eclectic First Reader for Young Children with Pictures*, by William H. McGuffey, 1836. Private collection.

through physical punishment and restraint. They deplored what they saw as the growing laxity of family government in the United States. Temperance preacher Herman Humphrey offered his views on childhood freedom in 1840:

> There is, if I am not deceived, a reaction in our unparalleled political freedom, upon our domestic relations. It is more difficult than it was half, or even a quarter of a century ago, for parents to "command their household after them." Our children hear so much about liberty and equality, and are told so often how glorious it is to be "born free and equal" that it is hard work to make them understand for what good reason their liberties are abridged in the family; and I have no doubt this accounts, in multitudes of instances, for the reluctance with which they submit to parental authority. The boy wants to be "his own man" long before his wisdom teeth are cut; and the

danger lies in conceding the point to him under the notion that our fathers were quite too rigid, and that a more indulgent domestic policy, corresponding with the "spirit of the age" is better. This may be the way to make *rulers* enough for a hundred republics; but not to make a single good *subject*.[9]

Despite Humphrey's call for a redoubling of parental control, during the 1840s medical experts, authorities on child care, and political leaders called for a more democratic approach to the nurture and education of children, one that encouraged parents to take into account a child's feelings and favored persuasion over punishment. The gentle new methods were thought to support the nation's republican spirit by teaching self-determination and individual responsibility. Beginning in the 1820s, an abundance of child-rearing manuals addressed to perplexed parents began to appear, offering advice about ways to deal with the conflict between the need for parental authority and the liberating influence of democratic ideals. Covering everything from hiccups to tantrums, these tracts espoused the use of gentle admonishments, positive reinforcement, and moral influence to elicit children's "cheerful obedience." Though parents were charged to maintain the order in their households, they were also advised to make their authority as unobtrusive as possible. "For instance, a child must be expressly forbidden to play with fire, to climb upon the tables, etc.," explained the eminent childhood authority Lydia M. Child. "But whenever it is possible, restraint should be invisible."[10]

A manifestation of the new currents of social democracy in American life, the progressive model of child rearing helped to nurture the continuing evolution of the country boy type. The figure reached its symbolic maturity in the second half of the nineteenth century when it became a commonplace element in literature and art, and a subject immediately recognizable as quintessentially American. *The Berry Boy*, painted by the New York artist John George Brown circa 1875, pictured a New England boy climbing over one of the region's ubiquitous stone walls after a berrying excursion (fig. 15). Farm mothers often sent children on berrying errands when their other chores were complete, and these "berrying parties" were a favorite choice of artists representing pastoral subjects. Brown chose to show a berry boy foraging on his own, and the expanse of the green vale behind him suggests the wide range of his wanderings. With a full bucket as an emblem of the richness of the harvest, the boy has discovered the places that are too steep for farming but full of nature's spontaneous offerings. Tan and fit, the boy personifies the physical and mental well-being that Americans associated with country life, especially during the second half of the century. An 1878 poem in *The Nursery*, a magazine for young children, celebrated the country boy as the epitome of health:

> *Joey was a country boy,*
> *Father's help and mother's joy:*
> *In the morning he rose early, —*
> *That's what made his hair so curly;*

FIG. 15   John George Brown, *The Berry Boy*, c. 1875. Oil on canvas, 23 x 15 in. George Walter Vincent Smith Art Museum, Springfield, Massachusetts.

Early went to bed at night,—
That's what made his eyes so bright;
Ruddy as a red-cheeked apple;
Playful as his pony dapple;
Even the nature of the rose
Wasn't quite as sweet as Joe's.[11]

In the context of prevalent concerns about the health of American children, pictures of healthy country boys working on the farm, engaged in vigorous play, and even making mischief came to function as indicators of the well-being of American democracy. The production of images like *The Berry Boy*, which connected country life with exercise and physical robustness, was also part of a broader preoccupation with health in the United States during the second half of the century. One symptom of this concern was the widespread popularity of "Muscular Christianity," a philosophy that called for the simultaneous development of physical and spiritual health. It rejected the Calvinist view that the denial of physical needs promoted moral virtue and claimed that a robust body was convincing proof of robustness of the spirit. The movement took hold in America as a counterpart to prevalent worries about the consequences of urbanization, which were nurtured by a plethora of newspaper and journal articles, advice books, and medical tracts that detailed the disastrous consequences of working in offices and factories. Preeminent American authors, including Ralph Waldo Emerson, Horace Bushnell, and Edward Everett Hale, touted the benefits of "the outdoor life" as a remedy for the enervating effects of urban life.

Medical experts and educators also promoted physical exercise as an essential adjunct to childhood schooling and an antidote to the debilitating physical effects of study and the classroom environment. Consumption, the leading scourge of the nineteenth century, was thought to affect most often studious and sedentary children, the "pale-faced, feeble-framed boys inclined to continue bending over their books."[12] A vigorous regimen of physical activity was seen as a method of keeping the illness at bay. In 1856, one sixteen-year-old in New England, James Edward "Ned" Wright, showed an anxiety about exercise that was typical for the period. Writing in his diary, he worried that he had not sustained the correct level of physical activity: "I don't think I have exercised enough this week, though I have used the dumb-bells occasionally," he mused. "I mean next week to pay more attention to this important subject, for I can't study hard without a proportionate amount of exercise, and with good health, I shall try to come out first in my class this term."[13] Unfortunately, Ned's preoccupation with fitness was not unwarranted, as his sister Fanny died of tuberculosis in 1865.

"Physical Health: To the Young People of America," an article published in 1865 in a leading children's journal, maintained that the nation's children were intelligent and

PHYSICAL HEALTH.

TO THE YOUNG PEOPLE OF AMERICA.

THE great war will end. Then what magnificent expansion! But what immense responsibilities! Soon they must rest upon you, — your manhood and womanhood. God and the nations will watch you.

A great and good nation is made up of great and good men and women. A strong building cannot be made of weak timbers.

A complete man is composed of a healthy body, a cultured brain, and a true heart. Wanting either he fails. Is his heart false? His strong head and body become instruments of evil. Is his head weak? His strong body and true heart are cheated. Is the body sick? His noble head and heart are like a great engine in a rickety boat.

Our Young Folks are strong and good.

I HAVE studied the life of the young among the better peoples of Europe. It is not flattery to say, that you, my young fellow-countrymen, have the best heads and hearts in the world. The great size of your brains is noticed by every intelligent stranger. The ceaseless activity of those brains is one of the most striking features of American life. American growth, as seen in railways, telegraphs, and agriculture, is tame and slow when compared with the achievements of our schools. And where else among the young are there such organizations for the spread of the Gospel, for temperance, for the relief of the sick and wounded?

But our Young Folks are weak.

Fig. 1.   Fig. 2.

John.   Thomas.

YOUR weakness is in your bodies. Here lies your danger. I see nothing which distresses me so much as the physique of the children in our public schools. Great heads, beautiful faces, brilliant eyes; but with that attenuated neck, thin, flat chest, and languid gait. Look at these two boys, John and Thomas. John is a native Yankee. I found him, without long searching, in one of our public schools. Thomas is an imaginary boy, composed by the artist.

FIG. 16   "Physical Health: To the Young People of America," from *Our Young Folks*, January 1865. Private collection.

virtuous, but weak. The text, accompanied by images of badly slumping "native Yankee" boys, described the imbalance that often occurred in the American child's physique (fig. 16). "The great size of your brains is noticed by every intelligent stranger. . . . The cease-less activity of those brains is one of the most striking features of American life," the author explained. "Your weakness is in your bodies. . . . Great heads, beautiful faces, bril-liant eyes; but with that attenuated neck, thin, flat chest, and languid gait." The author went on to describe the positions for sleeping and studying that provided the spinal sup-port essential for good health. Since he also considered American children to be "bad walkers," the author included detailed instructions on gait and bearing. Invoking youthful patriotism and a budding sense of enterprise to motivate improvements in posture and movement, the author reminded little readers that greatness lay ahead. "The great war will end. . . . Then what magnificent expansion!" he proclaimed. "But what immense responsibilities! Soon they must rest upon you."[14]

Paintings and other images in the second half of the century often made a connection between the robust healthfulness of country life and country boys' readiness for the call of enterprise. The illustrations and stories in books for children set dauntingly high standards for diligence, and many of these writings equated hard work and the moral fiber of the country boy. One informative tale introduced young readers to the world of rural finance and real estate. *Willie and the Mortgage: Showing How Much May Be Accomplished by a Boy* opened with a picture of "Willie" on a path in front of his ramshackle home (fig 17). His shoes, jacket, tie, and determined expression indicate he is setting out for the nearby vil-lage. With a basket on his arm and holding a net bag full of farm products, he is ready to market the fruits of his labor to help make the mortgage payments on the old pile behind him. The book's title gives away the climax of the story, of course, as Willie's hard work saves the family farm from receivership. The emphasis of such fables—and of images of industrious country boys like Willie—was not on innovation but on steady devotion to the gospel of hard work and its rewards.

Force and Skill, an 1869 painting by Charles Caleb Ward, presented a pair of youths sharing a farm task (fig. 18). Offering a double dose of country-style diligence, the painting depicts a boy who turns a heavy grindstone as his companion sharpens the blade of a knife. The painting's reference to cooperation and brotherhood had special meaning in the years immediately following the Civil War.[15] At the same time, in the context of the "magnificent expansion" of the postwar decade, the theme of collaborative labor—along with images that attested to the strength and ingenuity of the upcoming generation—emerged as important symbols of a reunified nation.

One foreign visitor gave a description that contradicted artists' portrayals of the virtuous character of the American country boy. In her account of life in the United States in the 1830s, British author Frances Trollope described a disturbing encounter with a skinny young rough who made a business of buying and selling chickens:

FIG. 17   Frontispiece from *Willie and the Mortgage: Showing How Much May Be Accomplished by a Boy*, 1870s. Private collection.

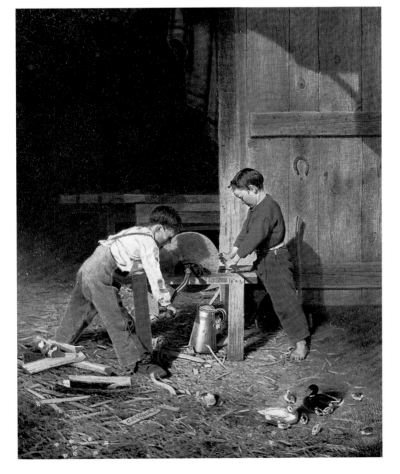

FIG. 18   Charles Caleb Ward, *Force and Skill*, 1869. Oil on canvas, 12 x 10 in. Currier Museum of Art, Manchester, New Hampshire. Gift of Henry Melville Fuller.

WILLIE loves to fish for trout,
In stream or purling brook,
Much better than to learn to read
In his new reading-book.
But, although dull he may appear
In reading, this is true,—
If he must take Fellows' Lozenge,
'Tis done without ado.

FIG. 19   Illustration from *The White Pine Illuminated Alphabet*, brochure, 1870s, with illustrations by an unidentified artist. Private collection.

I asked him how he managed his business. He told me that he bought eggs by the hundred, and lean chickens by the score. . . . And could easily double their price, and that his eggs answered well, too, when he sold them by the dozen. "And do you give the money to your mother?" "I expect not," was the answer, with another sharp glance of his ugly blue eyes. "What do you do with it, Nick?" His look said plainly, what is that to you? But he only answered, quaintly enough, "I takes care of it." . . . No human feeling seemed to warm his young heart, not even his love of self-indulgence, for he was not only ragged and dirty, but looked considerably more than half-starved, and I doubt not his dinners and suppers half fed his fat chickens.[16]

In spite of Trollope's disenchantment with the fledgling country businessman, during the nineteenth century the image of the country boy came to function as a guarantee for the quality and genuineness of different products. Beginning at mid-century, businesses hoping to expand their customer network took advantage of the wholesome connotations of the country boy to market a variety of commodities. One company, the New England Botanic Depot—purveyor of remedies for diphtheria, piles, scrofula, and other common complaints —showed it had grasped the potential of children to influence the purchasing habits of their parents. The company made its sales pitch in an alphabet book published as an advertising brochure in the 1860s (fig. 19). Interspersed with pictures of rustic children in a variety of bucolic settings, the company featured the country boy as the champion of "Fellows' Worm Lozenges." Shown fishing by a stream, the Botanic Depot's "Willie" knows when he must take his pill and—evincing the stoicism of his Calvinist forebears —"'Tis done without ado."

By mid-century, the new medium of photography gave middle-class Americans the opportunity to cast their own sons in the role of the country boy, bringing the spirit of democracy into the photographer's studio. Sitting for a photographer was usually a formal

FIG. 20   Unidentified photographer, Portrait of a boy, 1886. Collection of Priscilla Harris Dalrymple.

affair that involved dressing children in their Sunday best and paying considerable attention to the toilette. In a typical child portrait, a young man in the 1880s appears in a black jacket with elaborate lace trim at the neck and wrists; his velvet hat includes a tassel that drapes rakishly over the side (fig. 20). The studio setting is evident in the painted panel behind him and the obviously faux boulder where he rests his hand. A photograph from the 1860s shows the alternate, rustic kind of studio portrait that many photographers made available to clients. During this period, photographers used an expanded repertory of studio props, including swings, bales of hay, rowboats, fishing poles, fences, and painted country backdrops to create an attractively rural environment for country boy portraits. A typical example shows an abundantly tressed young subject sitting on a dock, with the requisite rolled trousers and fishing pole (fig. 21). Pretending to drop his line into the water painted on a panel behind him, the boy casts a dispirited look at the viewer, as if his patience with pastoral playacting is wearing thin. Another group of boys photographed in the country boy mode in the 1890s seemed to have a better time with their country boy charade (fig. 22). The playmates enjoy an outdoor game against an elaborate backdrop of the great outdoors—complete with farmhouse and fishing hole. The boy on the right who looks at the camera with a wide grin seems to take special delight in his complicity in the make-believe production.

Becoming a ubiquitous subject in American photographs, advertisements, and paintings, the figure of the country boy reached the apex of its popularity in the juncture between the end of the Civil War and the national centennial in 1876. During this period, Winslow Homer completed a series of eight paintings and two engravings portraying country children at school. The most animated of these was *Snap the Whip*, a painting depicting a group of boys playing a boisterous outdoor game (fig. 23). The image describes the happy emancipation of the noon recess, when children expended energies that had been kept in check during morning lessons. Snap the whip and other vigorous games gave boys an opportunity to develop their physical prowess, since a successful outcome required strength, speed, and the coordinated deployment of a variety of athletic skills. Of course,

FIG. 21   F. W. Guerin, *Country Boy Fishing*, c. 1866. Photograph, 25 1/2 x 21 1/2 in. Private collection.

FIG. 22   Unidentified photographer, *Playmates*, c. 1899. Library of Congress, Prints and Photographs Division, Washington, D.C.

FIG. 23 Winslow Homer, *Snap the Whip*, 1872. Oil on canvas, 12 x 20 in. The Metropolitan Museum of Art, New York. Gift of Christian A. Zabriskie, 1950. Photograph © 1999 The Metropolitan Museum of Art.

in the polite society of cities and the newly emerging suburbs, snap the whip was considered a sport too rough for schoolyard recreation.[17] Homer's image of boys free to engage in such a rollicking diversion embodied the abundant liberties of the country life, as well as the idea of national independence that was on every American's mind during the centennial decade.

Snap the whip—a game that worked by harnessing players' strength, speed, and momentum—functioned as a powerful symbol of the nation's accomplishments over the course of the century. Players at the center of the "whip" needed the size and power to anchor the revolving line of runners. In turn, the boys forming the line needed to accelerate enough and to keep their arms tight enough to generate the centrifugal force required to "snap" the outliers. Showing the figures on the left of the canvas as they fly off the whip and tumble to the ground, the painting seizes on the instant of most strenuous effort and the successful climax of the game. The garland of linked arms that was taut a moment ago has lost alignment, though some of the players are still running hard. The boy at the center opens his mouth, perhaps exhorting his companions to rally for another spin—but for now the momentum is lost. The young whippersnappers' torn jackets and patched pants mark them as veterans of the game, and other animated diversions seem sure to follow.

Snap the Whip was first displayed to the public at the Century Club in New York in the fall of 1872. A critic for the *New York Commercial Advertiser* praised the painting for its "drawing which puts our mind completely at ease, and action which is superb." Another reviewer, for the *New York Herald*, extolled Homer's entire country school series. "We know no works as thoroughly and distinctively American as those," he declared. "They will hand down to posterity pictures of Americans of the nineteenth century, possessing an individuality and marked by the strong idiosyncrasies of our people, not to be found elsewhere in the whole range of art." A year later, an engraving of *Snap the Whip* appeared in a two-page spread in *Harper's Weekly*, one of the most widely circulating magazines in the United States during the second half of the century. "Our beautiful double-page illustration this week, from the hand of Winslow Homer, is one that will delight the eyes of every school boy" announced the accompanying text. It would also "awaken pleasant memories for those who look back through intervening years to the days when their own thoughts were as free from care, and life sat lightly on their hearts."[18]

As the magazine's caption suggested, *Snap the Whip* evoked a sense of the passage of time, connecting it to the broader nineteenth-century American preoccupation with history books, agricultural and industrial schedules, almanacs, clockwork innovations, and other markers of time.[19] The painting contains a variety of elements that allude to the cycles of agrarian and human life, as well as the rhythms of the school day. The sprinkling of wildflowers in the painting's foreground sets the scene in the spring season, when country boys left school to help with plowing, planting, newborn animals, and the other farm chores that followed the winter respite. In addition, the suspenders the boys wear allude to their incipient manhood, since these were usually adopted after the age of seven or eight, when parents considered their sons ready to take on some of the adult farm work.[20] The presence of the red schoolhouse in the background, as well as the short shadows indicating a sun high in the sky, identify the recreation portrayed as a moment in the school's noon recess. The viewer's understanding that the boys soon will be called to return to their lessons—as well as of their imminent passage to adulthood—lends a sense of poignancy to their joyful but brief recreation.

Expanding out from the painting's engagement with the cycles of human and agrarian life, *Snap the Whip* also embodies an awareness of the years that had passed since the Civil War. Undoubtedly, such portrayals of farm children in the countryside served as a welcome respite for audiences weary of the somber images that Homer and other artists and photographers reporting from the field had supplied during the Civil War. *Snap the Whip* pictured the children of the soldiers who survived the campaigns at Antietam and Gettysburg, the citizens who would come of age in the centennial decade. Homer had already addressed this subject in a lithograph published in *Harper's Weekly* in 1870, which showed scenes from the years from 1860 to 1870 fanning out from a central "Wheel of Time" (fig. 24). Following a sequence of battle scenes, the image of a country family gathered for the harvest completes the circuit of the decade. Homer placed a symbol of

FIG. 24   Winslow Homer, "Wheel of Time," wood engraving, in *Harper's Weekly*, January 8, 1870.

renewal at the hub of the Wheel of Time, a baby who stretches out its arms as if to embrace the future.

For Americans caught up in the celebratory activities of the centennial decade, Homer's revolving Wheel of Time was also a reminder of the one hundred years that had passed since the American Revolution—as well as an invitation to speculate about the future of the United States. *Snap the Whip* portrayed country boys at a moment when citizens were acutely conscious of their own performance compared with that of the Founding Fathers. Through its focus on the exuberant well-being of the newest generation, *Snap the Whip* made a compelling argument for the health of the nation's republican traditions. Invoking the visual language of democracy, *Snap the Whip* drew on iconography associated with the republics of classical antiquity. The rhythmic sequence of figures across the canvas echoes the processional frieze of the Parthenon, while the figures at the center evoke images of winged Mercury, the boyish messenger god (fig. 25). The schoolboys' bare feet, finally, suggest the nudity of ancient athletes who competed in memorial games to commemorate fallen heroes—a poignant reminder of the Civil War dead.

When the nation's centennial approached, Americans engaged in a communal tallying of accounts, measuring accomplishments and shortcomings against the lofty standards that had been set by the revolutionary generation. Though Homer's image of boys playing during the noon recess marked the progress of Jefferson's agrarian vision for the new republic, the work also aligned itself with the nation's celebrated technological achievements

FIG. 25 Giambologna, *Medici Mercury*, 1580. Bronze, height 66 in. Museo Nazionale del Bargello, Florence, Italy.

and the fascination with machinery that infused American society during the nineteenth century. Writing in the 1870s, the renowned educator Jacob Abbot compared children to machines when he advised parents to allow children to let off steam through play and physical activity. "To give children food and then restrain the resulting activity," he declared, "is in conduct very analogous to that of the engineer who should lock the action of his engine, turn all the stop cocks, and shut down the safety valve, while he still went on all the time putting coal in the boiler."[21]

Abbot's analogy between children and the steam engine was part of the nation's widespread fascination with technology—as well as debates about the long-term consequences of mechanization. Musing about future generations of Americans, the prominent New York author and civic leader George Templeton Strong predicted there would be a melding of human and mechanical characteristics "tending toward development into a living, organic unit with railroads and steam packets for a circulating system, telegraph wires for nerves . . . and *New York Herald* for a brain."[22]

Of all the innovations that passed through the United States Patent Office during the nineteenth century, the steam engine was the device that captured the American imagination and the machine that artists and photographers invariably included in representations of the nation's most important accomplishments. *The Progress of the Century*, a print published by Currier and Ives in 1876, showed the machines powered by the steam piston that had transformed life across the United States during the nineteenth century, including the steamboat that dominated the nation's rivers and canals, the transcontinental railroad completed in 1869, and the steam press that allowed news to be printed and disseminated with unprecedented speed (fig. 26). In 1867, the eminent New England clergyman Samuel Osgood described in *Harper's New Monthly Magazine* the patriotic feelings the steam piston inspired at a low ebb during the Civil War:

FIG. 26   Currier and Ives, publishers, *The Progress of the Century: The Lightning Steam Press, The Electric Telegraph, The Locomotive, The Steamboat*, 1876. Lithograph, 10 x 12 15/16 in. Museum of the City of New York. The Harry T. Peters Collection.

I remember one day after a great deal of depression at public disaster, visiting a large cluster of workshops that gathered round a huge steam engine, not far from Harper's printing house. I went down into the basement and there saw the giant power lifting and dropping his ponderous shaft, and turning all those machines by his great force. The workmen in a mood of grim humor had put little flags upon his great head and arms and the monster seemed to be alive with patriotism. . . . I could have cried for joy or sung hallelujahs to the Lord of Hosts, for all was clear then. There, and everywhere through the loyal States, was that same mighty force working for us—the Providential arm of the nineteenth century.[23]

In the context of the American preoccupation with all things mechanical, as well as the prevalence of human-machine metaphors in nineteenth-century writings, it is significant that Homer's *Snap the Whip* showed children forming a dynamic phalanx that mimicked the mighty arm of a steam piston. Bound up with its reference to the technological revolution, however, the painting also embodied the sentimentalism about rural life that accompanied the rapid industrialization of the nation's once-pristine countryside. By the 1870s, one of the symptoms of the expansion of the factory system and urbanization was the stream of country youths leaving their hometowns and migrating to city clerkships. Homer and other American artists who traveled to rural communities in search of picturesque subject matter often lamented the sad appearance of depleted rural villages.

A picture of a country boy made at the end of the nineteenth century—in this version a painting of a youth leaving his rustic abode—was pronounced the favorite of the over-

FIG. 27   Thomas Hovenden, *Breaking Home Ties*, 1890. Oil on canvas, 52¼ x 72¼ in. Philadelphia Museum of Art. Gift of Ellen Harrison McMichael in memory of C. Emory McMichael.

whelming majority of visitors who toured the expansive art galleries at the World's Columbian Exposition held in Chicago in 1893 (fig. 27). The country boy portrayed in this painting, Thomas Hovenden's *Breaking Home Ties*, has grown into a young man, and he is shown preparing to take leave of his family. Surrounded by women whose melancholy expressions emphasize the sorrow of the parting, the youth is resolute. His steadfast expression and spanking new clothes testify to his readiness to pursue the social and economic opportunities that were considered the birthright of every male American. Many visitors at the Columbian Exposition responded emotionally to the narrative of *Breaking Home Ties*, indicating that they, too, had experienced the sadness of seeing their children move away. In an account of a visit to the fair, a reporter for the *Pittsburgh Press* wrote: "It did not surprise me to see tears running down many a motherly-looking face, and to hear one self-made man exclaim: 'By George, I'd rather have that than all the rest of the collection!'" Like the sad family members gathered around the departing country boy in Hovenden's painting, the emotions of the self-made men, mothers, and other citizens who saw *Breaking Home Ties* expressed the sense of farewell that went hand-in-hand with the displays of progress and modernity at the exposition. Audiences welcoming the technological wonders that ushered in the new century were also saying good-bye to the nation's cherished agrarian past, the "home ties" that had to be severed to make room for the onward march of enterprise.

Chapter 2

DAUGHTERS OF LIBERTY

In this land of precarious fortunes, every girl should know how to be useful.

LYDIA MARIA CHILD, *The Girl's Own Book*, 1834

In 1865, the last year of the Civil War, Seymour Guy painted *Unconscious of Danger*, a work that showed a boy and a girl standing on a high overlook (fig. 28). The boy's tousled hair and the girl's sagging stocking hint at the strenuous fun of the day's excursion, but the painting focuses on a moment of unexpected danger. Gazing downward, the boy steps toward the edge of a precipice as the girl extends her hand toward him. On the left of the canvas, a rocky beach visible far below reveals the extent of the drop. A contemporary critic described the painting's story to his readers: "It represents a young lad, unconscious of danger, while dreaming of the future, walking to the edge of a high ledge of rocks, while his sister is in the act of striving to bring him back," he explained.[1]

How was it that the art critic wrote with such certainty about the painting's narrative? Could he not just as easily have conjured up an alternative interpretation of the scene, one in which the little girl is in fact the "danger" the boy doesn't see? Stealing up behind him — perhaps her brother but maybe also her tormentor—could she be stretching out to give him just one little push? Though a darker reading might satisfy the post-Freudian preference for greater nuance, the critic's confident explanation of the painting's narrative was deeply rooted in the most fundamental beliefs of his society. His unequivocal situating of the actors in *Unconscious of Danger*—the risk-taking boy "dreaming of the future" and the vigilant girl ready to pull him back from the edge—embodied ideas about the distinct nature of males and females that journal publishers, newspaper editors, clerics, poets, educators, and medical authorities expressed throughout the century. The belief in the "separate spheres" of the genders in behavior, work, and creative expression shaped the boundaries of American society and influenced all aspects of daily life, from the arrangement of seating on trains and school curricula to the use of medicines and the design of furniture.

OPPOSITE: Detail of fig. 33.

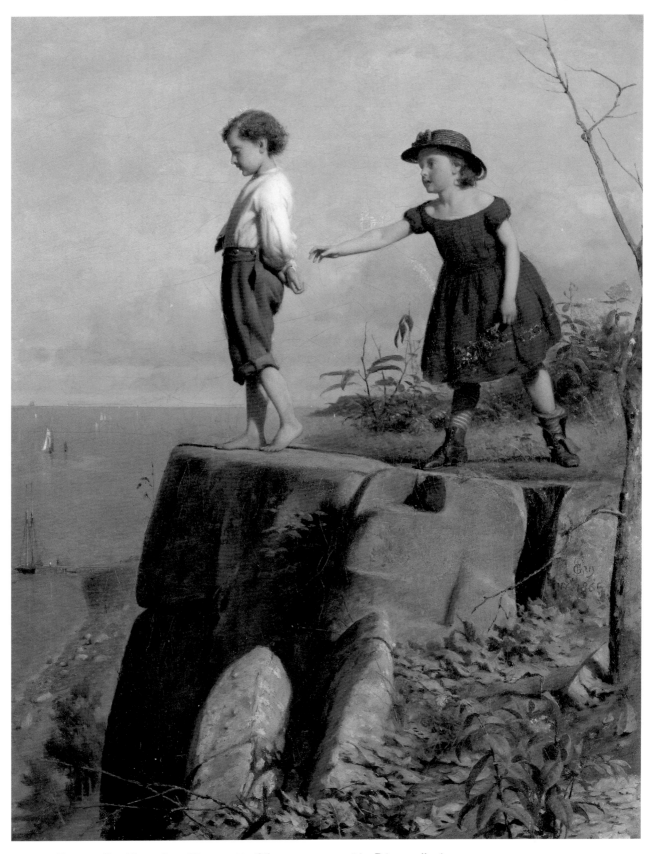

FIG. 28 Seymour Guy, *Unconscious of Danger*, 1865. Oil on canvas, 20 x 16 in. Private collection.

After the revolution of 1776, as American citizens sorted out new hierarchies of economic and social authority, the relationship of the sexes was one of the first to be clarified. Though the final form the new democratic order would take was not yet clear, the constitution promised a decisive break with the past and new rights for the disenfranchised. American women at the end of the eighteenth century were optimistic that there would be greater opportunities for their daughters and future generations of females. The prominent author Judith Sargent Murray, writing in Massachusetts in 1798, declared that she expected "to see our young women forming a new era in female history." Murray was not incorrect; females acquired new status during the nineteenth century, but it was not an era of expanded freedom for women. On the contrary, to a significant degree, American women lost the limited economic independence their colonial mothers and grandmothers had enjoyed and were placed on a pedestal at the center of domestic life.[2]

Framed by the peculiarities of the American political system, as well as by the expansiveness of the capitalist marketplace, American society during the nineteenth century became solidly bifurcated along gender lines. Males aligned themselves with an ethos of progress that celebrated self-interest, competition, and material gain. Females, on the other hand, emerged as the antidote for male egalitarian shenanigans. Rationality, piety, thrift, benevolent works, and the realm of virtue itself came to be seen as a woman's domain and the foundation of a separate sphere rooted in the routines of the home. Commended by politicians, artists, and ministers as creatures of "superior moral influence," women were diverted from the pursuit of political and economic equality in the name of a higher calling. They were appointed the guardians of democracy, a sacred trust that involved nurturing future citizens, providing moral encouragement for husbands buffeted by the tempests of entrepreneurial endeavor, and the usual panoply of household chores.

In her *Treatise on Domestic Economy*, eminent author and domestic management authority Catharine Beecher described the "lofty and fortunate" position of American women as the defenders of the nation's democratic institutions:

The success of democratic institutions, as is conceded by all, depends on the intellectual and moral character of the mass of the people. If they are intelligent and virtuous, democracy is a blessing; but if they are ignorant and wicked, it is only a curse, and is much more dreadful than any other form of civil government, as a thousand tyrants are more to be dreaded than one. It is equally conceded, that the formation of the moral and intellectual character of the young is committed mainly to the female hand. The mother forms the character of the future man; the sister bends the fibers that are hereafter to be the forest tree; the wife sways the heart, whose energies may turn for good or evil the destinies of a nation. . . . Then to American women, more than to any others on earth, is committed the exalted privilege of extending over the world those blessed influences, which are to renovate degraded man, and "clothe all climes with beauty."[3]

Of course, Beecher herself chose to remain single and carved out a public role as the nation's first expert in "domestic science" and an outspoken proponent of higher education for women. Other American women dared to defy the status quo, rejecting Beecher's claim that subordinate rank represented an "exalted privilege." In 1848, a convention of women seeking the right to vote presented a scathing assessment of women's assigned role through history. The "bill of rights" they set forth declared that the "history of mankind is the history of repeated injuries and usurpations on the part of man toward women, having in direct object the establishment of absolute tyranny over her. . . . He has endeavored, in every way that he could, to destroy her confidence in her own powers, to lessen her self-respect, and to make her willing to lead a dependent and abject life."[4] The convention's leaders riled the nation by arguing for a female identity that was distinct from family life and by asserting women's right to a public voice.

An editorial published in the *Lowell Courier* used humor to dismiss the claims of the "women folks" at the convention. It explained to readers that giving women the right to vote amounted to a complete inversion of the current and "natural" order of society. When women decided to insist on political equality, the article read, they "should have resolved at the same time that it was obligatory also upon [men] to wash dishes, scour up, be put to the tub, handle the broom, darn stockings, patch breeches, scold the servants, dress in the latest fashions, wear trinkets, look beautiful, and be as fascinating as those blessed morsels of humanity whom God gave to preserve that rough animal man, in something like reasonable civilization." The preposterous prospect of men dressed in women's clothing, darning stockings, and sweeping up encouraged readers to agree that political power and womanhood were mutually exclusive in the "reasonable civilization" ordained by God.

It was thus against a backdrop of struggle over the duties and rights of American women that pictures of the nation's little girls emerged as a noteworthy ingredient in the mixture of art and popular imagery that attended Americans in their everyday life (fig. 29). Always fewer in number than portrayals of country youths and depictions of boys preparing for or engaged in public life, images of American girls were nonetheless a pervasive presence on magazine covers, billboards, soap labels, calling cards, and in newspapers, stereographs, and art galleries. Representations of girlhood generally adhered to a narrow range of subjects: girls gathering flowers, playing with pets, sewing samplers, and engaged in other activities that represented the routines of home life—as well as the constraints on female behavior. The young ladies in these representations occupied an idyllic childhood realm of innocence and pleasurable pastimes, transcending the bitter debates over who should do the sweeping up in a democratic society. An integral component of negotiations between the genders that occurred during the nineteenth century, these works showed "daughters of liberty" who were ready and eager to take their place as managers of the home front. They also promised that the future triumphs of free enterprise and manifest destiny would go hand in hand with delicious dinners served on time.[5]

In their depiction of domestic virtues, the thematic repertory of images of American girls

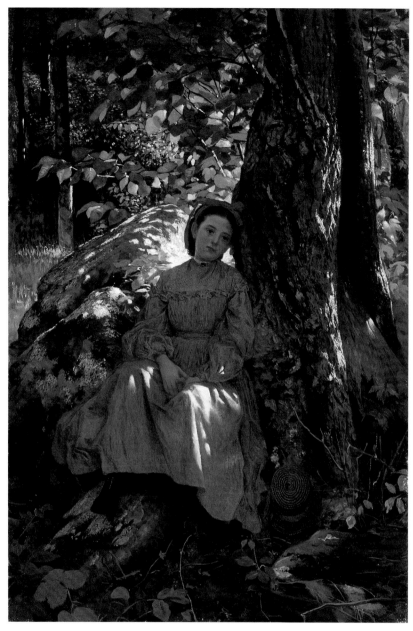

FIG. 29   John George Brown, *Resting in the Woods (Girl Under a Tree)*, 1866. Oil on canvas, 18 3/8 x 12 1/8 in. Collection of Jo Ann and Julian Ganz, Jr.

was closely related to the culture of self-improvement that energized nineteenth-century American society. Sparked by the religious revivalism of the Second Great Awakening during the 1820s and 1830s, public discourse was dominated by the idea of a nation undergoing a continual process of individual and national betterment. Improvement took a wide variety of forms—the establishment of public schools, abstinence from alcohol, religious observance, the expansion of industry, and support for technological progress. As the purveyors of moral influence, American females stood at the center of the self-

Pat Murphy from his window looks out,
To see what the villagers are about.

This boy is trying to get a notion,
Of the laws of centrifugal motion.

I'm sure you've played some roughish trick,
I think you'd better be off quick.

Ride away, Charley with all your might,
You and your horse make a pretty sight.

Jane has all her lessons learned,
And so that pretty prize has earned.

Jacky is blowing a furious gale,
To make his little vessels sail.

Pity the poor blind fiddler here,
Give him some cents, his heart to cheer.
19

FIG. 30 "Children at work and play," from *Little Folks' First Steps*, 1870s. Private collection.

improvement campaign. In imagery relating to little girls, the self-improvement campaign manifested itself in pictures of young ladies who were masters—or mistresses, as it were —of an assortment of admirable traits: cleanliness, kindness, filial piety, industry. In this context, portrayals of little girls carried with them the promise of social redemption, the vision of a future moment when the United States would resolve the petty conflicts that limited its growth and lead the world as a "redeemer nation."

Young seamstresses, little flower gatherers, and industrious mothers' helpers symbolized a nation developing its moral and physical energies, gathering its strength and directing it to the state-building tasks ahead. Such images were often presented in tandem with pictures of boys shown out and about sampling a variety of occupations—on the decks of seagoing ships, behind grocery store counters, stalking prairie game, and starting out in the newspaper trade. A page from a children's book of the 1870s showed how depictions of girls were often framed by their relationship to boys (fig. 30). One little boy experiments with centrifugal motion, while "Jacky" plays with his toy boats. "Charley" spurs his horse to ride away with all his might, as a mischief maker departs the scene of his crime. A counterpoint to the restless male energy around her, "Little Jane" stays at home to learn her lessons, in training for a life managing grown-up Charlies and Jackies.

The battalions of Little Janes that appeared in paintings, storybooks, photographs, and magazine articles had important implications for the growing order of market relationships. As American factories' need for a population of disciplined and obedient workers surged during the century, portrayals of little girls modeled the cooperative behavior that served industry's requirement for reliable employees. John Adams observed in 1800 that "manufactures cannot live, much less thrive, without honor, fidelity, punctuality, and private faith, a sacred respect for property, and the moral obligations of promises and contracts."[6] Though the virtues Adams described were part of the genteel standards of the revolutionary world, during the nineteenth century they became attributes allocated to the female portion of the citizenry.

Against the backdrop of the nation's growing "economy of manufactures" that depended increasingly on standardized parts and the efficiency of workers engaged in repetitive tasks, the vision of a unified army of American girls had potent cultural meanings. These pictures always displayed a certain variety in costume, setting, and style, but their adherence to a narrow range of types and activities linked them to the same ideal of consistency that nurtured the system of standardized parts. For contemporary audiences smitten by the idea of product reliability, the unchanging and static quality of images of little girls embodied Americanness just as convincingly as portrayals of energetic boys engaged in a variety of dynamic activities. Curiously, it was only toward the end of the century, when standardization became a pervasive feature of American industry, business, and public education, that portrayals of girls began to break away from the visual mold that had always shaped their identity.

A pair of prints published at mid-century by Nathaniel Currier illustrated the idea of female stability in relation to male mutability (figs. 31–32). After leaving their mothers' laps, the girl and boy strike characteristic poses as they move toward adulthood. Toting a rifle, the boy looks toward the man of affairs he will become. Heroic service in the military precedes a comfortable middle age. The man gesticulates energetically throughout the tableau, communicating to viewers about where he has been and where he will go. In contrast, the young girl is moored in place, assuming the fixed and neutral stance that she will maintain until her back is stooped by old age. Connected to the symbols of domestic

FIG. 31   Nathaniel Currier, publisher, *The Life and Age of Man: Stages of a Man's Life from the Cradle to the Grave*, c. 1850. Lithograph, Museum of the City of New York. The Harry T. Peters Collection.

FIG. 32   Nathaniel Currier, publisher, *The Life and Age of Woman: Stages of a Woman's Life from the Cradle to the Grave*, 1850. Lithograph, 9 x 12 in. Museum of the City of New York. Gift of Miss Minette Lang.

life—a doll, a bridal gown, a baby—she is the anchor around which her male companion revolves. The accompanying text describes the interactions with males that will rule her days "from cradle to grave."

> *In swaddling clothes behold the bud,*
> *Of sweet and gentle womanhood.*
> *Next she foreshows with mimic plays,*
> *The business of her future days,*
> *Now glorious as a full blown flower*
> *The heart of manhood feels her power.*
> *A husband now her arms entwine,*
> *She clings around him like the vine.*
> *Now bearing fruit she rears her boys*
> *And tastes a mother's pains and joys.*
> *Like sparkling fountain gushing forth,*
> *She proves a blessing to the earth.*
> *A busy housewife full of cares,*
> *The daily food her hand prepares*
> *As age creeps on she seeks for grace,*
> *Always to church and in her place.*

For most of the century, American girls were most frequently portrayed displaying or gathering flowers (figs. 33–35). The equation of females with the floral abundance of the earth was, of course, a ubiquitous theme in Western art since ancient times, but the trope also carried meanings that were specific to American culture. Part of a larger network of songs, poems, novels, and editorials representing American girlhood, these representations identified young females as a rooted, stable element, a part of the population that was always in place. A thematic current that ran beneath pictures of flower girls was, of course, the hypermobility of the United States citizenry, a pervasive topic in both national discourse and the published accounts of foreign visitors. In symbiosis with images that showed energetic males moving up the social ladder, moving west, and moving on with new business endeavors, representations of girls with flowers completed a vision of social equilibrium that echoed the regulating mechanisms of the American government. As men "dreaming of the future" bought, sold, invented, and explored, the vision of female stability served as the check and balance to the expansive energies of liberty.

The Ragan Sisters, a painting executed by Jacob Eichholtz in 1818, represents an early example of the American flower girl (fig. 36). The work depicts Mary and Elizabeth Barbara Ragan, the daughters of a prosperous merchant in Hagerstown, Maryland, who are shown outdoors in a garden setting. The girls have gathered flowers to decorate their bonnets, and these floral elements help to evoke the boundaries of the female sphere and

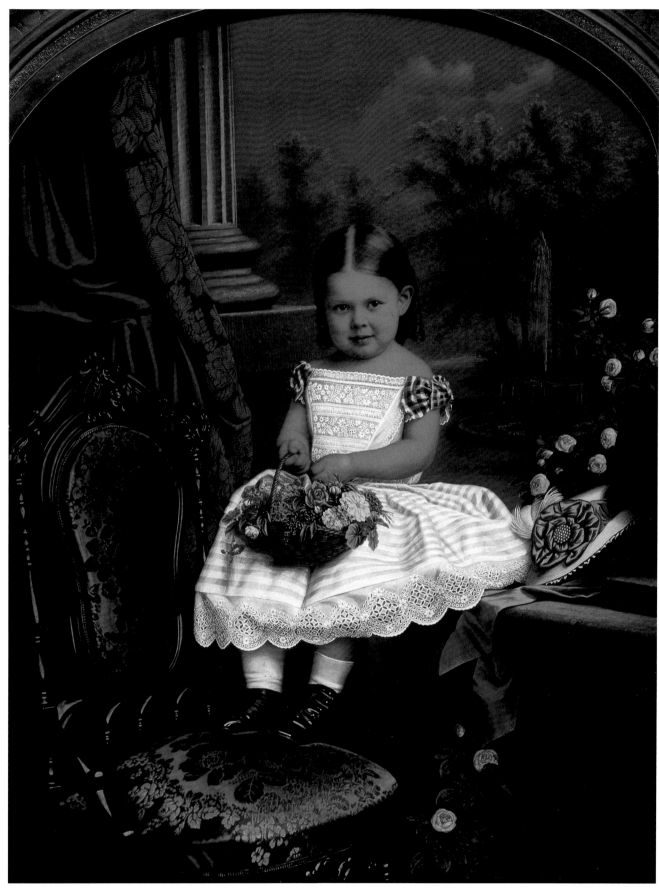

FIG. 33   F. A. Wenderoth, *Portrait of the Artist's Daughter*, c. 1855. Ivorytype with applied color, 21 1/2 x 16 1/2 in. George Eastman House, Rochester, New York.

F Fanny finding Flowers.

FIG. 34   Cornelia S. Pering, *Little Girl with Flowers*
(*Emily Mae*), 1871. Oil on canvas, 46¹/2 x 37 in. Private
collection.

FIG. 35   "Fanny Finding Flowers," from
A Treasury of Pleasure Books for Young People, 1865.
Private collection.

FIG. 36   Jacob Eichholtz, *The Ragan Sisters*, 1818. Oil on canvas, 59 1/2 x 42 1/2 in. National Gallery of Art, Washington, D.C. Gift of Mrs. Cooper R. Drewry.

the character of their household. As in many portraits of American girls with flowers, roses predominate in the bouquets the Ragan sisters have gathered. A cultivated flower that required careful attention to maintain, the rose was an emblem of the domestic comforts and decorations that were considered part of the female domain. Contemporary ladies' magazines that advised readers on the creation of pleasing decorative environments in their homes frequently mentioned the cultivation of flowers and floral arrangement as a cornerstone of the tastefully appointed interior. Considered the most beautiful and refined of flowers, the rose was most often suggested as an element for floral displays. At the same time, in the vocabulary of flowers that was commonly accepted in nineteenth-century society as a means of communicating about character or sentiment, the rose represented purity and grace, attributes thought to be essential in the nation's young womanhood.[7]

In addition to serving as a reference to gentility and virtue, the rose was traditionally used in American art as an emblem of fecundity and children. During the eighteenth century, women were often portrayed holding sprigs of roses, with the number of blooms indicating the number of children they had borne.[8] In this context, the Ragan sisters' bouquets allude to the girls' youth and also make a cheerful prognostication of their future sons and daughters—an ample harvest of offspring to match their family's wealth. The concentric circles of the rose's petals also echo the sisters' family relationships. At the center of the canvas, the girls' close embrace embodies the intimate bonds of siblings. It also refers to the broader orbit of affectionate ties that bind them to their parents, aunts, uncles, cousins, and the range of domestic connections that define the parameters of their world.

The only reference to an environment outside the *hortus conclusus* that contains and sustains the sisters is the book held by Elizabeth Barbara. In the context of the open air setting, the book, with its suggestion of study and indoor pursuits, seems somewhat out of place. While the book hints at the well-stocked library that was an essential feature of every gentleman's estate, it also indicates that the Ragan family may have shared the growing public interest in female education. The period when Eichholtz painted the Ragan sisters' portrait was a time of new educational opportunities for girls and young women, and a number of female academies opened in New England and the south to educate the daughters of the well-to-do. Thomas Jefferson, Benjamin Rush, and other revolutionary leaders had stressed the importance of an educated citizenry to the health of the republic, and their ideas on schooling included both males and females. Rush asserted that "the equal share that every citizen has in the liberty and the possible share he may have in the government of our country make it necessary that our ladies should be qualified to a certain degree, by a peculiar and suitable education, to concur in instructing their sons in the principles of liberty and government."[9] Directed by the advice of the Founding Fathers, the stated aim of most female academies was to prepare the nation's young ladies for their role as the mothers of future voters and leaders.

FIG. 37   Jacob Marling, *The May Queen (The Crowning of Flora)*, 1816. Oil on canvas, 30⅛ x 39⅛ in. Chrysler Museum of Art, Norfolk, Virginia. Gift of Edgar William and Bernice Chrysler Garbisch.

In devising a curriculum for American girls, educators grappled with the dilemma of serving capable students who were to be educated only "to a certain degree." Since, as one seminary student declared, "the Church, the Bar, and the Senate are shut against us," female academies created courses of study that targeted the needs of future sons and husbands. Girls typically studied reading, penmanship, arithmetic, geography, history, music, and bookkeeping in order to function as better tutors for their sons and domestic managers for their husbands.[10] Academy instruction was always presented to girls as a preparation for their role as the handmaidens of male industry; most educators studiously avoided the prickly subject of academic instruction as the basis for a claim to political power.

A painting from 1816 by the artist Jacob Marling, *The May Queen (The Crowning of Flora)*, embodied the curious dialectic between the push for female education and the insistence that girls be trained for nothing more than marriage and homemaking (fig. 37). The painting represents an outdoor ceremony at a girls' school in Raleigh, North Carolina, with pupils and instructors gathered near a building fronted with an elegant neoclassical portico. A newspaper in Lynchburg, Virginia, *The Echo*, gave an account of the event and Marling's record of it:

On the first day of May, the young ladies belonging to the Raleigh . . . academy assembled under the wide spreading trees which embosom their building, and proceeded to the election of a queen. Miss Mary Du Bose of Georgia was the successful candidate. She was conducted to the rural throne . . . [and] crowned with a chaplet of flowers. . . . [An] address to the queen was read by Miss Anne W. Clark of Georgia. . . . The echoes of the grove were awakened by the melody of music, and the mirthful scene impressed all so happily, that the students will long believe this day was not lost. Mr. Marling, so well known for his skill and taste in painting, was present, and sketched a likeness of the May queen, as she appeared in the ensigns of royalty.[11]

The fact that Miss Du Bose's crowning takes place outside the school building seems to affirm that the ultimate trajectory of her and her classmates' education lies outside the halls of academia or professional life. The "Crowning of Flora" was in fact a variant of traditional springtime celebrations that centered on girls ready for marriage and domestic life. Throughout the nineteenth century, May Day crownings took place in city parks and town squares across the land, and artists and publishers like Currier and Ives made flower-filled portrayals of May Day queens that were a favorite subject with American customers. In 1881, *The Nursery*, a journal for young children, published a poem that explained the selection criteria for May queens.

"When I was little," said Grandma Gray
"We used to welcome the month of May
With a song and a dance on the village green,
Choosing and crowning our May-day queen.
We used to choose of the prettiest girls,
The one who had the merriest eyes,
As clear and bright as the May Day skies . . ."
The one who had the sunniest curls.

The Raleigh Female Academy honored its pupils' accomplishments by basing its May Day selection of "Flora" on scholarly achievement and moral character. In the context of traditional May Day priorities and the hierarchies of the world beyond the classroom, however, the crowning of Mary Du Bose—as well as the image of Elizabeth Ragan's tentative grasp of her book—serve as reminders of the ultimate irrelevance of education for those excluded from the Church, the Bar, the Senate, and virtually all arenas of professional endeavor.[12]

In the hierarchy of the artistic subjects encompassed by paintings of the early nineteenth century, the identification of girls with flowers relegated them to the inferior place of floral and fruit still lifes. Prominent American artists preferred to devote their time to the elevated themes of history painting and landscape, which carried with them connotations of study in Europe and continuity with the works of old masters. Portraits and still lifes, marked by their connection to the marketplace and domestic decoration, were con-

The PASSION FLOWER *Belongs to the class*
MONADELPHIA *and order* PENTANDRIA.

FIG. 38 "Passion Flower," from *The Young Botanist*, by
J. L. Comstock, 1835. Private collection.

sidered the most plebeian of art subjects. "Flower painting belongs to the
decorative side of art, as floral subjects
themselves belong to the decorative
side of nature," explained one authority.
"And remembering this, it is easy to
understand why so few paintings of
flower subjects are altogether satisfactory,
or come within the range of thoroughly
good art."[13] Though they represented
a more complex undertaking than the
simple still life, paintings of little girls
with fruits and flowers occupied the
same subordinate artistic tier.[14]

A surge of national interest in botany
and the natural sciences after 1820 gave
additional relevance to pictures of
American girls with flowers and other
plants (fig. 38).[15] During the nineteenth
century, America became a nation of
"botanizers," and the study of plants
was considered particularly beneficial
for girls and young ladies. In addition
to the gentle exercise provided by field study, familiarity with plants brought with it practical knowledge that was a natural adjunct to women's role as family nurses and healers.
By mid-century, intrepid female specimen-gatherers were taking to the outdoors in
droves, equipped with plant guides, sample containers, and rough-weather gear. The distinguished botanist Amos Eaton, who gave public lectures throughout the northeast on
native flora, noticed that most of the botanical enthusiasts he encountered were female.
He remarked in 1822 that "more than half the botanists in New-England and New York
are ladies."[16]

The female role as the nation's plant specialists connected pictures of girls with
flowers to ideas about the close relationship between science, nature, and virtue. Spurred
by the teachings of Alexander von Humboldt and other contemporary naturalists,
Americans viewed science as a revelation of divine power—a discipline that could be
taught as a branch of applied theology. They also believed that familiarity with plant life
was a first step toward a broader understanding of the mechanisms of nature, including
physics, chemistry, and other subjects that were the foundation of technological innovation. Of course, it was considered unladylike for a female to exhibit too keen an interest

in any scientific discipline; a fascination with science was thought of as a particularly male characteristic. Women and girls were allowed the study of botany, however, since it helped future mothers prepare to support their sons' natural inclination toward building, engineering, and the mechanical arts that were thought to characterize America's "locomotive people."

When associated with the natural world outside the home, girls with flowers became the passive embodiment of purity, a quality defined precisely by a lack of agency. The eminent clergyman and author Horace Bushnell lauded women who assumed a modest unobtrusiveness, equating it with the quiet but inexorable influence of nature. "Let no woman imagine she is without consequence, or motive to excellence, because she is not conspicuous," he declared. "Oh, it is the greatness of woman that she is so much like the great powers of nature, behind the noise and clatter of the world's affairs, tempering all things with her benign influence only the more certainly because of her presence."[17] In his book *Women Suffrage: A Reform Against Nature*, published in 1869, Bushnell argued that the mingling of social responsibilities was "against nature" and that women were not suited to the "rough-hewing" work of government.

Although Americans extolled work as both a duty and a pleasure, the fact that most prominent nineteenth-century painters avoided depictions of female work altogether suggests that the subject had disturbing connotations that intruded on the rarefied world of art. Though paintings did not often take up the subject of girls working, the topic was frequently portrayed in popular theater, broadsides, magazines, advertisements, and photographs (figs. 39–40). The kind of work these sources represented most frequently was sewing, an activity that served as a genteel visual abbreviation for the full complement of household duties. Images of girls sewing tapped into a potent range of memories and associations in American viewers, including an awareness of the revolutionary past and ideas about the social connotations of different types of female work.

While the United States hurtled headlong into Progress, pictures of little girls sewing showed that, vested in tiny hands across the nation, the virtues of days gone by endured. "The Lesson on the Sampler," an 1881 illustration from the popular children's journal *Saint Nicholas Magazine*, portrayed the period before the American Revolution, when many women helped to support their families through sewing and spinning work (fig. 41). Sitting next to a spinning wheel and a grandfather clock—allusions to the industrious use of time—a pre-revolutionary housewife teaches her daughter how to sew. A representation of the border of the sampler frames the pair, showing the results of the girl's beginning efforts. At the top, the letters of the alphabet appear in detailed stitchery; at the bottom, the maker of the sampler identifies herself and the date: "Julia May's Sampler, February 17, 1740." For nineteenth-century audiences looking back more than a century through the image, the lesson on the sampler had to do with the rewards of work. Though the sewing machine and other technological advances had altered how mothers and daughters managed

THE SISTERS AT WORK.

THE LESSON ON THE SAMPLER.

FIG. 39   (above left) "The Sisters at Work," from *The Nursery*, 1871. Private collection.

FIG. 40   (left) M. B. Parkinson, *Little Girl Washing*, photograph 1898. Library of Congress, Prints and Photographs Division, Washington, D.C.

FIG. 41   (above right) "The Lesson on the Sampler," from *Saint Nicholas Magazine*, April 1881. Stanford University Libraries.

needle and thread in 1881, the illustration demonstrated that the learning rituals preparing American girls for adulthood had remained constant since colonial days. Domestic skills and virtuous habits, passed on from mothers to daughters in an unbroken chain, linked the homemakers of the past to those of the present and the future.

In addition to serving as generic symbols of industry of a female sort, pictures of girls sewing also functioned as specific reminders of the events leading to the American Revolution. During the 1760s, a British tax on American cloth production provoked colonists to the point of open rebellion and sparked a wave of boycotts against British cloth and other imported goods. Among the central forces opposing the tax were the "daughters of liberty," who organized spinning meetings to protest the outsiders' interference. In the turbulent pre-revolutionary environment, the production and wearing of homemade clothing became an act of open defiance against English administrators. Years later, long after British overlords had been routed from the land, cloth-making and sewing retained their iconic status as emblems of the nation's struggle for independence.[18]

If images of girls sewing reminded viewers of a time when the population was unified in its fight against outside domination, they also served as markers of new class hierarchies that separated segments of American society during the nineteenth century. As part of their training in refined pastimes, young ladies in middle-class and elite households were expected to learn to sew intricate embroidery, often in the form of samplers that displayed their range of skill in fine needlework. Embroidered decorations on samplers, aprons, pillowcases, and other household textiles testified about the needleworker's dexterity as well as the leisure time available to her, making them a token of the presence of household servants. They also referred to the sewer's other accomplishments, since, according to the arbiters of female decorum, girls could take up their "fancywork" only when all their duties had been discharged. In their treatise on home management, *The American Women's Home*, Catharine Beecher and Harriet Beecher Stowe admonished those who loved to sew that none had "a right to put a stitch of ornament on any article of dress or furniture . . . until she is sure she can secure time for all her social, intellectual, benevolent, and religious duties."[19]

In spite of sewing's broad cultural value, it did not appear as a subject in paintings by noteworthy artists, not only because male patrons probably preferred works portraying their own sphere of activities, but also because of sewing's emerging associations with factories and the subsistence work of the laboring classes.[20] When textbooks, children's novels, and popular magazines took up the subject, of course, it was usually framed as a hobby for females in respectable households. A lesson in *The Eclectic First Reader* published by William McGuffey in 1836 included a lesson titled "The Good Girl" (fig. 42). The good girl's polite request: "Mama, may I sew today?" banished any notion of the ragged urchins who stitched piecework in urban garrets. Though other lessons in McGuffey's textbooks showed that middle-class girls counted vigorous farmwork as part of their daily chores, "The Good Girl" showed sewing as an attribute of gentility. Supplementing

LESSON XVI.

The Good Girl.

Mama, may I sew today? Yes my child. What do you wish to sew?

I wish to hem a frill for your cap. Is not this a new cap? I see it has no frill.

FIG. 42   "The Good Girl," from *The Eclectic First Reader*, by William H. McGuffey, 1836. Private collection.

FIG. 43   Frontispiece from the *Lowell Offering*, 1845. Stanford University Libraries and Department of Special Collections.

the story about the good girl, the lesson included a lexicon of related words—"pray,"
"clean," "frocks," "lady"—that linked needlework to a vocabulary of politeness.

Although portrayals of sewing in children's journals and textbooks eschewed references
to the lower classes, the mill girl in the textile factory was the obvious counterpart to
well-to-do young ladies with time for fancywork. The textile industry was one of the fastest-
growing sectors of the United States economy, and its predominantly female work force
was the subject of considerable interest, controversy, and debate in the first half of the
century. During this period, business leaders asserted that girls and young women would
become a dominant part of the new industrial order, a shift from female domestic industry
to female factory production that Horace Bushnell described as the "transition from mother
and daughter power to water and steam power."[21] Textile factories offered nimble-fingered
girls the opportunity to earn a good salary, though it often meant twelve-hour workdays
and interactions with dangerous machinery. The renowned mills at Lowell, Massachusetts,
and Dover, New Hampshire, generally employed country girls from the age of twelve,
but others hired children as young as five. To field criticisms about the harmful effects of
such work, mill operators often required girls to participate in evening study hours and
regular "improvement circles."

Published images of mill girls in newspapers and magazines with national circulation
showed that America's fastest-growing industry was guided by the tempering female influence.[22] Some mills even produced their own publications, such as the *Lowell Offering*, which
featured poems and stories written by girls working at the Lowell Mill in Massachusetts.
A picture on the cover of an issue in 1845 presented the factory girl as the intermediary
between progress and tradition (fig. 43). The image pushes the monolithic mill buildings
into the background—next to a church and a schoolhouse—creating a frame for a mill
maid who stands in the middle distance. The girl displays an open book, a reference to the
intellectual pursuits that complement her work in the factory. She looks toward a bee skep
in the foreground, a symbol not only of the busy industry inside the mill but also of the
patient labor of agrarian life in the countryside outside the factory. Mediated by the mill
girl, the two elements—the factory and the farm—exist together in symbiotic equilibrium.

Beneath the mill girl's feet is the legend "Is Saul among the prophets?" This reference
to the teachings of the Bible acknowledges that some readers of the *Lowell Offering* would
scoff at the arcadian idyll portrayed on its cover. The question spurred the doubtful to
remember the New Testament account of the conversion of the Roman tax collector,
Saul. Struck from his horse by a light sent by a wrathful God, Saul took the new name
"Paul" and became one of Christ's most devoted apostles. Presuming to effect a similar
conversion in skeptical audiences, the journal was filled with poems and stories that attested
to the erudition and cultivated sensibilities of mill maidens. Many of these pieces were
republished in major metropolitan newspapers, accompanied by editorial comments and
letters from readers who experienced a surge of national pride on reading the "offerings"
of the country's hardworking factory girls.

1873.]   *Minnie's Bedtime.*   751

ducing, as she spoke, a piece of white mosquito-netting from her work-basket, and with a couple of hair-pins she fastened it to Minnie's curls. Minnie looked in the mirror and was well satisfied as to the result; and seldom does a mirror reflect a sweeter, fairer, or younger bride. Then the bridal procession moved out of the sitting-room and up the stairs, the soft little white hand of the bride clasping one baluster after another to assist her on her upward way, while the bridemaid behind bore the train of the bridal dress with becoming grace and gravity.

When they reached the chamber, Mrs. Gray lifted Minnie, and seated her on the side of the bed to take off her shoes and stockings.

"O mamma, do brides be —" Just there sleepy Minnie's mouth made another round O, and she applied the knuckles of both hands to her eyes in a vain endeavor to hold apart the lids that would keep drawing together. It was so long a pause, that both shoes and both stockings were off before she completed her question with "barefoot?"

"What is it, darling?" asked Mrs. Gray.

"Do brides be barefoot?" repeated Minnie.

Mrs. Gray laughed; and, cuddling both of the dimpled little pink feet in the palm of one hand, she said she had seen a great many brides, but never one before who had such cunning little feet, and she thought any bride having such would not mind going barefoot.

FIG. 44 "Minnie's Bedtime," from *Our Young Folks*, December, 1873. Stanford University Libraries and Department of Special Collections.

When not penning poetry for middle-class readers, the mill girls helped to manufacture fabrics that were ultimately transformed into dresses, shawls, pantaloons, petticoats, and aprons worn by girls like themselves. Pictures of girls interacting with clothing—selecting an outfit, dressed for special occasions, and playing dress-up—represented another common theme in girlhood imagery during the nineteenth century (figs. 44–46). Clothing often served in these portrayals as a symbol of the transition from childhood to adulthood, depicting the age when girls' youthful freedoms were replaced by the rigid protocols of adult life. At the time when boys began their encounters with the outside world by joining the army or heading west, girls were given their first corsets to wear. *The*

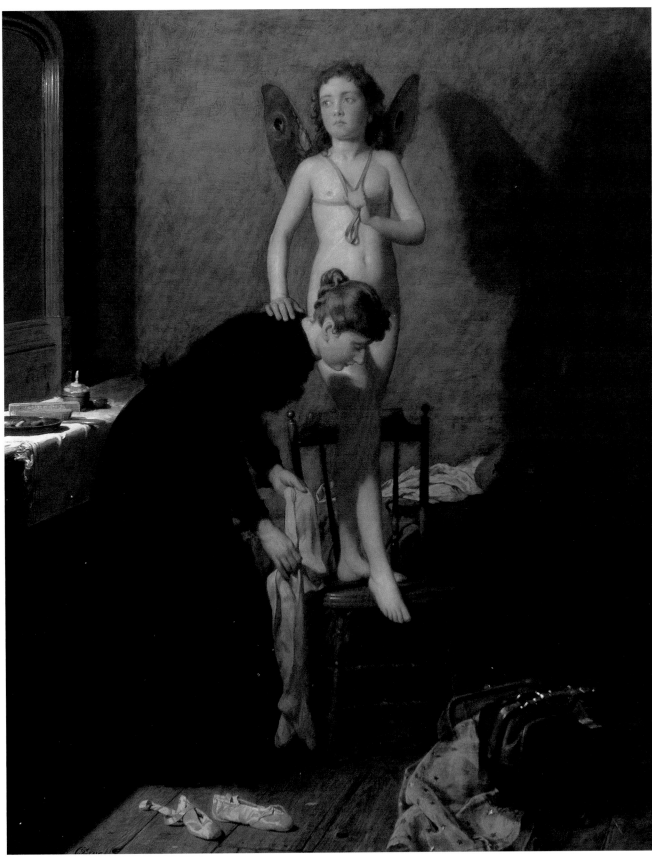

FIG. 45   Seymour Guy, *Dressing for the Rehearsal*, c. 1890. Oil on canvas, 34 1/8 x 27 3/8 in. Smithsonian American Art Museum, Washington, D.C. Gift of Jennie Anita Guy.

FIG. 46 "Good Sense Corset Waists," from *Lippincott's Magazine*, March 1891. Colby College, Waterville, Maine.

Party Dress, an 1872 painting by Eastman Johnson, took as its subject the anticipation of a girl preparing for a special occasion (fig. 47). Standing in a dark room looking toward the brightness of a window, the young lady waits patiently as a helpmate or sister adjusts her collar. The girl's expectant expression and the ministrations of her young companion suggest that the event marks one of her first appearances in a woman's attire. Her toilette complete, she is ready to attend the party where she will be introduced to young men of similar age and background who are suitable marriage prospects.

In spite of the painting's festive title, the darkness of the dressing room and the suggestion of something being tightened around the girl's neck imbue the work with a sense of foreboding. The crumpled doll that lies in the small rocking chair adds to the sense of an abandonment of the pleasures of childhood. Replacing it are the proprieties of womanhood, symbolized by the ungainly dress that envelops its wearer. The party dress is held

FIG. 47   Eastman Johnson, *The Party Dress (The Finishing Touch)*, 1872. Oil on composition board, 20 x 16 in. The Wadsworth Atheneum of Art, Hartford, Connecticut. Bequest of Mrs. Clara Hinton Gould.

out by multiple layers of stiff undergarments that distort the natural contours of the girl's body and impede easy movement, while also requiring a careful regimen of laundering and ironing to maintain their fullness. Propped up next to the fireplace behind her, the outline of a set of brass fire tongs mirrors the girl's triangular silhouette, a reminder of the duties she will soon take on as keeper of the hearth.

Nineteenth-century viewers' understanding of *The Party Dress* and other paintings of adolescent girls was influenced by a body of writings, much of it by women, that focused on girls' transition to adulthood. Many of these texts described the end of girlhood as a taming of female will, a period when girls were trained—sometimes through tragic circumstances—to give up youthful independence and embrace a life of obedience and submission. *Jack and Jill*, a novel by Louisa May Alcott, told the story of a high-spirited adolescent girl who is openly contemptuous of polite behavior. Providence intervenes in the form of a terrible sledding accident in which Jill is badly injured and almost crippled for life. During her long convalescence, she has time to reconsider her willfulness and make a resolution to reform. Surprised and delighted by her daughter's transformation from tomboy to deferential young lady, Jill's mother declares, "I'm not sure that I won't put you in a pretty cage and send you to the Cattle Show, as an example of what we can do in the way of taming a wild bird till it is nearly meek as a dove."[23] Alcott described her character's alteration with unmistakable ambivalence, explaining that "Jill had learned to love her cage now."[24]

In identifying her heroine with a caged bird, Alcott was employing an animal metaphor that was prevalent in visual representations of girls throughout the century. The theme first appeared in American paintings of the colonial period, when artists paired children with squirrels, blackbirds, and other animals caught in the wild. These works were partially inspired by European paintings of royal courts that maintained exotic menageries featuring cockatoos, monkeys, and other wildlife. Colonial artists also used wild creatures as emblems of America, referring through them to the taming of the wilderness and ongoing discoveries of new animals and plants. In his double portrait of the sisters Mary and Elizabeth Royall, John Singleton Copley included a hummingbird, one of the most tiny and exquisite representatives of the New World, perched delicately on his sitter's open fingers (fig. 48). Throughout the nineteenth century, artists continued to link children with all kinds of animals. Though boys were often shown with canine and feline companions—and often pictured as antagonists rather than friends—those most frequently depicted with animals were girls. These portrayals made flattering claims about female talents and virtues. At the same time, pictures of girls relayed conflicting messages about their subjects, associating them simultaneously with the freedom of nature and the confinement of domestication.

Alcott's use of the caged bird metaphor was also adapted by artists portraying girls and young women. In the 1860s, Seymour Guy, an artist renowned for his sensitive representations of girls, made a bird the focus of a small painting, *Girl with Canary (The New Arrival)*

FIG. 48   John Singleton Copley, *Mary Macintosh Royall and Elizabeth Royall*, c. 1758. Oil on canvas, 57³/₈ x 48¹/₈ in. Museum of Fine Arts, Boston. Julia Knight Fox Fund.

(fig. 49). The picture shows a canary in a cage, watched by a girl wearing a full-sleeved blue blouse. The scene takes place in an entry hall of an affluent household, a passageway where the public world cedes to the privacy of the home.[25] The "new arrival" is displayed in the middle of this transitional space on an elaborate Gothic table, a style that contemporary tastemakers associated with medieval churches, monasteries, and other venerable emblems of the Christian faith. Recalling the elaborate tracery of European cathedrals, the table's extravagant curves also conjure up the overstuffed comforts of rooms beyond our view, with the full draperies, plush carpets, and tufted armchairs that were the hallmark of the fashionable Victorian home. The girl, too, is overstuffed, with layers of thick undergarments exaggerating the contours of her torso.[26]

The girl's hat suggests that, like the bird, she has just alighted from outside and has just encountered the "new arrival." Her reaction is curiously subdued, defying viewers' expectations of surprise or delight. The expression on her face is masked by the shadow of her feathered chapeau, which casts a shadow over her eyes. As she contemplates the newest addition to the household, her hands provide a clue to her feelings about the encounter.

FIG. 49   Seymour Guy, *Girl with Canary (The New Arrival)*, 1860s. Oil on canvas, 12¼ x 9¼ in. Private collection.

two glad when
felt that killed
days floor mother
ago   about running

FIG. 50 "Lesson LXXXV," from *Pictorial Eclectic Primer*, by William H. McGuffey, 1849. Stanford University Libraries and Department of Special Collections.

With the fingers of her right hand, she reaches out to touch the bird as it leans forward expectantly. Her other hand is at her chin, an attitude that, in the repertory of poses and attitudes common in nineteenth-century theater, was used to indicate consternation or dismay. These two conflicting gestures communicate the girl's ambivalence toward her new companion; on the one hand, she welcomes the little bird; on the other, she seems to acknowledge it regretfully as a fellow inmate.

In constructing the narrative of Guy's painting, nineteenth-century audiences would have drawn upon stories and lessons familiar from popular literature for children. Textbooks frequently included stories about caged birds or children who felt sorry for birds in cages (fig. 50). In 1849, McGuffey's *Pictorial Eclectic Primer* published a lesson that described two boys walking in the woods who come upon a pair of baby birds in a nest.

"Let us take these birds into the house," says one of the boys. "We can put them into a cage." Fretting about the nestlings, his friend urges him to leave the birds alone. "Our parents would be very sorry if we were stolen and put into a prison," he insists. The short skirts of the young lady in *The New Arrival* indicate she is still a few years away from womanhood, but her melancholy contemplation suggests she understands the connection between the caged bird and her own impending maturity. One popular advice manual for newly married women, *The Young Wife; or Duties of Women in the Marriage Relation*, described the strictures of married life with chapters that set forth the meaning of "Domesticity," "Obedience," and "Submission." After laying out these daunting requirements, the author delivered the coup de grâce with a chapter on the duty of "Cheerfulness."[27] This section confirmed that young ladies thinking about marriage must consider the proposition most seriously, given the all-encompassing physical and mental commitment called for in new recruits.

Foreign visitors often remarked on the severity of the restrictions imposed on American women, as well as the singular autonomy enjoyed by American girls. Alexis de Tocqueville, Harriet Martineau, and other outside observers whose accounts were widely read in the

FIG. 51   Currier and Ives, publishers, after Lilly Martin Spencer, *Into Mischief*, c. 1857. Lithograph, 16 1/2 x 12 5/8 in. Library of Congress, Prints and Photographs Division, Washington, D.C.

United States and abroad were astounded by the liberties granted to girls, who were allowed to play with boys, engage in vigorous sports, and appear unchaperoned at social events. The observers noted that these freedoms lasted only until marriage, however, after which American females were deprived of the rights that even aristocratic Europeans considered fundamental in civilized society. Martineau remarked that the American treatment of women fell below "not only their own democratic principles, but the practice of some parts of the Old World." After giving examples of the paternalistic treatment that American males defined as "chivalrous," Martineau concluded that "indulgence is given her as a substitute for justice."[28]

Popular magazines and prints were filled with images of decorous American matrons and their youthful doppelgangers—little girls taking full advantage of their brief freedom with mischievous behavior (figs. 51–52). Of course, depictions of girlish naughtiness were inevitably accompanied by complementary images, text, or legends that warned about the

160   *Polly and the Pot of Honey.*   [March,

POLLY AND THE POT OF HONEY.

1872.]   *Polly and the Pot of Honey.*   161

VOL. VIII. — NO. III.   11

FIG. 52   "Polly and the Pot of Honey," from *Our Young Folks*, March 1872. Stanford University Libraries and Department of Special Collections.

consequences of impropriety. In 1879, the polite journal *Godey's Lady's Book* published "Out on First," an engraving that showed a young lady in a starched pinafore practicing baseball indoors (fig. 53). Inside a well-appointed sitting room, the pigtailed girl winds up for the pitch while an eager batter demolishes a window and glassware on a nearby table. The lady of the house opens the door of the room at the climax of the play, her hand raised in alarm. Representing the proper order of the household, the mother presumably will mete out the kind of punishment that will help her daughter remember the obligations engendered by refined attire and gracious surroundings.

   The Fruits of Temptation, a work painted in 1857 by Lilly Martin Spencer, who exhibited her works at the National Academy of Design, the Boston Atheneum, and other prominent eastern galleries, was one of the few paintings that took up the subject of girls' misbehavior (fig. 54). The picture shows a group of youngsters in a dining room, where a table is laden with platters of fruit and other delicacies. Spencer placed the figure of a naughty little

FIG. 53   James M. King after a drawing by F. O. C. Darley, "Out on First," from *Godey's Lady's Book*, June 1879. Private collection.

FIG. 54   Lilly Martin Spencer, *The Fruits of Temptation*, 1857. Oil on canvas, 28 x 22 in. Location unknown.

girl in lace pantalettes, busily scooping an abundant portion of delectables, at the center of the canvas. She is flanked by a boy who sits on the floor to devour his cache of melon and peaches, a cat who has jumped up on the table, and a thieving dog gnawing at a morsel on a chair top. On the left side of the room, an older girl ignores the mayhem around her as she looks into a mirror. The lady of the house, like her female counterpart in *Godey's Lady's Book*, holds up her hand in dismay when she opens the door and discovers the little rascals polishing off a repast clearly intended for guests.

Spencer's careful delineation of body postures and facial expressions made it easy for nineteenth-century viewers to piece together the painting's story. Left in the care of a servant girl while their mother prepares for visitors, the children of the family have run amok. As it plays up the humor of the children's tabletop scavenging, the painting and its title also invite the viewer to envision the next episode of the dining room debacle, a scene where the hostess will attempt to welcome her guests while the children moan with stomachaches. Spencer's audience would have been keenly aware of the dangers of eating too much or too fast, particularly in the case of young children, since digestive well-being was one of the most important health concerns of nineteenth-century America. Contemporary advice literature aimed at the nation's homemakers was filled with warnings about the variety of afflictions that resulted from overindulgence—symptoms that often came on without delay. "Very often, intemperance in eating produces immediate results, such as colic, headaches, pains of indigestion, and vertigo," cautioned one authority.[29] Indigestion, it seems, is the final "fruit of temptation" and nature's way of reasserting the proper order of the household.

Portrayals of naughty girls and other depictions relating to the notorious freedom of the American girl were qualified by images that communicated the idea of the taming and domestication girls underwent as part of their transition to womanhood. Pictures of girls training cats, dogs, and other animals symbolized their self-discipline and patience, as well as their ability to transfer those qualities to others. These images appeared in a wide variety of media throughout the century, including paintings, book and magazine illustrations, and lithographs showing determined girls asserting their influence over dogs and cats by teaching them to sit up and beg or accustoming them to wearing some kind of ridiculous hat (figs. 55–57). Framed by the presence of the nation's vast and untamed wilderness and the American reverence for the unchecked liberty of males "free, white, and twenty one," pictures of American girls as skilled animal trainers had cheering implications not only for the winning of the west but also for temperance campaigns and other social reform efforts.

The nefarious counterpart of the girl patiently teaching her pet to sit was, of course, the unruly boy who took pleasure in mistreating animals. Schoolbooks and popular literature abounded with pictures and stories of boys kicking dogs, juggling kittens, and pulling wings off flies, accompanied by admonishments urging restraint and compassion. In the context of boys' notoriously cruel treatment of animals, representations of girls' gentle goodness as trainers took on even greater meaning as a symbol of their ability to soften the rough edges of male behavior. Of course, taming adult subjects represented a task considerably more complex than teaching Rover to speak. A print published by Nathaniel Currier pictured one of the challenges young ladies might face when, as married women, they shifted their attentions to mature subjects—as well as the sad consequences when training failed (fig. 58). *The Drunkard's Progress: From the First Glass to the Grave* shows an enthusiastic tippler as he wends his way from congenial toasting to "Desperation and crime." Centered beneath the arc of his life is a weeping woman, the wife who has proved to be no match for her husband's dissolute habits. *The Drunkard's Progress* presented one of the many kinds of beasts that roamed the nation's sidewalks and parlors, untamed creatures who could be handled only by women of stout heart and steely resolve.

In a work executed in 1871, *Elizabeth with a Dog*, the iconoclastic artist Thomas Eakins adopted the convention of animal training for his painting of a young friend, Elizabeth

LESSON 5.

dog	bee	eat
log	dee	fun
how	has	gun
his	can	bun

Here is a dog. See how he
stands on his hind legs.
He has a bun on his nose.
He will eat it if he can get it.
How very still he stands.

LESSON LXXXVI.

pie	nice	word	whose
stay	says	chair	fancy
dine	head	straw	master
speak	name	known	Edward

Sister Mary, come here
and see Fido.

He is sitting up, and has
a hat on his head.

He looks like a little boy
in the chair. It is only Fido.

FIG. 55   (above left) "Lesson 5," from *Little Child's Home ABC
Book*, c. 1880. Private collection.

FIG. 56   (left) Rice and Buttre, engravers, "Who Speaks
First?" from *Godey's Lady's Book*, 1851. Stanford University
Libraries and Department of Special Collections.

FIG. 57   (above right) "Lesson LXXXVI," from *Pictorial
Eclectic Primer*, by William H. McGuffey, 1849. Stanford
University Libraries and Department of Special Collections.

FIG. 58   Nathaniel Currier, publisher, *The Drunkard's Progress: From the First Glass to the Grave*, 1846. Lithograph, 9⅝ x 12⅞ in. Library of Congress, Prints and Photographs Division, Washington, D.C.

Crowell, whom he depicted instructing her little poodle to sit on its hind legs (fig. 59). The artist's handling of the subject is entirely unconventional, however, since it imbues the young woman with a power and independence at odds with most contemporary depictions of American girls. Elizabeth fixes her dog with a forceful look as she points her finger in a gesture of command. Sitting on the floor and wearing a hat that echoes her poodle's fluffy topknot, she is equated with the world of animals and nature. The keen intelligence of her gaze, however, sets her apart from the docile creature who obeys her, as well as from society's expectations for female passivity. The schoolbooks that lie on the floor beside her also introduce the idea that her authority is connected to a developing intellectual acuity. With the poised attitude of one accustomed to giving commands and being obeyed, the girl eyes her dog with the intensity of a marksman drawing a bead on a target. The subject of the painting is indeed the force of Elizabeth's will, and its centering of a girl's awareness of her power served to challenge the prevalent idea of a feeble female "influence" as the counterpart to male potency and dynamism.

Eakins's portrayal of a young woman learning to command paralleled other pictures that represented the nation's growing engagement with the issue of women's rights at the end of the nineteenth century. As greater numbers of women sought the right to vote and equal opportunities in education and professional life, paintings and popular imagery presented different interpretations of female independence. *The Age of Brass: Or the Triumphs of Women's Rights*, a lithograph published by Currier and Ives in 1869, depicted a possible finale to the nascent female power Eakins explored in his portrait of the young Elizabeth Crowell. It foretold the coming of a future "Age of Brass," where ladies crowd around the

FIG. 59   Thomas Eakins, *Elizabeth with a Dog*, 1871. Oil on canvas, 13 3/4 x 17 in. San Diego Museum of Art. Museum purchase and a gift from Mr. and Mrs. Edwin S. Larsen.

ballot box to get their share of the new freedoms while men take care of the young ones (fig. 60). The women's new power manifests itself as an assortment of outlandish outfits, hats, hairdos, and impolite behaviors. One shapely suffragette hikes her skirts high on her knees while she puffs on a cigar. To her left, a mannish voter wears a gentleman's top hat and tail coat and a sausage-shaped coiffure. On the right, an angry matron shakes her fist at her husband, who holds their swaddled infant in his arms.

The rude spectacle of women voters relishing the abundance of their new freedoms recalls the tabletop rummaging of *The Fruits of Temptation*. Like Spencer's vision of domestic disorder, *The Triumphs of Women's Rights* makes plain the consequences of what was presented as women's overindulgence in political liberties. Not only have these new liberties

FIG. 60   Currier and Ives, publishers, *The Age of Brass: Or the Triumphs of Women's Rights*, 1869.
Lithograph, 8 3/4 x 13 7/16 in. Library of Congress, Prints and Photographs Division, Washington, D.C.

addled women's taste in fashion and sense of maternal duty, they also have produced a
class of female candidates that bodes ill for the electorate. A flyer on a table calls the
assembled to "Vote for Sheriff Miss Hangman," while a sign at the center of the scene
reads: "Vote for the Celebrated Man-Tamer Susan Sharp Tongue." Developing more
fully the female talent for training that Elizabeth Crowell and other girls displayed, the
man-taming Susan Sharp Tongue and her colleagues have replaced womanly beneficence
with more assertive techniques for managing the male body politic. Newly enfranchised
members of a society where freedom is a finite commodity, the rabble of women of the
Age of Brass belly up for their turn at the table of democratic opportunity.[30]

Pictures of American girls—flower maidens, little seamstresses, and patient dog trainers
—take on their full meaning when considered alongside the dire view of women activists
taken by Currier and Ives. Together, these images asserted that there was no middle ground
between the communal harmony that was thought to be a by-product of female virtue
and a divisive free-for-all where males and females competed for limited political and
economic resources. Throughout the nineteenth century, Americans remained reluctant
to even envision in art a society energized by empowered citizens of both sexes, and for
the "daughters of liberty," the claim to the right to vote was deferred until the second
decade of the next century.

Chapter 3

Children of Bondage

I was born in Tuckahoe, near Hillsborough, and about twelve miles from Easton,
in Talbot County, Maryland. I have no accurate knowledge of my age, never having
seen any authentic record containing it. By far the larger part of the slaves know as little
of their ages as horses know of theirs, and it is the wish of most masters within
my knowledge to keep their slaves thus ignorant.

FREDERICK DOUGLASS, *Narrative of the Life of Frederick Douglass,*
An American Slave, 1845

Around 1826, the Pennsylvania artist Robert Street painted the children of Commodore John Daniel Danels, a wealthy Baltimore shipowner (fig. 61). The five Danels children sit in a well-appointed parlor where they amuse themselves by blowing bubbles. At the top of the group, the oldest boy holds an open book and looks away from the play of his siblings. He is flanked by two younger brothers wearing elegantly fitted jackets and ruffled shirts. One of the pair smiles benevolently as the other is ready to release a bubble he has blown from a small pipe. The two youngest children sit at the bottom of the group, holding out their hands to catch a bubble floating in midair. Their gestures call attention to an African-American youth lying on the floor at their side, holding a saucer containing the soap for the bubbles that are the source of the fun. He, too, is well dressed, though the simple cut of his collar and jacket confirm his lesser status. The angle of the black youth's upturned face, in turn, leads the viewer's eye across the room to his counterpart, another African-American boy who stands on the threshold of the parlor's open door.

A scene of domestic contentment and prosperity, the painting of the Danels children is unremarkable in the context of the portraits of its time except for the inclusion of the two African-American children who enfold the Danels siblings on the right and left. Blacks were a rarity in early-nineteenth-century American paintings and a subject that would have drawn the attention of contemporary viewers. The manner in which the African-Americans were represented in Street's painting—as both participants in and

OPPOSITE: Detail of fig. 80.

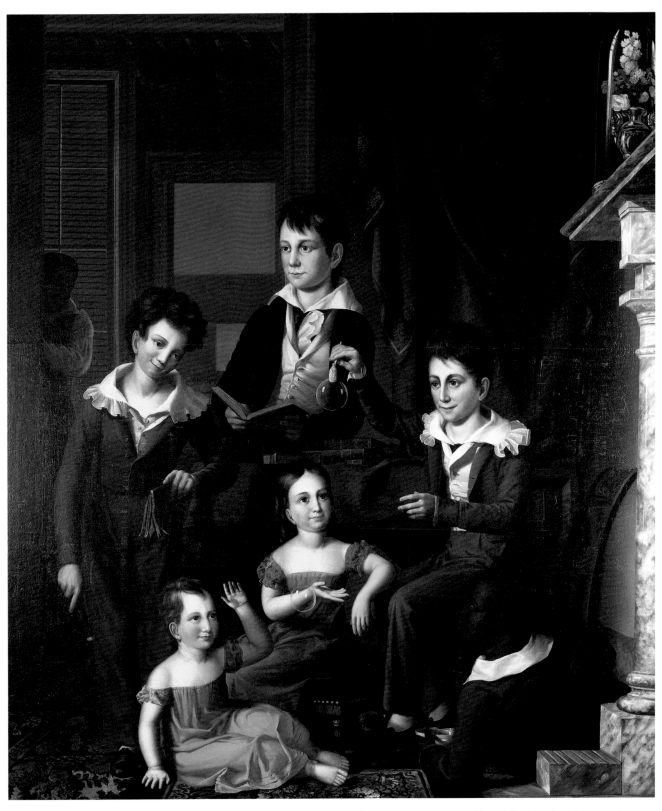

FIG. 61   Robert Street, *Children of Commodore John Daniel Danels*, c. 1826. Oil on canvas, 69 1/2 x 59 3/4 in. The Maryland Historical Society, Baltimore.

onlookers of the family's spontaneous game—was also a noteworthy feature. Presenting a group of whites framed by African-Americans, the Danels portrait alluded to the kinds of relationships whites and blacks experienced in everyday life, as well as citizens' beliefs about the significance of those connections.

Later in the century, as the United States was poised on the brink of civil war, Abraham Lincoln warned the nation that its future depended on citizens' ability to reach consensus about the place of African-Americans: "A house divided against itself cannot stand."[1] Painted just before the issue of slavery erupted as a national controversy in the 1830s and 1840s, the Danels portrait pictured the symbiosis of white and black Americans. Though the African-Americans clearly play a subservient role in the Danels household, the black youth on the right has an integral part in the bubble-blowing game. In contrast to eighteenth-century portraits where an impermeable line between white masters and black servants was affirmed by the subjects' posture, costume, and setting, the pose of the African-American boy in the Danels portrait contradicts the established visual protocol for such works. Relaxing with one elbow akimbo, he completes the family circle that centers around the two bubbles hanging in midair.

The boy's physical proximity to the Danels children was not in itself noteworthy, since blacks lived intimately with whites in both Northern and Southern households. Still, the painting's literal foregrounding of the subject was unusual for its period. Considering the increasingly restrictive laws regulating the relationship between whites and blacks in the first half of the century, Robert Street risked criticism by introducing blacks into his painting at all. His patron Commodore Danels may have been unusually open-minded on such matters, however. Since we know that Danels traveled to South America to join the Columbian navy when that country was fighting for independence from Spain, he may also have been attuned to the struggles for liberty taking place around him at home in Baltimore. The city had a large population of free blacks and was surrounded by the slavery-based plantations of wealthy Maryland planters. In the decades when the Danels portrait was executed, the number of slaves in the South was expanding rapidly, the methods of slave management were becoming increasingly oppressive, and, more and more, citizens were compelled to think about the place of blacks in their midst.[2] Through Street's portrayal of white and black children together, the commodore may have expressed his hopes for a happy resolution to the growing interracial animosity. At the same time, the bubbles at the center of the composition—symbols of the ephemeral nature of childhood—seem to allude to the tenuous aspect of any notion of racial harmony.

The Danels portrait includes another element that disrupts the painting's vision of childhood happiness. The bubble blowers in the foreground are watched by a second black child, one who remains isolated from the group (fig. 62). Neither in the room nor outside it, the figure of the boy who lingers in the doorway makes a different kind of forecast about the future of blacks in the United States. The child's place on the thresh-

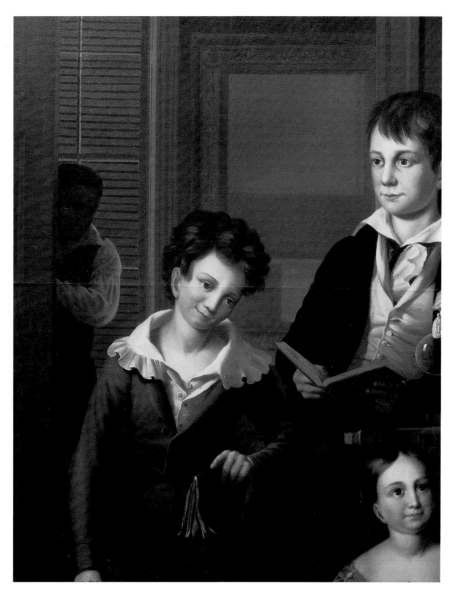

FIG. 62   Detail of fig. 61.

old resists pat conclusions about the favorable outcome of the current racial controversies. There is no telling whether he is slave or free, on his way in or on his way out, making him an apt symbol of a period consumed by debates on where slaves and former slaves belonged in a democratic society. In an open letter of 1826, a group of Baltimore freedmen addressed white residents of the city to vent their frustrations over what they saw as their untenable position in the community: "We reside among you, and yet are strangers; natives, and yet not citizens; surrounded by the freest people and most republican institutions in the world, and yet enjoying none of the immunities of freedom."[3]

Just a few years before the Danels portrait was painted, Thomas Jefferson gave his opinion that the best place for African-Americans was outside the nation's borders. As part of his recommendation that slavery be gradually abolished, the revered former president also advised that all black children should be deported to Africa or Haiti. Though it is impossible to reconcile Jefferson's deportation plan with his rallying cry for liberty in the Declaration of Independence of 1776, his scheme represented an attempt to deflect what he saw as a grave threat to the republic's democratic institutions. He presented the presence of blacks in the United States as a practical rather than a moral concern, drawing on his own experience as a slaveholder and Virginia planter to calculate costs for the purchase of slaves to be deported and for outbound shipping. In an 1824 letter to Jared Sparks, a New England civic leader and future president of Harvard, Jefferson proposed selling land taken from Indians to pay for the cost of exporting all children born to African-Americans each year—"the whole annual increase"—leaving their parents to die off in the natural attrition of time. Since Jefferson was himself the father of at least one child by a slave in his household, he was calling for the implementation of a plan that would have banished his own progeny from the United States.[4]

> Suppose the whole annual increase to be sixty thousand [children], fifty vessels, of four hundred tons burden each, constantly employed in that short run, would carry off the increase of every year, and the old stock would die off in the ordinary course of nature, lessening from the commencement until its final disappearance. In this way no violation of private right is proposed. . . . I am aware that this issue involves some constitutional scruples. But a liberal construction, justified by the object, may go far, and an amendment of the constitution, the whole length necessary. The separation of infants from their mothers, too, would produce some scruples of humanity. But that would be straining at a gnat, and swallowing a camel.[5]

Jefferson's astonishing deportation scheme proved to be economically and logistically unworkable, but others shared his worries about the future consequences of slavery, especially the possibility of widespread rebellion. In 1831, the highly publicized slave insurrection led by Nat Turner seemed to confirm whites' worst fears. A slave preacher in Virginia, Turner led an armed band of fellow slaves from house to house in Southampton County, where they massacred sixty white men, women, and children. Northern and Southern newspapers were filled with graphic accounts of the carnage and editorials speculating about the reasons for the violence. Spurred by fears of a wave of slave conspiracies, whites called for strict containment of the black population. In the following decades, a spate of increasingly harsh federal and state laws blocked African-Americans' access to economic and social power. Congress prohibited blacks from serving in the militia or working as mail carriers, and most states passed laws to prohibit blacks from testifying against whites in court, from marrying whites, and from entering a state in search of employment. Only five states allowed blacks to vote, and one of those—New York—made voting rights contingent on discriminatory property-owning stipulations. The group of new states admitted to the Union at mid-century imposed even more severe restrictions on blacks, including laws that prevented them from entering into legal contracts or purchasing real estate.

Laws that truncated African-American participation in the nation's political and economic life were accompanied by paintings, theater performances, and other cultural productions that helped to complete the quarantine of black citizens from the rest of the body politic. The visual imagery of elite and popular culture drew on an extensive repertory of derogatory stereotypes built up since colonial times. Paintings and prints, which both inspired and were inspired by portrayals in contemporary literature and theater, characterized African-Americans as lazy, dimwitted, ugly, sly, and susceptible to every kind of vice. Artists who thought it expedient to steer clear of blacks' notorious sensuality chose childhood themes, which resonated favorably with white viewers who believed in blacks' essentially childlike nature.[6]

The appreciation for unflattering portrayals of African-Americans evolved into a vehicle for communal solidarity as the nation struggled for cohesion during the nineteenth century. In particular, the black child was pictured as an amusing subject beneath the status of virtually everyone, allowing it to serve as an inside joke that united disparate classes, regions, and political groups. For a citizenry cleft by sectional rivalries and economic and social inequities, the sharing of prejudice against blacks—particularly when it manifested itself as a seemingly harmless joke about funny little pickaninnies—served as a healing national ritual for whites. In addition, nineteenth-century artists manipulated the figure of the homely and silly black child in ways that called attention to the superior qualities of white subjects. Contrast with white behavior and mores was usually the point of such images, though black children often displayed redeeming virtues of honesty, pluckishness, or cheerfulness.

A painting from 1813 by the German immigrant artist John Lewis Krimmel demonstrated that the visual convention of the pickaninny—the happy if dimwitted black child —was already in place in the early decades of the nineteenth century. *The Quilting Frolic* depicts a gathering of Northern townspeople that includes an African-American servant girl at the center of the occasion (fig. 63). Smiling widely at the guests who have just arrived, she absentmindedly offers tea to a harried young woman who is clearly too busy to pause for refreshments. The portrayal of the servant girl's lack of common sense alludes to one of the most typical faults assigned to black children, and the figure of the giddy black fiddler on the right of the canvas confirms that the defect is not one that will disappear with maturity. The musician fiddles away as the guests move to greet their hosts, interrupting their polite hellos with a cascade of music. Of course, African-Americans were thought to have a great proclivity for musical entertainments, and Krimmel showed the African-Americans muddling the niceties of the occasion in their childish eagerness to start the "frolic" segment of the evening. Their lack of polish flatters the rather common country rabble around them, as well as Krimmel's sophisticated Philadelphia audience.

By mid-century, Northern viewers' perception of African-American subjects was

FIG. 63   John Lewis Krimmel, *The Quilting Frolic*, 1813. Oil on canvas, 16 7/8 x 22 3/8 in. Courtesy of Winterthur Museum, Garden, and Library, Winterthur, Delaware.

affected by a new awareness of the circumstances of slaves on Southern plantations. The publication of firsthand accounts of slave life by white authors and former slaves shocked the non-slaveowning world with descriptions of the dark side of plantation life, including the abuse and neglect of slave children.[7] The autobiography of Frederick Douglass, a slave who escaped to the North in 1838, was one of the most widely read slave narratives, with eleven thousand copies selling within three years of the book's publication. Though Douglass did not suffer harsh punishments as a child on a Maryland plantation, his account of the meager amenities afforded to slave children appalled his many readers.

> I was seldom whipped by my old master, and suffered little from anything else than hunger and cold. I suffered much from hunger, but much more from cold. In hottest summer and coldest winter, I was kept almost naked—no shoes, no stockings, no jacket, no trousers, nothing on but a coarse tow linen shirt, reaching only to my knees. I had no bed. I must have perished with cold, but that, the coldest nights, I used to steal a bag which was used for carrying corn to the mill. I would crawl into this bag, and there sleep on the cold, damp, clay floor, with my head in and my feet out. My feet have been so cracked with the frost, that the pen with which I am writing tonight might be laid in the gashes. . . . Our food was coarse corn meal boiled. This was called

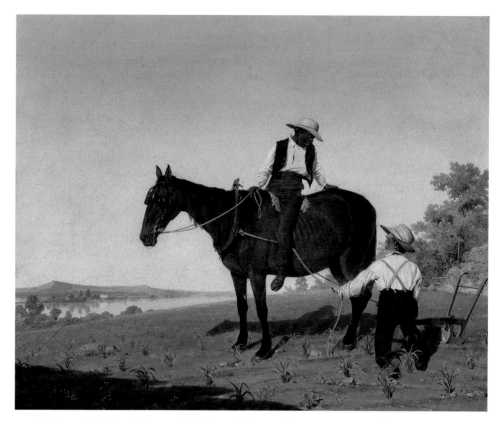

FIG. 64   James Goodwyn Clonney, *In the Cornfield*, 1844. Oil on canvas, 14 x 16⅞ in. Museum of Fine Arts, Boston. Gift of Martha C. Karolik for the Karolik Collection of American Paintings, 1815–1865.

mush. It was put into a large wooden tray or trough, and set down upon the ground. The children were then called, like so many pigs, and like so many pigs they would come and devour the mush; some with oyster shells, others with pieces of shingle, some with naked hands, and none with spoons. He that ate fastest got most; he that was strongest secured the best place; and few left the trough satisfied.[8]

By the 1840s, accounts like the one by Douglass helped to catapult the issue of slavery to the forefront of national and state politics and to divide the citizenry into pro-slavery and abolitionist camps. The annexation of slaveholding Texas in 1844 rallied support on both sides of the controversy, bringing a new level of vehemence to the conflict. In that year the artist James Goodwyn Clonney exhibited at the American Art-Union in New York a painting depicting two children—one white, one black—in a rural landscape (fig. 64). Titled *In the Cornfield*, the painting addressed the subject that was on every American's mind, portraying an interracial exchange taking place amid a sprouting corn crop that stretches into the distance. Preparing to start their plowing work, the white youth attends to the mechanics of the operation, hitching a rope to the plow, while his African-American companion sits on the plow horse and waits. The painting reverses the customary visual hierarchy defining the relationship between whites and blacks, since the white boy is placed in the position of a social inferior. On his knees in the dirt, he looks up as if posing a question to the black youth who sits astride.

In the Cornfield played on its audience's familiarity with stock figures of blacks in contemporary theater. The ineptitude of African-Americans performing simple farm chores was a favorite subject in the blackface minstrel shows that became wildly popular at mid-century. Emerging just as abolitionist and pro-slavery forces were squaring off in the northeast and in newly admitted states along the western frontier, minstrel performances featured white actors in ragged clothes and cork soot makeup who sang and told jokes and stories in black vernacular. The words of the minstrel song "Going Ober De Mountain," showed how blacks made a mess of even rudimentary farm work:

> *Dis nigger went to feed the sheep.*
> *He gib them green tobacker leaf,*
> *He went some water for to get,*
> *And carried it in a corn basket.*
>
> *He went to shell corn in de shed,*
> *He shelled his shins all bare instead,*
> *He went to feed de horse at de barn,*
> *He put himself in de trough for corn.*[9]

While "Going Ober De Mountain" equated the African-American with menial labor, barnyard animals, and corn, Clonney's *In the Cornfield* conveyed the idea that white citizens' preoccupation with slavery had inverted the proper order of American politics. It suggested that the welfare of a black minority was in command of the ballot box, with more important concerns of the white majority following behind. Though the social shadings of the painting may be invisible to modern audiences, the artist understood that his image of a towheaded country boy genuflecting before a seated "darky" would discomfit even staunchly abolitionist viewers—tapping into the sense of solidarity that emerged when white citizens of all classes and regional affiliations confronted African-Americans. *In the Cornfield* hinted that voters had been hornswoggled by campaign rhetoric devoted to debates about the place of blacks and now had no choice but to "plow the corn" of politics hitched to questions about slavery.[10]

Other artists played with the reversal of white and black roles as Clonney had done with his portrayal of boys in a cornfield. A lithograph executed by Edward C. Clay in 1839 pictured the nightmare that some white citizens feared would be the ultimate result of abolitionist efforts (fig. 65). *The Fruits of Amalgamation* presented a scene of domestic harmony, with a mother nursing an infant as she sits next to her husband and their older child. Their home is elegant, with richly upholstered furniture, fine carpets, and artwork displayed on the wall. Despite the veneer of normalcy of the household, close inspection reveals that the mistress is white and the master is black, a situation that white audiences

FIG. 65   Edward C. Clay, *The Fruits of Amalgamation*, 1839. Lithograph. American Antiquarian Society, Worcester, Massachusetts.

would have seen as a sickening travesty of middle-class decency. Puffing on a cheroot, the black "gentleman" takes his ease in his dressing robe as he peruses a newspaper called *The Emancipator*. He is watched by the scion of the family, a boy with stereotypically thick lips and woolly hair. The boy and his infant sibling are the abominable "fruits of amalgamation," mixed-race monsters who have no place in respectable society.[11]

In addition to serving as the visual punch line in parodies about interracial marriage, images of African-American children were used in other ways to show where blacks belonged. In the 1850s, Lilly Martin Spencer, an artist famous for her paintings of American children, invited viewers to share a visual joke about African-Americans' supposed love of finery (fig. 66).[12] The little girl represented in the print titled *Height of Fashion* amuses, not only because she is dressed in the clothes of an adult, but also because by her color she is de facto excluded from the white world of style and refinement. The coquettish tilt of her head and fetching smile show her talent for mimicry of white manners. The idea of careful observation is reinforced by the makeshift monocle, apparently fashioned from refuse metal or cans, that she holds in front of her eye as she looks out at the viewer. At the same time, the obvious fakery of the optical contraption calls audiences' attention to the sham of the "lady" in front of them. The white fur of the pet the girl holds in her arms, providing a striking contrast to her dark skin, underscores the idea of the African-American predilection for "putting on the dog."

In portraying a young girl's aspirations to elegance, Spencer's *Height of Fashion* drew on

FIG. 66 Lilly Martin Spencer, *Height of Fashion*, c. 1854. Oil on canvas,
32 3/8 x 24 in. Location unknown.

a well-established tradition of depicting blacks with ridiculous social pretensions, which
included representations of subjects decked out in outlandish and garish outfits attending
"Negro Balls" and other festive occasions. A lithograph published in New York in 1837
showed the "Philadelphia Fashions" of that year as interpreted by an African-American
couple (fig. 67). The triple flounces of the woman's sleeves and the multiple tiers of embell-
ishments on her bonnet are evidence of an abject ignorance of respectable attire. Her
companion's outfit, with ill-fitting velvet jacket, lace cuffs, and laughable white gloves, is
also an example of the vulgar fashions that blacks were thought to crave. Like Spencer's
overdressed miss, the pretentious dandy holds up a monocle to his eye—in this case to get
a better look at whites who are ogling him. Peering out at the viewer, he tells his ornately
dressed companion, "I look at dat white loafer wot looks at me. I guess he from New
York." Apparently, in the early decades of the nineteenth century, New Yorkers' reputation
for rudeness was already so well established that even African-Americans were allowed
to remark on it.

FIG. 67 *Philadelphia Fashions*, 1837. Lithograph published by H. R. Robinson, New York. The Library Company of Philadelphia.

FIG. 68 William Matthew Prior, *Three Sisters of the Coplan Family*, 1854. Oil on canvas, 26³/₄ x 36¹/₂ in. Museum of Fine Arts, Boston. Bequest of Martha C. Karolik for the Karolik Collection of American Paintings, 1815–1865.

It is revealing to contrast works that ridiculed blacks with a pretense to respectability with a contemporary portrait of three African-American girls that may have been commissioned by the sitters' family (fig. 68). In 1854, the artist William Matthew Prior portrayed the daughters of an African-American pawnbroker in Boston. An itinerant New Englander who produced paintings for several middle-class black clients, Prior showed the Coplan girls—Eliza, Nellie, and Margaret—in dress and setting indistinguishable from similar portrayals of white children. The girls are simply and neatly dressed, with lace trim on their undergarments and hair tied up with ribbons. Sitting next to a window opening to a sun-filled sky, they hold the usual emblems of female virtue: flowers, fruit, and a book. The artist carefully noted the rich color of the sisters' skin and their thick dark hair—features that set them apart from their white neighbors. There is none of the condescension or derision, however, that usually went hand-in-hand with attributes of blackness. Undoubtedly in alignment with Mr. Coplan's aspirations for his daughters, the painting pictured the Coplan children as respectable members of the Boston community.

While Spencer and Prior were making portrayals that sidestepped the issue of slavery, abolitionists were producing pictures and stories about black children as a strategic element of their anti-slavery campaigns. Many of these works were addressed to white children, who were seen as a means to influence the attitudes of their parents—as well as the key to the future of slavery itself. The presence of African-American subjects in schoolbooks and children's magazines reflects the pervasiveness of the struggle over slavery and abolitionists' resolve to leave no portion of the citizenry uninformed about their cause. Since the South did not have a significant publishing industry, it was easy for Northern opponents of slavery to dominate the readership for children's books and magazines.

The Anti-Slavery Alphabet, published in 1846, targeted young children who were beginning to read (fig. 69). "You are young, 'tis true. But there's much that you can do," the authors explained in the preface. The book included an abolitionist verse for every letter of the alphabet, educating pupils simultaneously about vocabulary and the evils of slavery:

I is the Infant, from the arms
Of its fond mother torn
And, at a public auction, sold
With horses, cows, and corn.
J is the Jail, upon whose floor
That wretched mother lay,
Until her cruel master came,
and carried her away.
K is the kidnapper, who stole
That little child and mother
Shrieking, it clung around her, but
He tore them from each other.

FIG. 69   Letters A, B, C, D, from *The Anti-Slavery Alphabet*, Philadelphia: Printed for The Anti Slavery Fair, 1846. Private collection.

For older readers, *The Child's Anti-Slavery Book* presented stories and pictures about the South's "peculiar institution." One tale described the misadventures of Little Lewis, a slave boy who is eager to learn to read. The story opens with Lewis straining to recognize the letters of the alphabet in a primer given to him by a kindly white child. "'A,B,C,' said Little Lewis to himself, as he bent eagerly over a ragged primer," the narrative begins. "'Here's anoder A, an' there's anoder, an' there's anoder C, but I can't find anoder B. Miss Katy said I must find just so many as I can. Dear Little Miss Katy!'"[13] Little Lewis is later sold at a slave auction, and an accompanying illustration shows a cigar-smoking slave trader squeezing the child's arm to gauge its strength (fig. 70). The expression of saintly resignation on Lewis's face shows he is prepared for the many hardships that await him before he ultimately reaches freedom in the North.

The best-known abolitionist text was, of course, Harriet Beecher Stowe's *Uncle Tom's Cabin*, which sold more than three hundred thousand copies following its publication in 1852. The book's highly dramatized account of the brutalities of slavery caused a nation-wide sensation and ignited a wave of protest against slaveholding. The impact of *Uncle Tom's Cabin* was such that, for the rest of the century and well after, its characters served as templates for portrayals of African-Americans in literature, theater, and the visual arts. Children played a pivotal role in *Uncle Tom's Cabin*, both as personifications of virtue and

FIG. 70   "Little Lewis Sold," from *The Child's Anti-Slavery Book*,
published by Carlton & Porter, New York, 1859. Private collection.

as mirrors of adult shortcomings. Topsy, the recalcitrant, larcenous slave child who has
been abused by her first owners, embodied the degrading effects of slavery on both the
slaveholder and the enslaved. However, though she learned to lie and steal to survive
brutal circumstances, Topsy also responded to kindness and showed that compassionate
training could redeem her. For decades after the publication of *Uncle Tom's Cabin*, pictures
and stories about little pickaninnies modeled after Stowe's Topsy proliferated.

In 1860, pro-slavery forces responded to the abolitionist campaign with a children's
reading book that posed an alternative to Beecher's interpretation of plantation life (fig.
71). *The Southern Primer*, published in Richmond, Virginia, presented the lists of capital
letters, vowels, and consonants that were ubiquitous in American schoolbooks. The primer
also included a brief but pointed lesson on the peaceful routines of the cotton field: "Let
us take a walk this fine day. We will go and see the field hands pick the snow white bolls.
Hark! Hear their songs from all parts of the field as they pick, pick, pick, and fill their sacks
with the soft down. See! There are the huts where they all live. One, two, three, four, five,
six. Six nice huts."

With the outbreak of the Civil War in 1861, some of America's most prominent artists
produced images of African-American children. Winslow Homer made childhood subjects
one of his specialties during the 1860s and 1870s, and he proved especially adept at avoiding
the overt stereotypes that characterized popular images of African-Americans. A contemporary critic praised Homer for the "originality" of his depictions of blacks when compared with those in popular magazines, which were "overrun with pitiable caricatures of
negroes."[14] Although his works allowed African-Americans a dignity and interiority
uncommon in the works of his contemporaries, however, Homer often merely reformulated

WORDS OF FIVE LETTERS. 27

Sheep	swims	stalk	check	ditch	beans
geese	birch	catch	truck	hedge	night
lambs	lurch	latch	drink	wedge	light
jambs	teach	hatch	brink	kedge	sight
grass	sting	watch	heard	ledge	white
brass	sling	match	beard	lodge	spite
frock	makes	patch	sleep	swamp	might
clock	bakes	birch	beast	cramp	spank

The Cot-ton Field.

Let us take a walk this fine day. We will go and see the field hands pick the snow white bolls. Hark! hear their songs from all parts of the wide field, as they pick, pick, pick, and fill their sacks with the soft down.

See! there are the huts where they all live. One, two, three, four five, six. Six nice huts

FIG. 71   From *The Southern Primer; Or Child's First Lessons in Spelling and Reading*, 1860. Private collection.

racist conventions. Using his keen eye for visual nuance, the artist was able to reinforce his representations of blacks with the weight of a meticulously fashioned realism.

Army Boots, a painting Homer executed in 1865, presented a pair of black youngsters inside a Union tent (fig. 72). Many African-Americans came to the Union side as "contraband," escaped slaves who were claimed as war prisoners by Northern troops. Males were accepted as "boots"—the term for new recruits—and most were given menial jobs such as tending animals or shoeshine duty. Homer's smiling youths seem to be content with their assignment to the footwear brigade, though the artist chose to portray them resting in their sleeping quarters rather than helping with the many camp chores that were delegated to those of lowest rank. The sunlight that streams through the tent fabric sets the hour as work time, while the pair of dusty boots featured prominently in the foreground points to duties not yet completed. Inside a space strewn with their belongings, the boys' sprawled postures and easy grins hint at a benevolent laziness fundamentally at odds with the spit-and-polish discipline of military life.[15]

FIG. 72 Winslow Homer, *Army Boots*, 1865. Oil on canvas, 14 x 18 in. Hirshhorn Museum and Sculpture Garden, Smithsonian Institution, Washington, D.C. Gift of the Joseph H. Hirshhorn Foundation, 1966.

FIG. 73 "Little Joe, the Contraband," 1860s, sheet music cover published by Horace Waters. Private collection.

Although Homer was praised for the originality of his portrayals of blacks, the theme of African-American bootblacks in the Union army was a common topic in Civil War imagery, stories, and music (fig. 73). One popular song, "Little Joe, the Contraband," told about a boy who ran away from his master in Virginia to join the Union side:

And who are you, my merry boy
With blacking brush in hand.
Oh, I's a happy darky, sah!
I's Joe de Contraband.
I's born in ole virginny, sah,
I a hut on massa's land;
And sere's where Joe lib seben years
Afore he's Contraband.
And now we works, and gets de pay!
We owns ourselves! We's free!
We's gwin to hab a house some day,
To lib in! Yas we be!
My daddy fights for Uncle Abe,
Mammy works on de land,
Dis chile he bracks the gemmens boots,
Becase he's contraband.[16]

The theme of the Union shoeshine boys retained its popularity well after the conflict between the states ended, when the subject became a vehicle for sentimental portrayals of white paternalism and ideas about black childishness. In 1872, the children's journal *Our Young Folks* published a story about "Tobe," a runaway slave boy who is given the job of caring for a Union officer's favorite boots. After Tobe's party is lost behind Confederate lines, a rebel soldier demands he turn over the boots he has been charged to protect. Even when threatened with a revolver, the loyal Tobe clings doggedly to the footwear of "Massa Cap'n." Predictably, Tobe is shot by the exasperated rebel before he and his band are run off by Union soldiers and the captain's return. The popular illustrator Sol Eytinge produced a depiction of the moment before Tobe dies, when the captain finds him clutching the bloodstained boots (fig. 74). The words beneath the image are Tobe's last: "Mass Cap'n, I done de bes' I knowed,—I kep' de boots!"[17]

The book *Hand Shadow Stories* encouraged Northern children to invent their own reenactments of contraband adventures. Published in 1863, the texts showed young readers how to place their hands together in front of a candle or lantern to make the figure of "Sambo the Contraband" in the shadow cast on the wall (fig. 75). Accompanied by illustrations instructing readers about creating shadow pictures of geese and donkeys, the book's spectral image of Sambo had a chilling authenticity. Presenting the subject with eyes

"MASS CAP'N, I DONE DE BES' I KNOWED,—I KEP' DE BOOTS!"

FIG. 74   "Mass Cap'n, I Done De Bes' I Knowed, —I Kep' De Boots!" from *Our Young Folks*, 1872. Private collection.

FIG. 75   "Sambo," from *Hand Shadow Stories*, 1863. Boston: Taggard & Thompson. Private collection.

14

SAMBO.

SAMBO THE CONTRABAND.

 IT is a black man!" said Addie.

"Yes," said her mother. "His name is Sambo. He was a slave once, but came north, where, by working hard, saving his money, and the kindness of the people in the village where he lived, was able to buy a small cottage and garden, and a cow.

"By and by he lost all his property, and could get no food for his cow. He was very honest, and did not like the name of thief; but after thinking it over in a number of ways, he said that his cow must either die, or he must go to his neighbor's barn and get hay for her. One night he went, and began to pitch off some to take home. At the same time he was talking aloud to himself, saying, 'Honesty is the best policy, but my cow shall not die.'

"At last, his honesty made him pitch the hay back on the mow, saying, 'Honesty is the best policy, and my cow shall die.' But then the thought of his poor cow

FIG. 76 Winslow Homer, *Contraband*, 1875. Watercolor, 8 x 5 in. The Canajoharie Library and Art Gallery, Canajoharie, New York.

looking up and an open mouth, the Sambo hand shadow conjured up the breathless desperation of a fugitive slave. The book's publishers may have noted the disturbing realism of the image, which may explain why the accompanying story did not elaborate on the subject of slaves escaping. When a child in the narrative asks what the word "contraband" means, the woman narrator replies: "My darling . . . You are too young to know why the black men are so called. When you are older, I will tell you all about it."[18]

The production of pictures of contrabands continued after the war, when Winslow Homer turned again to the subject. His 1875 watercolor titled *Contraband* was displayed at the American Society of Painters of Watercolors in February 1876, and viewers probably felt very much at home with the familiar theme (fig. 76). Homer diffused the frightening connotations of runaway black men by presenting the subject as a young boy. Sitting next to a young man in a Zouave uniform, the little contraband seems ready to accept a drink from the man's canteen. Outfitted in their startling red caps, blue jackets, and baggy red pants, the Zouaves were the elite troops of the Union army and a favorite subject of pictures and stories in the Northern press. They were renowned for their bravery and military skills, though the high visibility of their uniforms made them a favorite target of Confederate sharpshooters.[19] By juxtaposing the ragged contraband with a soldier who represented the glory of Union manhood—and whose uniform was derived from North African tribesmen—Homer called attention to the drama implicit in such a meeting. The artist left the background of the picture dark and undefined and provided only minimal delineation of the foreground, as if he knew he could rely on his audience's familiarity with the subject to fill in the details. Making no attempt to hide the fact that the work was his own reconstruction of events long past, the artist used the blankness of his painting to allow symbolic connections to insinuate themselves into viewers' awareness.

Homer used the same child model he used in *Contraband* in several other paintings he made the same year, inviting audiences to make narrative connections between the works. The artist's portrayals of the young contraband in *Weaning the Calf, The Unruly Calf, The Busy Bee, Taking Sunflower to Teacher*, and other works seemed to follow the boy as he adapted to life after slavery (figs. 77–80). Performing a variety of farm tasks in an idyllic rural setting, the Civil War runaway distances himself from his, and the nation's, turbulent past. The happy ending of the sequence is implicit in the subject of the watercolor *Taking Sunflower to Teacher*, which recalled the prohibition of even rudimentary forms of education for slaves—a notorious offense of Southern planters that had been singled out for special criticism in the Northern press before the war. Relying again on viewers' willingness to participate in what had become a national myth by the 1870s, Homer evoked with his simple image and its suggestive title the many new benefits—including access to public education—that were thought to have accrued to emancipated blacks after 1865.

In 1876, Homer continued his exploration of African-American children in the postwar environment. A painting he titled *The Watermelon Boys* took the subject of black children

FIG. 77   Winslow Homer, *Weaning the Calf*, 1875. Oil on canvas, 24 x 38 in. The North Carolina Museum of Art, Raleigh. Purchased with funds from the State of North Carolina.

FIG. 78   Winslow Homer, *The Unruly Calf*, 1875. Oil on canvas. 24 1/4 x 38 1/2 in. Location unknown.

adapting to new circumstances one step further, showing a pair of black boys in an easy friendship with a white companion (fig. 81). The three youngsters are feasting on fruit, a repetition of the playful fruit pilfering that was a ubiquitous subject in nineteenth-century representations of the American country boy. Where country boys typically were shown stealing green apples or cherries, however, the booty of Homer's trio is a large watermelon with crimson flesh that enlivens the painting's otherwise subdued palette. The watermelon had functioned as an emblem of blackness in the United States since the first half of the century and it featured prominently in racist depictions that proliferated after the Civil War. Minstrel performances often included jokes and skits about watermelon-loving blacks

FIG. 79   Winslow Homer, *The Busy Bee*, 1875. Watercolor and gouache on paper,
10¹/₈ x 9¹/₂ in. Private collection.

who could not resist the temptation of the fruit. An actor with Buckley's New Orleans
Serenaders, a widely known minstrel troupe, was so taken with the "grotesque outfit" of an
African-American watermelon street vendor in Savannah in 1856 that he bought the peddler's clothes, cart, and donkey and created "The Watermelon Man," an act he continued
to perform to popular acclaim until his retirement in 1895.[20]

Although the watermelon in *The Watermelon Boys* was an icon of racism, the inclusion
of the white child in the group raised the work above the level of mere stereotype. The
painting boldly introduced the subject of racial integration, an issue that was a minefield
of controversy in the postbellum period. Few artists were willing to venture into this per-
ilous territory, and those who did often did so tentatively by representing chance encounters
between white and black children. Setting such meetings in the realm of childhood disconnected them from prevalent fears about interracial marriages, the potential for black
domination of the labor market, and other scenarios that played on white imaginations in
the postwar period.

FIG. 80 Winslow Homer, *Taking Sunflower to Teacher*, 1875. Watercolor on paper, 7⅝ x 6³/₁₆ in. Georgia Museum of Art, University of Georgia, Athens. Eva Underhill Holbrook Memorial Collection of American Art. Gift of Alfred H. Holbrook.

FIG. 81   Winslow Homer, *The Watermelon Boys*, 1876. Oil on canvas, 24 1/8 x 38 1/8 in. Cooper-Hewitt, National Design Museum, Smithsonian Institution, New York. Gift of Charles Savage Homer, Jr. Photograph by Michael Fischer.

FIG. 82 "Flibbertigibbit," from *Our Young Folks*, March 1871. Private collection.

FIG. 83 "Going Halves," from *Our Young Folks*, April 1867. Private collection.

Two illustrations published in *Our Young Folks* a short time after the war showed black and white children testing the waters of interracial friendships (figs. 82–83). In an image titled "Flibbertigibbit," a pair of black and white farm boys watch while their two small dogs meet, sniffing and wagging their tails. The boys are similar in age and stature, and the playful stance of their canine companions bodes well for a new friendship. The text immediately qualifies what the artist portrayed as a meeting of equals, however. "There never was anything more like a monkey and less like a boy than Flibbertigibbit," the story began, telling about a boy "who would have been a perfect treasure to an Ethiopian minstrel troupe" because he was a marvel of perpetual motion—dancing, performing somersaults, and jumping like a wild animal. It was not the fault of the white children if they could not interact with this human tornado or if his unceasing gyrations made it impossible for him to attend school.

The image that accompanied the short story titled "Going Halves" in an 1867 issue of *Our Young Folks* showed a white boy in a natty sailor outfit feeding a stick of candy to a ragged black child. As if in acknowledgment of the problems inherent in such an exchange, a dog at the white child's feet bares his teeth and snarls at the black youngster. Like the illustration, the story was filled with conflicting elements of bigotry and optimism about the possibility of racial harmony. Presented as the true account of an exchange observed by the narrator, the tale related the good deed of Percy, a "dear, bright, blue-eyed boy" who, despite the cruel taunts of a neighborhood ruffian, offered half his candy to "Darkey," a neighborhood child.

> Percy, as I said before, is a bright blue-eyed fellow, who is always willing to give a portion of his candy, cake, or apple to a friend; but he deserves particular credit for "going halves" this summer afternoon; for Percy is also extremely sensitive, and, to say the least of it, it wasn't pleasant to hear Johnny McCafferty shouting at the top of his voice, "Ha-a! Givin candy to a nagur! Givin candy to a nagur!" . . . Percy waxed indignant, and shook his little round fist at Johnny McCafferty. "Johnny McCafferty," said he, "you just hush! He's no more of a nigger than you are, *under his skin*. And now I won't give you a piece." . . . Darkey opened his mouth, and it wasn't small,—no, to tell the truth, it was large, very large (Percy seemed rather taken aback by the prospect at first, but stood his ground with the air of a boy who had resolved to do what is right . . .). "Golly, that's good and sweet," said Darkey, smacking his lips; but just then I heard the voice of his master. "You young scamp," cried he, from his parlor window, "haven't you been to the butcher's yet? You were sent half an hour ago. Just you wait, sir,"— and the window went down with a bang.[21]

If *The Watermelon Boys*, "Flibbertigibbit," and "Going Halves" attempted to portray harmonious relationships between whites and blacks, the habit of discrimination that was pervasive in both Northern and Southern societies proved hard to break. It is significant that, in an engraving based on *The Watermelon Boys*, Homer included the figure of an irate farmer menacing the boys from over the fence. Though the figure is absent from the painting of the same scene, the backward glance of the African-American boy in the middle of the canvas and the centrality of the watermelon retain both the suggestion of impending trouble and the idea of the persistence of racist ideas in American culture. The youth of the watermelon boys and the verdant landscape around them set the stage of an Edenic garden, with the fruit they share a symbol of an impending fall from grace. Sitting next to a long fence that bisects the landscape, the white and black boys who are "going halves" on the watermelon will grow to manhood in a society divided along racial lines, where attempts to even conceptualize a multiracial polity will be foiled by the absence of a visual or verbal language of unity.

Photographs of a group of emancipated slave children who were brought to the North in 1863 explored the theme of racial integration that Homer took up in *The Watermelon Boys*. Though both Homer's painting and the photographs of former slaves represented a space where whites and blacks intersected, the photographs showed mulatto children who physically embodied an interracial connection. Contemporary audiences, who saw the

FIG. 84   M. H. Kimball, *Emancipated Slaves*, 1863. Photograph with printed captions. The New-York Historical Society.

images when they were reproduced as engravings in *Harper's Weekly*, were astonished to see apparently white children who had been rescued by missionaries from slavery in the Deep South (fig. 84). The caption beneath one of the photographs identified the subjects as "Emancipated Slaves, White and Colored." During the Civil War, the group traveled on a public tour to Philadelphia and New York to raise money for an educational fund for former slaves in Louisiana. To complement the public appearances of the former slaves, organizers also produced and sold a collection of small "carte de visite" photographs of the group. These images, which presented the children in a variety of combinations and poses, usually focused on the subjects with the most distinctly Caucasian features, often eliminating or relegating to the background those who were obviously of mixed race.[22]

The interest in the mulatto children from Louisiana was part of an ongoing discussion about the markers of racial identity that engaged white Americans before, during, and after the war.[23] The former slaves Rosina Downs, Rebecca Huger, and Charles Taylor were

FIG. 85   Currier and Ives, publishers, *The Old Barn Floor*, 1868. Lithograph, 17¹³/₁₆ x 23¹⁵/₁₆ in. Museum of the City of New York. The Harry T. Peters Collection.

"as white, as intelligent, as docile, as most of our own children," and their pictures compelled a national audience to consider whether race was an element of appearance or something essential that permeated the blood. Reinforced by the image of black children who looked white, American ideas about childhood innocence and tractability seemed to trump the issue of race. The accompanying article in *Harper's* expressed indignation that the children had been refused lodging at a Philadelphia hotel, although the hotel owner was acting according to the definition upon which white Americans in both North and South agreed, namely that any amount of African blood conferred blackness. The white-black children brought audiences to the uncomfortable place where notions about childhood nurture and Christian benevolence toward the disadvantaged collided with discrimination based on spurious constructions of race.

Artists' interest in black children reached its peak during the Civil War and Reconstruction years, when the subject emerged as a symbol of the humanitarianism of the Northern cause. Many of these works adopted musical themes, clinging to the old visual conventions of contented slaves on the plantation even in the radically changed environment of the postwar period. *The Old Barn Floor*, a lithograph published by Currier and Ives in 1868, depicted an African-American banjo player and child inside a barn, with white observers appearing on the periphery of the scene (fig. 85). As the banjo player smiles in approval, the child waves his arms in gleeful abandon and lifts his feet. The title of the print invites viewers to imagine the sound of the boy's footwork as he executes one of the athletic dances for which African-Americans were renowned. Flying through the paces of dances that audiences may have known as the "Buck and Wing," or the "Buzzard Lope," the boy is watched by a farmer and his wife who pause in the middle of chores suggested by the neat farm buildings between them. A dog wandering through the barn bisects the space between white and black, consigning the African-American revelers to a place next to the stables, where a horse chews contentedly on a mouthful of hay. Through its engaging musical subject and careful delineation of the separate spheres of the races, *The Old Barn Floor* offered a pleasing forecast for the postbellum years, a visual idyll appropriate for wall decoration in respectable homes, North and South.

A Virginny Breakdown, painted by the Virginia artist John Adams Elder, presented a musical subject from a Southern perspective (fig. 86). Executed a few years after 1877, the official end of Reconstruction, the painting invited viewers to assess the results of the Northern efforts to break up the old order of Southern society after the Civil War.[24] The painting's setting is a rural cabin, a dwelling that resembles one of the "neat huts" that made up plantation slave quarters in the days before the war. At the center of the canvas, a pair of boys—one dancing, the other playing a mouth harp—entertain family members with a Virginia Breakdown, a popular dance that was a mainstay of antebellum plantation fetes and slave-quarter festivities.[25] A grandmotherly woman on the right of the canvas inclines her head with keen interest while a younger woman holding a baby gazes thoughtfully into space, as if musing on dancers and musicians of times gone by. Representing the past, the present, and the future, the multiple generations of the family meld together through the power of music. The performance engages even the newest family addition—an infant on his mother's lap—who raises his hand toward the youthful dancer in a gesture of benediction.

Virginny Breakdown used the themes of childhood and music to answer the question posed in editorials throughout the North and South during the postwar decade: What will the former slaves do with their freedom? The painting focused attention on the two youths at the center of the canvas, subjects who represent the segment of the population that stood to benefit most from Reconstruction policies. The Freedman's Bureau and other political and social institutions charged with reconstituting Southern society made African-American children the foundation of many of their campaigns, which included the creation of an extensive system of schools for freedmen. Though the boys in *Virginny Breakdown* are the first generation of Southern blacks born in freedom, the painting shows that little has changed since slavery days—while also handing them the blame for their failure to improve. In an era when many Americans were keenly interested in acquiring tasteful domestic amenities—upholstered furniture, window drapery, fine carpeting—the rude cabin serves as an indictment of the family's lack of enterprise. Farm acreage and tools beckon in the doorway—symbols of the land allotments that Reconstruction leaders claimed would help to lead Southern blacks out of oppression. Still the slaves of their own sensuous natures, the boys dance away precious work time—caught in the thrall of

FIG. 86   John Adams Elder, *A Virginny Breakdown*, c. 1880. Oil on canvas, 18½ x 22¼ in. Virginia Museum of Fine Arts, Richmond. The Virginia Art Fund. Photograph by Ron Jennings, © Virginia Museum of Fine Arts.

music. At a moment when Americans around the country were asking what the struggle of Reconstruction efforts and the blood of the Civil War dead had accomplished in the end, *Virginny Breakdown* offered a bitter response: nothing.

Elder's painting made its point by connecting with a decades-long tradition of portrayals of black children dancing and making music. In the 1840s and 1850s, the acclaimed artist William Sidney Mount of Long Island produced several depictions of African-American children in music-related situations.[26] One of his first such works was *Dance of the Haymakers*, a painting from 1845 that showed a group of farm laborers frolicking (fig. 87). The hay strewn on the ground at the entrance of the barn and the shadows cast by an afternoon sun set the scene at the end of the workday, evoking the idea that the haymakers have earned their rustic entertainment through the sweat of their brows. At the periphery of the merriment, an African-American boy keeps time with the fiddler's melody, tapping on the barn door with a pair of drumsticks. The sharp turn of his head shows he is carefully watching the haymakers' performance and his lifted heel echoes the men's exuberant footwork. Though he stays outside, the youth is literally knocking to get in, using the Morse code of drumming to communicate between the black and white worlds.

FIG. 87   William Sidney Mount, *Dance of the Haymakers*, 1845. Oil on canvas, 24 x 29 in. The Long Island Museum of American Art, History, and Carriages, Stony Brook, New York. Gift of Mr. and Mrs. Ward Melville, 1950.

It is significant that the boy has drumsticks but no drum, a detail that recalls the variety of controls that were imposed on African-Americans' ability to make music and other kinds of noise during the nineteenth century. Many Southern states prohibited drumming by slaves, because plantation owners feared their workers would use it as a means of communication to organize insurrections. A statute enacted in Georgia in 1845 prohibited slaves from using any kind of loud instrument, although they circumvented the law by using sticks, bones, and hand clapping. While slave owners feared slaves would use music to assemble conspirators, they nevertheless forced them to sing while laboring in the fields as a means of tracking workers' whereabouts.[27]

In his autobiography, published in the same year that Mount painted *Dance of the Haymakers*, the former slave Frederick Douglass described the melancholy purpose of music on Southern plantations, an account that contradicted most contemporary visual and literary portrayals of blacks making music. He described being deeply disturbed by the songs he heard as an enslaved child in Maryland:

They told a tale of woe which was then altogether beyond my feeble comprehension; they were tones loud, long, and deep; they breathed the prayer and complaint of souls boiling over with the bitterest anguish. Every tone was a testimony against slavery, and a prayer to God for deliverance from chains. . . . I have often been utterly astonished, since I came to the north, to find persons who could speak of the singing, among slaves, as evidence of their contentment and happiness. It is impossible to conceive of a greater mistake.[28]

Although Douglass portrayed music as a medium through which slaves lamented their lot, white artists invariably pictured African-American music makers as a merry band, with childhood subjects adding to the idea of musicians' carefree existence. In a painting from 1856, *The Banjo Player*, William Sidney Mount depicted a cheerful youth playing the banjo, an African-derived instrument that by mid-century had become an icon of the minstrel show (fig. 88). With his toothy grin, the banjo player displayed the cheerfulness that audiences expected of black performers. Mount also, however, depicted his sitter with an attention to individual features and form that challenged the standardized black features—coal-dark skin, bulging eyes, and inflated lips—of popular convention. Mount's sitter may have been a member of one of the "Ethiopian" minstrel troupes that capitalized on the popularity of blackface performers by offering a selection of songs and dances in an exaggerated African-American dialect. Though blacks were always the butt of the joke at these shows, Mount's sympathetic representation resisted the usual protocol. The boy's confident posture and the sensitive placement of his fingers on the banjo strings mark him as the master of his domain, while the gold chain at his pocket and his elegant waistcoat vouch that audiences have paid him well for his musical skill.

At the end of the century, Henry Ossawa Tanner, an African-American artist, took up the subject of the banjo player, exploring as Mount had the connection between musical artistry and the place of blacks in American society (fig. 89). Tanner's painting from 1893, *The Banjo Lesson*, portrayed a barefoot boy holding a banjo and seated on the lap of a grandfatherly older man. Pictured in a sparsely furnished room, the man and the boy sit near pots and pans, an eating table, hat and coat, and other objects that refer to the routines of everyday life. Within this intimate domestic space, the banjo lesson embodies the family bond between pupil and teacher. The boy's focused expression and the tilt of his head reflect the effort of learning the banjo's intricate strumming technique, while the older man assists by pressing his fingers to the banjo's neck to produce the correct notes. The banjo was considered particularly unforgiving of inexpert handling, a subject endlessly exploited in the raucous satires of contemporary blackface minstrelsy, as well as in a Currier and Ives lithograph from the 1880s (fig. 90).

The nostalgic mood of *The Banjo Lesson* may have been an expression of the artist's homesickness and resignation to a life of exile. Tanner executed the painting soon after moving to Paris, where he spent the rest of his life as an expatriate. He had been a student of Thomas Eakins at the Pennsylvania Academy of Fine Arts and the second African-American to gain admission to the school, but Tanner chafed at the limitations that racial prejudice imposed on his artistic career in the United States. He rejected the African-

FIG. 88   William Sidney Mount, *The Banjo Player*, 1856. Oil on canvas, 36 x 29 in. The Long Island Museum of American Art, History, and Carriages, Stony Brook, New York. Gift of Mr. and Mrs. Ward Melville, 1955.

FIG. 89   Henry Ossawa Tanner, *The Banjo Lesson*, 1893. Oil on canvas, 48 x 35 in. Hampton University Museum, Hampton, Virginia.

PUBLISHED BY CURRIER & IVES.   COPYRIGHT 1886 BY CURRIER & IVES, N.Y.   115 NASSAU ST. NEW YORK.

THE DARKTOWN BANJO CLASS - OFF THE KEY.
"If yous cant play de music, jes leff de banjo go!"

FIG. 90   Currier and Ives, publishers, *The Darktown Banjo Class—Off the Key: "If Yous Can't Play de Music, Jes Leff de Banjo Go!"* 1886. Lithograph, 9 $^{13}/_{16}$ x 13 $^{7}/_{16}$ in. Museum of the City of New York. The Harry T. Peters Collection.

American genre subjects that his supporters believed would bring him success and established himself as a painter of biblical scenes. *The Banjo Lesson* was in a sense the artist's backward glance at the land of his birth, a recognition of the artistic and social legacy that had both drawn and pushed him to Europe.

The melancholy, elegiac quality of *The Banjo Lesson* connects the painting to an important development in ongoing debates about "the Negro problem" in the United States at the end of the nineteenth century. Tanner painted the work soon after data from the national census of 1890 began to circulate, information that was interpreted as showing that the black population in the United States was declining relative to whites. Reputable authorities around the nation, including scientists, economists, and historians, promoted the census statistics as proof of Charles Darwin's theories about the "survival of the fittest." In the late 1850s and 1860s, the publication of Darwin's *Origin of Species* had inspired a wave of racist predictions about the longevity of different racial groups in the United States, and the decline in the black population relative to whites in the last decades of the century was accepted as final scientific evidence of the flawed biology of blacks. With African-Americans apparently on the road to extinction, many white citizens felt they had been liberated from the menace of a growing black presence. In an article published in the *North American Review* in 1891, James Bryce, a British scholar who specialized in American institutions, affirmed the triumph of Darwinian principles. "In proving that the colored population grows more slowly than the white, the census just taken relieves . . . a source of anxiety," he explained. "It is now clear that the negro, regarded as a factor in

FIG. 91 *George Thatcher's Greatest Minstrels: "Hello! My Baby,"* 1899. Lithographic poster by the Strobridge Litho Company. Library of Congress, Prints and Photographs Division, Washington, D.C.

the whole community, is becoming far weaker; nor is the prospect likely to be arrested."[29]

In the context of the new information about the status of the black population, *The Banjo Lesson* is more than the artist's individual farewell to his homeland. It is also a meditation on the passing of a way of life, even as it offers the possibility of regeneration. In selecting the topic of his painting, Tanner was certainly aware of the links between his portrayal of African-American banjo players and the contemptuous stereotypes that persisted throughout the century—and were growing even more prevalent as the century drew to a close (fig. 91). A deeply religious man who wanted to convey moral lessons through his paintings, Tanner used *The Banjo Lesson* to confront racist practices, as well as to offer an alternate interpretation of black character and destiny. In a nod to the popular stage, the artist created a spotlight to surround his figures, making a glowing circle around them on the floor. The quality of the light acknowledges the connection between the subject and the antics of minstrel performances, but it also creates a consecrated space resembling the illuminated circles that surrounded Christ and his beatified followers in European liturgical imagery.

Through the sanctified light and reverential mood of his painting, Tanner signals that something other than the usual slaphappy tomfoolery is afoot. The boy and his teacher enact a solemn covenant as the knowledge of music is passed from one generation to the next. A portrayal about black Americans painted by a black American, *The Banjo Lesson* represents the African-American as the Artist, a figure with a priestlike power to transport his audience to a realm that transcends the routines of everyday life.[30] In the guise of catering to white expectations, *The Banjo Lesson* affirmed the longevity of the black race —though it pointedly excluded the upcoming generation from the goals and pursuits of American progress. Tanner's portrayal of a boy learning to play the banjo conceded that the legacy of the past was inescapable, but it also demonstrated that African-Americans had learned to sustain themselves in the rituals of creative endeavor.

Chapter 4

RAGAMUFFIN

It should be remembered that there are no dangers to the value of property or to the permanency of our institutions, so great as those from the existence of such a class of vagabond, ignorant, ungoverned children. . . . They will vote. They will have the same rights as we ourselves, even though they have grown up ignorant of moral principle, as any savage or Indian. They will poison society. They will perhaps be embittered at the wealth and luxuries they never share. Then let society beware, when the outcast, vicious, reckless multitude of New York boys, swarming now in every foul valley and low street, come to know their power and use it!

CHARLES LORING BRACE, *Eleventh Annual Report, Children's Aid Society,* 1864

In the spring of 1864, Eastman Johnson exhibited a painting titled *The Young Sweep* at the Metropolitan Fair in New York (fig. 92). Johnson was one of many artists who sent works to the fair, which was organized to raise money for Union troops fighting in the Civil War. *The Young Sweep* represented an uncomfortable subject for Northern audiences as the conflict wore on. Many had criticized Lincoln for issuing the Emancipation Proclamation, fearing that freed slaves would flood the North in search of work and land. Because of the surge in immigration at mid-century, New York, Boston, Philadelphia, and other Northern cities already grappled with significant levels of unemployment, homelessness, and the social unrest that accompanied these problems. Although those in the North were increasingly confident about a victory for the Union, they were also deeply concerned about its effects on the social equilibrium of Northern cities.

The Young Sweep portrayed a black street urchin, a symbol of the needy masses ready to converge on New York. When an anti-draft riot broke out in the city in 1863, an angry mob made an orphanage for black children the target of its fury. "Hundreds and perhaps thousands of the rioters, the majority of whom were women and children, entered the premises and in the most excited and violent manner they ransacked and plundered the building from cellar to garret," reported a *New York Times* account. "After the entire building had been ransacked, and every article deemed worth carrying away had been taken—and

OPPOSITE: Detail of fig. 109.

FIG. 92   Eastman Johnson, *The Young Sweep*, 1863. Oil on paper board, 12¼ x 9⅜ in. Private collection.

this included even the little garments for the orphans, which were contributed by the benevolent ladies of this city—the premises were fired on the first floor. . . . There is scarcely one brick left upon another of the Orphan Asylum."[1] That the rioters would purposely seek out the most defenseless members of the city's dispossessed was evidence of the degree of animosity that festered between groups jockeying for position in the city's labor market.

The Young Sweep pictured one of the waifs outside the reach of New York's "benevolent ladies." His soot-smudged face and worn sweeping brush speak of the harsh conditions of his work, while the heavy blanket he totes under his arm hints at makeshift sleeping arrangements. Most chimney sweeps were vagrant children working under the supervision of employers who sought out sweeping jobs and gave their charges a portion of the payment. The boy's defensive posture and somber gaze confirm that he is not the master of his own services. The tension of his pose also suggests the variety of hazards that could beset a boy adrift on the streets of New York, from abusive keepers and hunger to the menace of hostile police. Like a protective camouflage, the darkness of the sweeper's skin and clothing allows him to meld into the shadowy corner where he waits for his next assignment.

Significantly, there is nothing in Johnson's portrayal of the chimney sweep—an engaging smile or the presence of a respectable adult—that would allow viewers to construe a hopeful future for the boy. Isolated by his youth, race, and poverty, the young black urchin represented the bottom of the pile of American society. More broadly, however, he also stood for the growing numbers of the disenfranchised, including immigrants, native-born whites, and freedmen, proliferating in America's cities during the second half of the century. For well-to-do audiences who saw The Young Sweep as part of an excursion to the Metropolitan Fair, the painting served as a sobering reminder of the vast, disparate rabble outside the exposition gates—vagabonds, paupers, riffraff, and hoodlums with time on their hands and nothing at all to lose.[2]

Johnson's chimney sweep was an example of a new theme emerging in American art, one that appeared only rarely in galleries, books, and journals until the second half of the nineteenth century. Where images of country boys, American girls, and black children on plantations dealt with beliefs about gender roles, race, and democracy that had been prevalent since the days of the revolution, the street child was a novel subject. For most Americans, the realization that a mass of impoverished "street arabs" roved the nation's cities was shocking and incomprehensible. Citizens were astonished by statistics published in newspapers and journals that revealed the exponential growth of American cities during the nineteenth century—and troubled by the fact that much of it was driven by skyrocketing rates of immigration. More than 1.5 million European immigrants arrived in the United States between 1840 and 1850. During the 1850s an additional 2.5 million immigrants came to the United States, and most settled in the large cities of the northeast. Half of the population of New York was foreign born in 1860, representing a variety of nationalities

—Irish, German, Italian, French, and English. Most immigrants were unskilled laborers and families that arrived penniless with no immediate prospects for employment.[3]

The swelling ranks of the poor in American cities challenged citizens' traditional faith in the easy availability of the nation's resources and raised doubts about the long-term economic security of all Americans. Walt Whitman, lecturing in 1879 on unemployment and labor unrest, revealed that he had been amazed by the sight of three vagrant men "of respectable personal presence" scavenging for bones and scraps to sell. Whitman warned his listeners, "If the United States, like the countries of the Old World, are also to grow vast crops of poor, desperate, dissatisfied, nomadic, miserably-waged populations, such as we see looming upon us of late years—steadily, even if slowly, eating them like a cancer of lungs or stomach—then our republican experiment, notwithstanding all its surface-successes, is at heart an unhealthy failure."[4]

Portrayals of street children began to creep into visual and literary media in the 1830s and 1840s, long after civic authorities first began to deal with large-scale child homelessness. In 1836, two short stories about a "little chimney sweep" were published in McGuffey's *Eclectic First Reader*, a text widely used in schoolrooms across the country. Pupils were introduced to a poor boy who, though less fortunate than his middle-class counterparts, still shared their moral standards. "No," declared the sweep as he spied a client's gold watch on a table. "I cannot take this watch. I would rather be a sweep and always be poor, than steal." After mid-century, the street urchin became an accepted subject for artists specializing in scenes of city life and others looking to add variety to their repertoire. For audiences disturbed by newspaper accounts documenting the growing problem of poverty in American cities, pictures of vagrant children helped them to fathom the troublesome issue of scarcity in a land of abundance.

After 1848, American viewers' acceptance of newsboys and other ragged street types was accelerated by the Gold Rush, when farmers, bankers, and clerks flocked to California's mountains in search of instant wealth. During this period, citizens across the country were inundated by pictures and stories about "rough and ready" miners striking it rich in California's gold fields. Where painted and photographic portraits previously had been the exclusive domain of the well combed and well dressed, images of Gold Rush miners showed respectable citizens in dirty and ragged clothing. In the iconography of prospecting that fascinated Americans through the end of the century, shabby clothes came to symbolize imminent prosperity—or, at the very least, evidence of admirable self-reliance and hard work. The Gold Rush accustomed Americans to the idea that men who had been professors and merchants in the east could appear in threadbare pants and shirts (fig. 93). The Gold Rush stories of writers like Bret Harte also popularized the idea that the grizzled occupants of mining camps were decent, god-fearing folk, despite their lack of refinement in attire or manners. Both literary and visual portrayals of the Gold Rush promoted the idea that access to wealth and power had spread across a wide range of American society.

FIG. 93   Charles Christian Nahl, "The Miner's Sunday," from *Pen Knife Sketches; or, Chips Off the Old Block*, by Alonzo Delano, 1853. Private collection.

Just as Americans were considering new kinds of pictures associated with Gold Rush mining, chimney sweeps, newsboys, flower sellers, and street musicians emerged as acceptable subjects for paintings displayed in prominent galleries, as well as in illustrated newspapers, magazines, and books. These sources offered a safe introduction to the nation's population of impoverished citizens, one of the most conspicuous and feared elements of the metropolitan environment. The causes and consequences of poverty were the focus of intense public debate throughout the century, and the range of portrayals embodied the spectrum of attitudes toward the problem. Some artists portrayed street children as innately vicious, handing them responsibility for their own misery because of some moral or physical defect. Poor children were also depicted as the passive, innocent, and eminently reformable victims of unfortunate circumstances. A third version represented the waif as a go-getter whose ambition and ability were honed by adverse fortunes. Each visual interpretation was indirectly related to a proposed solution to the problem of child poverty—from building more prisons and organizing houses of refuge to adopting a laissez-faire attitude that would allow "nature" to portion out equitably society's resources.

In their depictions of street children, artists usually represented boys who performed some kind of menial but "honest" work. Newspaper sellers and bootblacks were the types most frequently represented, followed by chimney sweeps and vendors of matches and flowers. Occasionally, artists also portrayed rag and bone pickers, the "ragamuffins" who sorted through city refuse heaps looking for bits of salable material. Girls were infrequently included in the visual assortment of street waifs. Until the end of the century, gender biases tended to prevent girls from taking up the most coveted street jobs like newspaper

FIG. 94   R. A. Muller after Briton Riviere, "Charity," from *St. Nicholas: Scribner's Illustrated Magazine for Girls and Boys*, 1875. Private collection.

FIG. 95   "Girls' Dormitory," from "New York House of Refuge," *Appleton's Journal*, March 18, 1871. Private collection.

or shoeshine work, so the idea of a female waif working her way up out of the slums was filled with unpleasant connotations. American audiences considering such images had been primed by city chroniclers' chilling descriptions of impoverished girls forced into prostitution. "No one can walk the length of Broadway without meeting some hideous troop of ragged girls, from twelve years old down, brutalized already almost beyond redemption by premature vice," disclosed one authority. "And such a group is I think the most revolting object that the social diseases of a great city can produce. A gang of blackguard boys is lovely by the side of it."[5] Respectable artists tended to steer clear of this charged subject. When destitute girls did appear in paintings and other representations, they were often portrayed as very young—almost toddlers—or in situations that made their virtue explicit (fig. 94). Other depictions disconnected homeless girls from the disturbing implications of street life altogether by showing them at work in houses of refuge (fig. 95).

David Gilmour Blythe, a self-taught artist from Pennsylvania, was one of the first to specialize in portrayals of street children. Blythe's idiosyncratic paintings offered his audiences a peek at the inner workings of the metropolis. Instead of picturesque depictions of urban bustle, however, the artist exposed the unmentionable back alleys and squalid neighborhoods where the dregs of the city lingered. He focused his efforts on the vagrant population of Pittsburgh, where he created a series of more than twenty paintings of indigent boys. These displayed none of the treacly sentimentality that would come to characterize representations of street children later in the century. On the contrary, Blythe exaggerated the nastiness of the city's wretched youth, accentuating both their physical unattractiveness and their despicable behavior. These works served as a depressing catalogue of youthful vice—truancy, greed, drunkenness, gluttony—recalling the stern Calvinism of the colonial period, when even children were seen as naturally inclined toward depravity. The artist's curious willingness to take on such disturbing subjects in the first place may have had more to do with his own misanthropic character than his anticipation of the public's taste for such works.[6]

A Match Seller shows a young vendor pausing to eat a piece of fruit, perhaps part of a payment given by the artist in exchange for modeling (fig. 96). The boy's full basket of matches is a token of his unhappiness; its unsold inventory indicates either the start of another wearisome work day or one that has ended with too few sales to sustain him. The match boy's sallow complexion speaks of meager fare as well as the suffocating effects of Pittsburgh's famously polluted air. After a tour in the 1850s, a British traveler described the city as a place where all vegetation was choked by smoke and coal dust from nearby factories. "The fresh green leaf and the delicate flower being begrimed, ere they have fully unfolded themselves, by the smoke and soot with which the whole atmosphere is impregnated."[7] Like Pittsburgh's struggling flora, the impoverished match seller represents one of the costs of doing business—the inevitable attrition of anything unable to adapt to the accelerating pace of enterprise.

The match boy sells a household commodity produced by America's growing city-based manufacturing system, the "economy of manufactures" that the Founding Fathers had feared would uproot the nation's agricultural enterprise and, by extension, its democratic institutions. Alert to the dangers inherent in the expansion of urban influence, Thomas Jefferson warned citizens never to let industry replace the country's network of self-sufficient farms. "While we have land to labor, then," he urged, "let us never wish to see our citizens occupied at a workbench, or twirling a distaff." The match seller exposes the existence of an impoverished urban underclass beneath even "workbench" laborers, a signal of the failure of Jefferson's vision for the American republic. Gnawing an apple that hints at the demise of the revolutionary generation's dream of an American Eden, the little peddler certifies that the metropolis, with its dens of vice and extremes of rich and poor, has been allowed to take root in American life. Furthermore, Blythe's portrayal of this dark subject resists any suggestion of resolution of the profound social problems inherent in the image. The match seller's deadened eyes and hunched, defensive posture imply that he will remain society's burden for the full measure of his years.

Blythe's exposés of city life connected him to many Americans who voiced fears that citizens' single-minded quest for profit would lead to the erosion of loyalty to republican government, local communities, and family. Describing the "anxious spirit of gain" as a defect of the American character, a prominent New York minister lamented in 1845 that "enterprise is our only enthusiasm."[8] The adulation of enterprise encouraged rash speculation in a variety of financial schemes, resulting in dizzying cycles of economic expansion and contraction throughout the century that shook the public's faith in the nation's financial and political institutions. Clergymen, political leaders, and reformers responded to economic

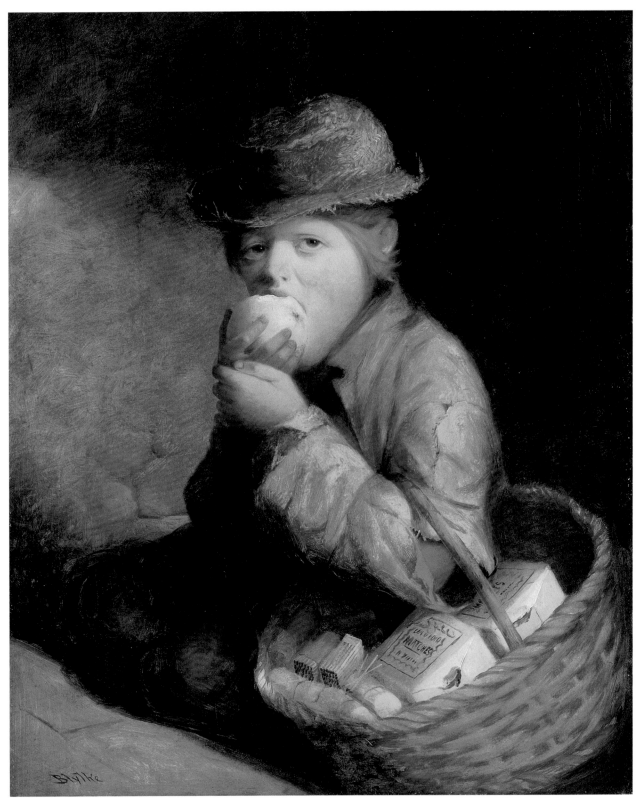

FIG. 96   David Gilmour Blythe, *A Match Seller*, c. 1859. Oil on canvas, 27 x 22 in. North Carolina Museum of Art, Raleigh.
Purchased with funds from the State of North Carolina.

mayhem by demanding legislation that would balance the liberty of buyers and sellers with the communal responsibilities of citizens in a democracy.

In addition to their references to the flaws of the American national character, Blythe's paintings of urchins also pointed to the determining power of biology in individual moral and physical development. The street children he depicted have distorted facial features that, in the context of nineteenth-century culture, conveyed to viewers the idea of their ultimate unredeemability. Though we have no direct evidence that the artist accepted the teachings of phrenology, many Americans of the period embraced the idea that a person's mental abilities and proclivities could be read through the bumps and projections of the skull. Phrenology's popularity rested on its ability to make a person's character readable to those educated in its method, providing a means to explain—and ascribe credit or blame for—an individual's particular circumstances in life. Even Americans who were skeptical about the discipline were constantly exposed to it; during the nineteenth century twenty thousand phrenologists practiced in the United States and phrenological analyses were a common feature of public lectures, advertisements, and self-help literature.[9]

On examination, the crude features of Blythe's urchins provided much to worry the experts (figs. 97–98). The children who wear caps cannot disguise the low-slung aspect of their skulls, a sign of vicious character, and the crowding out of elevated qualities that were thought to reside at the top of the head, including benevolence, spirituality, and con-scientiousness. The relative smallness of the eyes of Blythe's subjects was also a significant factor in phrenological terms, since this was the area where qualities pertaining to a sense of order and facility of expression were located. Certainly, facial regularity and physical appearance in general were important factors for administrators making selections of children considered for admission to juvenile houses of refuge. Those with unusual or unharmonious features were often rejected in favor of more attractive candidates. "A fair face or fine form not infrequently gives one boy an advantage over others," explained a superintendent at New York's House of Refuge in 1848. Those "to whom nature has been less lavish of her gifts," when admitted to the refuge, were likely to "remain much longer than they ought, exposed to the corrupting influences of the institutions."[10]

The News Boys depicts a pair of unattractive city toughs unlikely to gain admission to one of Pittsburgh's benevolent institutions (fig. 99). Nevertheless, in spite of their aesthetic shortcomings, the two are better prepared to turn a profit on the routines of urban life than Blythe's pitiful match seller. These young entrepreneurs are making some kind of financial arrangement or speculation, perhaps a wager on a horse race or another public event announced in the newspaper they are consulting. The boy on the right seems to be a veteran of the process; he holds out a fistful of dollars as he eyes the other boy's small coin smugly. He appears to be saying something and the grin that puckers his face hints at coarse language and shady plans. The boy on the left, younger and more conventionally dressed, is less confident about the transaction. He looks up questioningly at his colleague,

FIG. 97   David Gilmour Blythe, *The Oatmeal Eater*, 1856–1858. Oil on canvas, 27¹/₈ x 22¹/₈ in. The Schumacher Gallery, Capital University, Columbus, Ohio.

FIG. 98   David Gilmour Blythe, *The Urchin*, c. 1856. Oil on canvas, 25 x 30 in. The Duquesne Club, Pittsburgh, Pennsylvania.

FIG. 99 David Gilmour Blythe, *The News Boys*, c. 1846–1852. Oil on canvas mounted on academy board, 29 3/4 x 25 3/4 in. Carnegie Museum of Art, Pittsburgh, Pennsylvania. Gift of Haugh and Keenan Galleries.

who, we have the feeling, will get the better of the deal. The cigar that is close to singeing the younger boy's hair adds to the air of menace in the scene.

In picturing a pair of newsboys, Blythe presented a subject that American viewers considered uniquely representative of the national character. By mid-century, newsboys were a ubiquitous feature of city life in the United States and had become the new emblem of American entrepreneurialism and ingenuity. Their emergence was tied to the development of a large-scale metropolitan press in the United States, which replaced earlier political and mercantile sheets during the 1830s. Rather than marketing to a customary list of subscribers, newspapers found it profitable to let street urchins do the soliciting. In return for a small premium on each sale, little vagrants hawked their wares incessantly at strategic downtown intersections. A writer in the 1870s described newsboys in reverent terms: "As

FIG. 100   Edward Mitchell Bannister, *Newspaper Boy*, 1869. Oil on canvas, 30⅛ x 25⅛ in. Smithsonian American Art Museum, Washington, D.C. Gift of Jack Hafif and Frederick Weingeroff.

you look at the Newsboys, one thing will strike your attention. There is no appearance of vice amongst them. Nothing skulking, nothing mean, nothing vicious lurks in the aspect of the true Newsboy. No redness of the eyes, no bloated face, no pallid debauchery. His eyes are open and candid, and his air as free from the braggart as the coward. Honor to the self-reliant, self-maintained, honest Newsboy."[11]

Blythe's portrayal ran counter to more typical newsboy imagery, which typically represented the children as worthy mascots for the nation's esteemed newspaper business (fig. 100). American readers supported a staggering variety of newspapers and took great pride in the number of dailies available and their latitude of commentary. Because of their strategic role in supplying timely political and economic information to the "common man," newspapers were perceived as instruments of democracy. In 1832, Daniel Webster declared that "the press . . . suppresses everything which would raise itself against the public liberty; and its blasting rebuke causes incipient despotism to perish in the bud."[12] Throughout the century, artists used the newspaper as a symbol of democracy and the free flow of ideas that was considered an essential feature of republican government (figs. 101–102). At the same time, the newspaper industry was lauded by the American public as a model of innovative business practices that made it one of the fastest-growing sectors of the economy during the nineteenth century.

Notwithstanding the lofty reputation of newspapers as the guardians of democracy, Blythe's depiction of the newsboys' financial transaction affirmed that the industry had its roots firmly in the marketplace. Many large metropolitan presses began as advertising sheets promoting city development, and newspapers were one of the most important tools of entrepreneurs seeking to bring settlers into new communities. Along with railroad lines and supportive legislation, newspapers played an essential role in sparking the exponential growth of American cities during the nineteenth century. Captain Henry King, editor of the St. Louis *Globe-Democrat*, explained the process: "The printing press preceded all the usual agencies of society. It did not wait for the rudimentary clutter of things to be composed and organized," he declared. "The spirit of adventure thrust it ahead of the calaboose, the post office, the school, the church, and made it a symbol of conquest."[13]

Blythe's grim view of the denizens of Pittsburgh was part of a broader uneasiness about "the spirit of adventure" that tugged at the American conscience at mid-century. The period was marked by an unprecedented expansion of credit, resulting in frenzied building-lot speculation in cities along the Atlantic and in the Ohio and Mississippi valleys. At the same time, when gold was discovered in California, a flood of gold seekers surged to the Sierra foothills, adding to the sense of wild speculation blazing across the land. For many citizens, it seemed the rules that previously governed the marketplace had vanished, and with them the reliability of traditional economic, political, and personal relationships. In the 1860s, Blythe created his own apocalyptic vision of the adventure run amok, a blasted landscape littered with drilling rigs, smokestacks, bones, and advertisements for

FIG. 101   William Sidney Mount, *The "Herald" in the Country (Politics of 1851—or, Who let down the bars?)*, 1853. Oil on panel, 16⁷/₈ x 12⁵/₈ in. The Long Island Museum of American Art, History, and Carriages, Stony Brook, New York. Gift of Mr. and Mrs. Ward Melville, 1955.

FIG. 102   Richard Caton Woodville, *Politics in an Oyster House*, 1848. Oil on canvas, 16 x 13 in. The Walters Art Museum, Baltimore, Maryland.

FIG. 103   David Gilmour Blythe, *Prospecting*, 1861–1863. Oil on canvas,
12 1/8 x 9 1/8 in. Location unknown.

"options" (fig. 103). The artist's urchins are the acolytes of this new order—the domain of
the "go-getter," where newsboys working out small-time collusions mirror the adult world
of powerful merchants, financiers, and city bosses. At the bottom of the heap are match
sellers and others without ambition, skill, or luck, who are left to fend for themselves in a
society unencumbered by outmoded conceptions of fair play.

Although Blythe was one of the first American artists to address the subject of the
street child, his paintings—which confronted the viewer and challenged middle-class
complacency—were too prickly and idiosyncratic to serve as models for others. Other
artists who portrayed the urban poor found it expedient to devise a more pleasant perspective. Many adhered to the formula of the English "fancy picture," which portrayed
charming beggar children, including flower girls, street musicians, and chimney sweeps
(fig. 104). Images of street children in the European tradition became something very
different in the context of American culture, however. Behind all American representations
of city life was the idea that American cities should not have the same kinds of problems

FIG. 104   John Russell, *Love Songs and Matches*, 1793. Pastel on paper
laid on canvas, 35 1/2 x 27 in. Holburne Museum of Art, Bath, England.

as those of the Old World. In Europe, where society had rigid social distinctions, images
of street types served as a confirmation of class hierarchies. One of the chief tenets of
American democracy, on the other hand, was the belief that all citizens enjoyed ample
opportunities for success. Artists gave full play to this notion when fashioning pictures of
little boys and girls in urban slums, cobbling together an odd mixture of the emblems of
democracy with visual types Americans had traditionally denounced as symbols of Old
World oppression.[14]

In spite of its humble subject, the oval-shaped format of Henry Inman's *News Boy*
placed the image firmly in the elevated realm of art (fig. 105). The painting depicts a newsboy standing next to a stone sphinx whose silent gaze serves as a rebuke to the clamor of
newsboys around town. The sphinx decorates a stairway leading to the elegant Astor House
Hotel in New York, acting as a symbolic guardian segregating the world of news and
commerce from the privileged sphere attained by those who had mastered the game.
While the *News Boy* acknowledges the separation of rich and poor in the American city,
the picture is also ripe with symbols of the boy's future prospects. Standing in a prime

location for spotting customers, the boy engages the viewer with an inquiring expression, his thumb ready to peel off a paper and net another sale. Though he is still at the bottom of the stairway of success, the boy's useful occupation and workmanlike attitude link him to the city's expanding industry. At the same time, the magical sphinx watching him alludes to the luck required for economic and social transformation in New York. Even admission to a well-outfitted asylum that poor children nicknamed the "Astor House" depended on the vagaries of fate (fig. 106). Only a fortunate few were able to secure a coveted bunk for the evening at the institution, which offered newsboys and other urchins a supper ticket and night lodging. The newsboy's proximity to the sphinx is an auspicious portent, a clue that good fortune may soon help him to acquire one.

In addition to paintings of newsboys that were displayed in elite galleries, similar images were also disseminated in illustrated magazines and city guide books. In 1843, the illustrator F. O. C. Darley created an image of the ragged newsboy for a lithograph published in *In Town and About*, a collection of stories describing the street life of Philadelphia. A bedraggled newsboy is shown hawking the latest edition along a cobbled street lined with tidy dwellings and stores (fig. 107). The accompanying narrative struggled to convey the broader significance of the image:

> The dragon teeth of tyranny have often caused the earth to crop with armed men, and the nineteenth century, thirsting for information and excitement, finds its Ganymede in the newsboy. He is its walking idea, its symbol, its personification. Humanity, in its new shape, is yet young and full of undefined energies, and so is he. The first generation of his race not having outgrown their business, is as yet too imperfectly developed even for the meditations of the most speculative philosopher that ever extracted glowing sunbeams from the refreshing cucumber; but as nature does nothing in vain, it is but fair to infer that the newsboy is destined in one way or another to fix the period which gave him birth, in the niche of history.

Although such prose was difficult to decipher, it was easy to convince readers steeped in the Puritan tradition of hard work that the poor newsboy was someone to be admired rather than pitied. Protestant doctrine encouraged the idea that privation was good preparation for adulthood, and children who had to learn how to make do were often better off than those who grew up coddled in the bosom of the family. In 1843, Darley's image of a newsboy peddling his way to prosperity achieved its own kind of success when it reappeared in the July 1843 issue of the widely read journal *United States Magazine and Democratic Review* (fig. 108). Reworked by the renowned artist and printmaker Nathaniel Currier, the image of the industrious street urchin passed muster for publication in a respected periodical devoted to analysis and commentary on the most important events and ideas of the day.

While hardworking newsboys were favored as the new icons of American egalitarianism, artistic portrayals also dealt with other city children, those most obviously disenfranchised

FIG. 106   M. Wostt, "Newsboys Getting Their Lodging and Supper Tickets," from "The Poor Boy's 'Astor House,'" *St. Nicholas: Scribner's Illustrated Magazine for Girls and Boys*, 1876. Private collection.

FIG. 107   F. O. C. Darley, "The News-Boy," from *In Town and About* (Philadelphia, 1843.) New York Public Library.

FIG. 108   Nathaniel Currier, "The News Boy," from *United States Magazine and Democratic Review*, July 1843. Private collection.

from the nation's economic and social systems. Many street images represented the youngest and most desperate urchins, the trash scavengers or "ragamuffins" who sorted through city refuse heaps searching for bones, rags, wood chips, and scraps of metal that could be sold to peddlers. The economy of rubbish was unpredictable; on some days the children netted a meager profit and other days turned up nothing—particularly when inclement weather made scavenging difficult. Despite the unpleasantness of the work, it was not without redeeming social value. A report for the New York Children's Aid Society called scavenging work "filthy, laborious, and dangerous to the morals, but . . . honest."[15]

In 1869, Eastman Johnson produced a small painting of a "ragamuffin" who was typical of New York's trash brigade (fig. 109). The khaki tones of his outfit and the pith-helmet-like shape of his cap conjure up visions of Livingstone and Stanley and their highly publicized contemporary expeditions to the Dark Continent. Arms behind his back like a good member of the regiment, the little ragamuffin has navigated successfully through the heart of the metropolis. His aplomb deflects the viewer's pity, making him just the type to win the hearts of the clergymen, benevolent ladies, and educators who made selections of children for houses of refuge. Charles Dickens, visiting a Boston institution in 1842, described the special accommodations that persons of means made possible for the youngest wards. "Some [orphans] are such little creatures, that the stairs are of lilliputian measurement, fitted to their tiny strides," he observed. "The same consideration for their years and weakness is expressed in their very seats, which are perfect curiosities, and look like articles of furniture for a pauper doll's house."[16]

For many viewers and readers, the appeal of benign street types like Johnson's ragamuffin was tied up with pride in the nation's lack of social hierarchies. The ragamuffin was a suitably egalitarian counterpart to the children of the well-to-do frequently represented in paintings and other imagery of the period. The physical weakness and snobbery of children brought up in the hothouse atmosphere of upper-class city homes was also a persistent theme in contemporary popular literature. One sardonic critique appeared in the

FIG. 109   Eastman Johnson, *Ragamuffin*, c. 1869. Oil on canvas, 11¹/₂ x 6³/₈ in. Private collection.

late 1850s in *Harper's New Monthly Magazine*, which featured a series of articles chronicling the misadventures of "Master Charlie," the pampered child of a prosperous family. A boy of little intelligence and even less common sense, Master Charlie demonstrated the enervating effects of good breeding. He makes the acquaintance of several streetwise young ruffians, who inevitably cheat him and subject him to sound drubbings. An image in the series portrays the delicious denouement of one such encounter, with a despondent Charlie sporting a black eye next to his long curled locks and an arm dangling in a sling above his lace-trimmed pantalettes (fig. 110). Though Johnson's wee ragamuffin was not the sort to dish out comeuppance to the richly deserving Master Charlie, his earnest presence tapped into the disdain for artifice and humbug that many had come to believe was a special feature of the American national character.

While the image of the respectable ragamuffin inverted middle-class notions about the proper order of society, it was also the kind of picture that Johnson's wealthy customers might hang in their sumptuous parlors. In *Christmas Time (The Blodgett Family)*, a painting executed in 1864, Johnson portrayed an elegant home in one of New York's finest neighborhoods, the residence of William T. Blodgett and his wife and children (fig. 111). Surrounded by gold-framed paintings, a Persian carpet, and finely paneled walls, Blodgett watches his son, William Blodgett, Jr., as he plays with a Christmas toy. The boy is approximately the same age as Johnson's ragamuffin, and his brown suit invites comparison with the rustic ensemble of his impoverished doppelganger. The elder Blodgett's contemplative expression suggests that he may be remembering Christmases past and his own more modest childhood. Blodgett had made his fortune by building up a varnish business into a lucrative manufacturing concern, and the rich appointments of his home testified to the acumen that earned him a place at the center of New York's civic affairs. For Blodgett and other self-made men in New York society, paintings of street types like the young ragamuffin served as reminders of their humble origins, as well as a confirmation of their commanding view of the multitudes beneath them.[17]

The philanthropic activities of Blodgett and other New York elites were an integral part of the circuit of genteel activities through which members defined their status. Those who aspired to be models of society placed assistance to destitute children particularly high up in the hierarchy of good works. Not only did it establish the elevated moral credentials of city leaders, it also made good political and financial sense for captains of industry to promote the well-being of future voters, workers, and consumers. Johnson's young ragamuffin, reassuringly free of troubling ethnic characteristics and still young enough to be innocent of hardened vice, is a candidate ready for the charitable interventions of public-spirited ladies and gentlemen. He was the type who would respond readily to the basic occupational instruction and moral guidance offered at the houses of refuge funded by the prominent. Though it was uncertain whether the ragamuffin might ultimately emerge as a future Carnegie, clerk, or laborer at a varnish factory, his innocence and round-faced healthiness indicated that he would give a good return on society's investment of time and money.

Charlie's last acquaintance resulted disastrously. "Does your Pa live here?" asked his new friend.—"Yes."—"Has your Pa ever been in the Tombs?"—"No."—"My Pa has been there more'n a week; and he can go there just when he's a mind to. My Pa can lick your Pa; and I can lick you." And he did "lick" him.

CHARLIE'S KNIFE.

THE NICE BOY'S KNIFE.

MASTER CHARLIE AFTER BEING LICKED.

FIG. 110 "Master Charlie's Sidewalk Acquaintances," from *Harper's New Monthly Magazine*, August 1857. Private collection.

FIG. 111 Eastman Johnson, *Christmas Time (The Blodgett Family)*, 1864. Oil on canvas, 30 x 25 in. The Metropolitan Museum of Art, New York. Gift of Mr. and Mrs. Stephen Whitney Blodgett, 1983. Photograph © 1984, The Metropolitan Museum of Art.

FIG. 112 Augustus Kinnersley, "Ragged Dick," from
Ragged Dick, by Horatio Alger, Jr., 1867. Private collection.

Viewers' appreciation of pictures like *Ragamuffin* was enhanced by a profusion of popular
stories that showed the American public that street children followed middle-class standards of behavior. Published in 1867, Horatio Alger's *Ragged Dick*, which told the story of
a street boy a few years older than Johnson's ragamuffin, was one of the best-selling books
of this genre (fig. 112). While Ragged Dick's relentless optimism in the face of adversity
seemed too good to be true, Alger insisted in the preface of the book that the characters
in the story were based on real people "sketched from life." The author introduced Ragged
Dick as a waif of sterling character, one who "would not steal, or cheat, or impose upon
younger boys, but was frank and straightforward, manly and self-reliant." The narrative
traced Dick's peregrinations through the city as he guided a country boy named Frank
Whitney past all the dangers of lower-class city life. In the course of their meandering
through a labyrinth of cheats, pickpockets, good-time girls, and traffic, Dick's instructions
to his naive companion were constant and detailed. As he listened to these sermons on
streetwise deportment, Whitney returned the favor by introducing his ragged friend to
the rudiments of refinement, encouraging Dick to keep regular hours, improve his speech,
and reform his careless spending habits. Ragged Dick took readily to these etiquette

lessons since, as a model youth, he cared more about respectability than wealth or prominence. By the end of the book, luck and pluck prevailed and Dick departed from the nomadic life of the street, taking his place among persons of comfortable means.[18]

While serendipity and perseverance allowed Ragged Dick to escape a life of poverty, the numbers of unfortunates who surrounded him in the book made it evident that there was not room for all on the highway to success. This was a less cheerful layer of meaning that lay beneath idealized depictions of bootblacks, sweepers, and ragpickers. In "The Gospel of Wealth," an article published in *North American Review* in 1889, steel magnate Andrew Carnegie confidently dispatched the idea that all Americans were entitled to an equitable allocation of resources:

> The problem of our age is the proper administration of wealth, that the ties of brotherhood may still bind together rich and poor in harmonious relationship. The conditions of human life have not only changed but revolutionized in the past few hundred years. . . . The contrast between the palace of the millionaire and the cottage of the laborer with us to-day measures the change which has come with civilization. This change, however, is not to be deplored, but welcomed as highly beneficial. It is, nay, essential, for the progress of the race that the houses of some should be homes for all that is highest and best in literature and the arts, and for all the refinements of civilization, rather than that none should be so. Much better this greater irregularity than universal squalor.[19]

In Carnegie's view, the "proper administration of wealth" put the management of capital in the hands of the most capable and portioned out to these managers a bigger slice of the pie for the service. As he and other business leaders encouraged Americans to dream of prosperity, they also introduced the idea that it was fitting for a portion of the nation to make do with mere subsistence—though this "Gospel" urged all citizens to adopt a disciplined attitude toward work. Ragged Dick described the new egalitarianism as it applied to those in the lowest echelon: "To succeed in his profession, humble as it is," he explained, "a bootblack must depend on the same qualities which gain success in higher walks of life." While they represented different ends of the economic spectrum, Carnegie and Ragged Dick shared the belief that even those working in low-paying jobs could take pride in their high professional standards.

Though Ragged Dick was native-born, American viewers often connected portrayals of city urchins to the masses of immigrants who had come to the United States in search of a better life. Artists frequently portrayed street children who were members of specific immigrant groups, including Italian musicians, French flower girls, and Irish bootblacks. Most representations of urban waifs, however, avoided explicit references to the newcomers flocking to American harbors, a subject that was a lightning rod for argument and dissent. As the volume of immigrants to the United States soared after 1820, Americans complained bitterly about the alien habits and beliefs of the new arrivals—though the

FIG. 113   John George Brown, *Jersey Mud*, c. 1885–1890. Oil on canvas, 23 1/4 x 15 3/4 in. Collection of Mr. Walter and Mrs. Lucille Rubin.

nation's manufacturing sector flourished with the infusion of cheap labor. Business leaders even encouraged immigration during the economic boom that followed on the heels of the Civil War. By the last decades of the century, the United States' most important manufactories, including the iron and textile industries, were powered mainly by immigrant workers. In turn, the boom-and-bust cycles of the nation's speculative economy led to periods of unemployment and often homelessness for immigrant laborers and their families.

The native-born blamed immigrants for a score of ills, from cholera epidemics and crop failures to a decline in national moral standards. In 1858, a tract published by the Boston Industrial Aid Society described immigration as a "vast influx of foreign pauperism, ready-made and hatched abroad, ignorant, squalid and degraded, alien to our institutions, habits, and laws."[20] During the severe and lengthy economic depression that began in 1873, labor unrest that spread across the country was attributed to foreign-born agitators. Significantly, pictures of urban urchins, which frankly acknowledged the yawning gap between the nation's haves and have-nots, gained their widest popularity in the same period. These images were addressed to viewers unnerved by the financial tremors shaking American society and the threat of the insurgence of the lower orders. In an uncertain economic climate, the ability to appreciate or buy an image of an urchin was in itself an indication of an established place in the social hierarchy, a soothing affirmation for those whose businesses teetered on the brink of receivership.

The acknowledged master of the street-child genre during the last decades of the century was John George Brown, who earned the sobriquet "Boot-Black Raphael" for the type of painting that became his trademark. Brown was well known in artistic circles as a prospector of picturesque street characters; for models he sought out fair-complexioned, dark-haired urchins who were the visual equivalents of "Ragged Dick" and other insolvent literary heroes. At the Tenth Street Building where Brown and many other artists kept studios, a critic for the New York art scene reported that there was "constant traffic up and down the

FIG. 114 John George Brown, *The Last Edition*, c. 1890–1910. Oil on canvas, 44 x 32 in. Carnegie Museum of Art, Pittsburgh. Gift of Mr. and Mrs. Henry J. Heinz II.

stairs of street urchins, charwomen and derelicts come to pose for a fee. Though Brown asked his models to wash before posing, the smell in the corridors at times rivaled the odor of W. J. Hayes' do-it-yourself hobby of taxidermy."[21]

Beginning in the 1860s, Brown turned out a quantity of paintings of street waifs performing a variety of tasks that served genteel society: shining shoes, sweeping sidewalks, and selling newspapers (figs. 113–114). He displayed these works in exhibitions in Boston, Cincinnati, and Chicago, as well as at the National Academy of Design, the Brooklyn Art Association, and other prominent galleries in New York. These street types were painted in a highly realistic style that became increasingly meticulous and detailed during the 1870s and 1880s. This aspect of

Brown's paintings gave them a distinctly reportorial aspect, even though their contrived narratives were blatantly fictional. Still, Brown backed up the genuineness of his depictions by claiming intimate knowledge of the street child's experience. "I do not paint poor boys solely because the public likes such pictures and pays me for them," he insisted, "but because I love the boys myself because I was once a poor boy."[22]

Some indigent children earned a living making curbside recitations of poetry, speeches, and autobiographical tales, and Brown often focused on this subject in his paintings. Many little storytellers found that their own troubled, if necessarily brief personal sagas afforded the best chance of snagging passersby. *A Tough Story* shows an aspiring young thespian trying out his tale on three of his dusty colleagues (fig. 115). Counting on his fingers—maybe the episodes of his tale or the years of his life—he seems to be in the middle of his narrative. His pensive expression, coupled with the worn elbows of his jacket and his smudged bare feet, verify that his lot has been a sorrowful one; his listeners' threadbare clothing confirms that they too have tough stories to tell. Still, the boys' well-fed appearance and the snug circle in which they are enclosed suggest that camaraderie has helped them to weather the worst privations of street life.

For urchins with special talent, autobiographical storytelling became a steady source of

FIG. 115   John George Brown, *A Tough Story*, 1886. Oil on canvas, 25 x 30 in. North Carolina Museum of Art, Raleigh. Purchased with funds from the State of North Carolina.

income and the means for leaving the streets altogether. The story of one ragged raconteur, Johnny Morrow, was so successful that it was published in 1860 as *A Voice Among Newsboys*. The facts of the boy's life or his memory of it were a bit muddled, however. Though the records of the New York's Children's Aid Society stated that Morrow came from an Irish family that had immigrated to the United States at the height of the potato famine, the boy claimed in the book to be of English and Scotch descent. He described his early childhood as a peaceful idyll in a prosperous household, complete with a "hired man," a rose garden, and a cat named "Puss." The unexpected death of his mother and his father's subsequent remarriage were the catalysts of an unfortunate series of events that ended with the family's destitution. The truthfulness of the whole account came into question when Morrow divulged a different version of his mother's death to a newspaper reporter. "My real mother would have been alive now, I think, if my father hadn't drunk so much," he remarked. "When he was drunk he used to quarrel with her, and beat her. When she died she was black and sore all over, *and she died.*"[23]

Morrow's revelations confirmed that he was not in fact a middle-class boy fallen on hard times, but the ensuing controversy about his social provenance undoubtedly helped to increase the sales of his book. As with all works portraying street children, the issue of the boy's class and ethnic background was an important component. Many authors and artists represented waifs as temporarily diverted members of the respectable classes, as Morrow did for his own history when he tried to cover up his actual origins. Brown, in *A Jolly Lot* and other paintings, instead chose to depict a multiethnic environment, with groups of disparate children bound together by common work. For audiences fretting about the growing voting power represented by distinct and seemingly unified immigrant groups, Brown's works divested newcomers of their worrisome solidarity. The artist divided his subjects into cheerful multiethnic bands made up of what one art critic described as the "German, Irish, Irish-American, English or Jewish types of character," as well as black and Italian youths.[24] In these havens of diversity, bootblacks kept company with other bootblacks, sweepers convened with sweepers, and those of similar age but unidentified occupation united together as "A Jolly Lot" (fig. 116). By diffusing immigrant groups that were known to live in urban clusters into the nation's vast melting pot, *A Jolly Lot* and similar images addressed the prevalent concern that the immigrant communities might ultimately refashion the despised social order they had left behind in the Old World, with all of its inequities and oppressions. *A Jolly Lot* contradicted such notions, suggesting instead that entirely new communities were coalescing out of the froth of immigration, with members sharing the ethos of hard work. Implicit in the painting, too, this ethnic and racial mingling was occurring at some remove from the realm of polite society.[25]

Brown's charming pictures of sleeping street children similarly defused conclusively the threat posed by the nation's young homeless. A typical example, *Tuckered Out*, shows a weary bootblack who is all softness and vulnerability, from his shiny curls and well-filled cheeks to his rosy open mouth (fig. 117). Gazing at such an image, viewers were vulnerable to the full force of the artist's persuasive power. Fixed in Brown's painterly crosshairs was a depiction of the nation's worst failings: a representative of the "outcast, vicious, reckless multitude" of street boys that reformer Charles Loring Brace said would "poison society." Manipulating his audience's fears with a showman's consummate skill, Brown made all trace of menace vanish. In its place, he conjured up a delectable vision of cuteness disconnected from worries about the need for urban reforms. The boy's round face and blooming complexion make it plain that street life agrees with him, and his "tuckered out" state reveals nothing more than a job well done. To be sure, the bootblack's ragged condition spoke of hard work with minimal compensation, alluding to social asymmetries that were a common feature of the capitalist metropolis. As Brown portrayed it, however, the problem

FIG. 116 John George Brown, *A Jolly Lot*, 1885. Oil on canvas, 32¼ x 44¼ in. Private collection.

FIG. 117 John George Brown, *Tuckered Out*, c. 1888. Oil on canvas, 24¼ x 16⅛ in. Museum of Fine Arts, Boston. Bequest of Maxim Karolick.

could be polished away with elbow grease as a rapidly growing nation stirred itself to arrive wide awake in time for the new century.

Like Brown, the photojournalist Jacob Riis created images of street children neutralized by sleep (figs. 118–120). The author of *How the Other Half Lives* (1890), a hard-hitting exposé of New York's slums, Riis presented dozing "street arabs" as one of the many shocking sights of life in urban tenements. *How the Other Half Lives* was based on Riis's work as a reporter for the *New York Tribune* and the Associated Press news bureau. His talent for creating dramatic stories epitomized the sensationalism that came to characterize the city's newspapers after the 1880s. Replacing the sober commentary of older "journals of opinion" with features that aimed to provoke strong emotions—horror, pity, reverence —the new dailies dispatched their reporters to seek out the unique and thrilling. In this climate, the deplorable state of New York's poorest neighborhoods represented a subject ripe for the public's consideration. Riis took New York slums as his special reportorial territory, making it his personal crusade to spread the word about the dismal conditions he found there and to initiate reform efforts.

Along with his altruistic activities, Riis also understood well the topics that helped to increase newspaper circulation and the sales of his book. Adept at creating the most compelling sequence of information, he placed his best material—the chapters that dealt with impoverished children—at the heart of *How the Other Half Lives*. "The Problem of the Children," "Waifs of the City's Slums," and "The Street Arab" gave accounts of the dire predicament of the slums' youngest residents, accompanied by wrenching photographs of these subjects. The images of sleeping waifs were the most riveting feature of these exposés, showing heaps of children slumped together for warmth and protection. Any notion of the viciousness of these children was banished by the sight of their vulnerability and weariness. The text that accompanied the pictures of the little sleepers explained that they were, in fact, true Americans writ small (and poor):

> [The Street Arab's] sturdy independence, love of freedom, and absolute self-reliance, together with his rude sense of justice that enables him to govern his little community, not always in accordance with municipal law or city ordinances, but often a good deal closer to the saving line of "doing to others as one would be done by"—these are the strong handles by which those who know how can catch the boy and make him useful. Successful bankers, clergymen, and lawyers all over the country, statesmen in some instances of national repute, bear evidence in their lives to the potency of such missionary efforts. There is scarcely a learned profession, or a branch of honorable business, that has not in the last twenty years, borrowed some of its brightest light from the poverty and gloom of New York's streets.[26]

In addition to calling attention to the plight of children who were never tucked in at night, Riis's vicarious tenement tours complemented the growing industry of urban tourism that developed toward the end of the nineteenth century. Traditionally, Americans had viewed

FIG. 118   Jacob Riis, *Street Arabs in Sleeping Quarters (a church corner, Mulberry Street)*, photograph, c. 1889. Museum of the City of New York. The Jacob A. Riis Collection.

FIG. 119   Jacob Riis, *Street Arabs in Sleeping Quarters (Areaway, of Mulberry Street)*, photograph, c. 1890. Museum of the City of New York. The Jacob A. Riis Collection.

FIG. 120   Jacob Riis, *Street Arabs in Their Sleep Quarters*, c. 1890. Photograph printed by copy negatives. Museum of the City of New York. The Jacob A. Riis Collection.

the nation's cities as devoid of the kind of cultural and historic attractions that drew them to the cities of Europe. By the 1870s, however, those with the means for pleasure excursions found that New York, Chicago, San Francisco, and other American cities had many interesting features that made them worth a visit. For many, the most memorable part of a city tour was a stop in a lower-class neighborhood, particularly those with strong ethnic identities. Elite sightseers filed through Chinatown restaurants and joss houses, synagogues, and areas where the predominant language was German. The more intrepid travelers also ventured into cities' poorest sections, where child beggars and derelicts filled the streets and crime was rampant. This part of the tour was usually accompanied by a police escort who watched over the well-to-do as they peeked into sweatshops, saloons, and miserably crowded dwellings. In turn, a lucrative new industry of guidebook publications, tour agencies, and transportation services evolved around the business of city tourism and the creation of interesting urban itineraries.[27]

Like a police escort, the text of *How the Other Half Lives* mediated between readers and the terrible stories and pictures they encountered. Disturbing images of slums were tinctured with spoonfuls of encouragement. After a discussion of a "frightful" life insurance scheme that aimed to profit from the brevity of orphans' lives, Riis changed his tack: "It is with a glad sense of relief that one turns from this misery to the brighter page of the helping hands stretched forth from every side to save the young and the helpless," he mused. "New York is, I firmly believe, the most charitable city in the world." These hopeful words were reinforced by a photograph of toddlers in nightgowns saying their prayers at the Five Points House of Industry (fig. 121). In this way, Riis expertly aligned even the cruelest images of urban squalor with reminders of the nation's fine qualities, using little guttersnipes as compelling examples of "independence, freedom, and absolute self-reliance."

Riis's photographs demonstrated that the problem of the human detritus inhabiting the American city, represented by the heaps of street children accumulating in city corners like so much rubbish, was no longer a problem confined to a small segment of urban society as it had been in David Gilmour Blythe's day. On the brink of the new century, New York —America's largest and most prosperous city—staggered under the burden of a divided population. The fortunate half reaped the harvest of material abundance touted by Carnegie as its natural right. The other half, identified by Riis as ne'er-do-wells, immigrants, child bootblacks, and ragpickers, made do with meager rations and the castoffs of their betters.

By 1900, Riis's photographs of street children had been reproduced in newspapers and journals from Vermont to California, and a broad range of Americans had been compelled to consider their significance. Many citizens interpreted these images as confirmation of the nation's precocious maturity and the missteps inherent in its passage from infancy to adulthood. The existence of little ragamuffins and sweepers effectively punctured the dream of a prosperous and unified agrarian nation, and through them Americans grew

FIG. 121   Jacob Riis, *Prayer Time in the Nursery—Five Points House of Industry*, photograph, c. 1889. Museum of the City of New York. The Jacob A. Riis Collection.

accustomed to the fact that they had deviated from the agenda set forth in 1776. Still, in an environment where pictures of rambunctious country boys flourished as symbols of the nation's democratic character, images of the nation's impoverished youth also represented a rebellion against the constrictions of the society outlined by the revolutionary genera- tion. Portrayals of street children acknowledged the deep rifts in American communities and, like a declaration of independence from the past, introduced the idea that the nation could survive on terms the Founding Fathers never envisioned—with all the cynicism and regret that went hand in hand with the tarnishing of a dream.

Chapter 5

THE PAPOOSE

*When you have learned a little more about [Indians] my daughter, you will find they
are not all bad. Although naturally cunning and revengeful, yet they have some good
traits of character which their white bretheren would do well to imitate. A ungrateful Indian
is seldom or never known. A pleasant word or kind act is treasured up for years, perhaps.
—Love for parents, and respect for the aged are prominent characteristics of the Indian;
traits always lovely in the young.*

MRS. LOVECHILD, *Talk About Indians*, 1849

Although nineteenth-century Americans were fascinated with the subject of childhood,
and pictures of different kinds of American children filled popular galleries and illustrated
magazines and books, Indian children were a rare subject in the imagery of the period.[1] For
most of the century, even artists who focused on Indian themes gave native children only
the most cursory treatment. Textbooks and juvenile journals occasionally touched on the
subject of white children's Native American counterparts, but they usually kept to the history of battles, treaties, and the broad aspects of Indian-white relations. The white perception that America's original inhabitants were a people doomed by progress to extinction
discouraged portrayals of a thriving new generation of Native Americans. At the same
time, the remote and sequestered aspect of many native settlements made it difficult for
artists to observe their family life. Those who lived with Indians over extended periods of
time and made extensive visual records of their ways still dealt only briefly with children,
the people that the natives themselves considered the heart of their nation.[2]

In spite of the often strained relations between Indians and European settlers, the earliest
colonists approved of the close bonds between Indian adults and children. Eighteenth-
century observers recorded the Indians' intense affection for the tribes' youngest members,
including one early writer who remarked, "The mothers love their children with an extreme
passion, and although they do not reveal this in their caresses, it is nevertheless real."[3]
Later explorers visiting Indian encampments in the far west made similar observations,

OPPOSITE: Detail of fig. 130.

FIG. 122 Benjamin West, *Penn's Treaty with the Indians*, 1771. Oil on canvas, 75 1/2 x 108 3/4 in. Courtesy of The Pennsylvania Academy of the Fine Arts, Philadelphia. Gift of Mrs. Sarah Harrison (The Joseph Harrison, Jr., Collection).

but they generally overlooked the role of children in the daily activities, ceremonies, and rituals of Indian life. This lack of attention to Indian children is particularly noteworthy in light of the meticulous documentation that artists and other visitors made of most other aspects of tribal life, including the hierarchies of leadership, burial customs, warfare and hunting practices, the gathering of staple foods, and religious rituals.

When white American artists included Indian children in their work, they usually added them as peripheral elements to enliven scenes portraying the activities of adults. This practice was popular at the time of the American Revolution, when Benjamin West represented a seminal event in early American history with his *Penn's Treaty with the Indians* (fig. 122).[4] The painting, from 1771, depicted a gathering of Delaware Indians and Quaker settlers that was thought to have taken place in Pennsylvania in 1682. At the time West painted it, the event was celebrated as evidence of white newcomers' equitable treatment of native peoples and the settlers' fair claim to Indian lands. West presented the meeting of whites and Indians as a symbiotic exchange between civilized colonists and the people of the forest. On the left of the canvas, William Penn in the characteristic Quaker tri-cornered hat opens his arms in a gesture conveying sincerity and generosity. Opposite him, an Indian chief responds with an open hand. West placed at the center of the canvas the transaction that will cement the new relationship between the newcomers and the

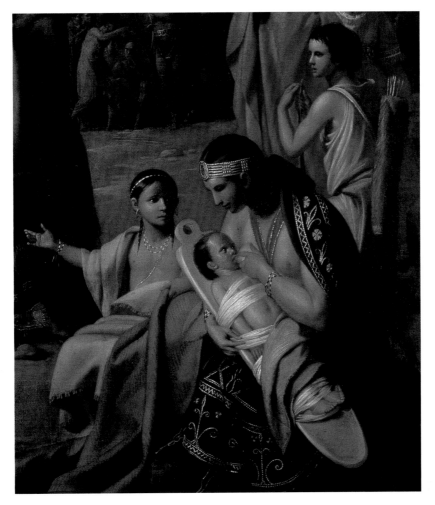

FIG. 123   Detail of fig. 122.

original inhabitants of the territory in the form of a bolt of cloth that a young Quaker presents to the tribespeople.

Accompanying the trade goods that attest to white people's fair claim to new territory, an Indian family group on the right of the canvas augurs well for what Indians will become as a result of their new relationship (fig. 123). Three noble Indian children and their elegant mother introduce the possibility of intermarriage between the two peoples. Standing respectfully behind his elders, a young brave modeled on the toga-clad youths of classical antiquity leans against his bow. A Delaware girl with braided pigtails seems to be explaining the exchange to her mother, who holds a fair-skinned infant in a papoose. The girl and her mother have already accepted a bolt of fabric from the Quakers, an indication that the treaty makers are at the end of their negotiations. The fabric passes around the papoose and over the girl's knees to the ground, where it touches the full quiver of arrows the chiefs have laid down. The intertwining symbols of domestic life, commerce, and peace foretell the success of Penn's new settlement.

West's cheering portrayal of the relationship between Delawares and Quakers in Pennsylvania presented idealized Indian children who embodied Thomas Jefferson's vision of Indian assimilation. In *Notes on the State of Virginia* and other writings, Jefferson advanced the idea that many of the Indian tribes were intelligent peoples eminently suited to adapting to white customs and habits. In the 1780s he wrote that "proofs of genius given by the Indians of N. America place them on a level with Whites in the same uncultivated state."[5] In part, Jefferson's ideas about Indian "genius" were a rebuttal to the criticisms of Georges-Louis de Buffon, Cornelius De Pauw, and other prominent representatives of the European Enlightenment who asserted that North American peoples, flora, and fauna were degenerate forms of Old World stock. For Jefferson and other revolutionary intellectuals confronting European elites, the transformation of the nation's Indians was to be the first triumph of American democracy and proof of the viability of the new republic. Jefferson told the Delaware, Mahicans, and Munsees, "You will become one people with us, and we shall all be Americans."[6]

As Jefferson reacted to his Enlightenment peers in Europe, he may also have been influenced by the colonial practices of the Spanish Empire in the New World. Despite Spain's reputation for cruelty in its treatment of native peoples, it had devised a system that preserved, converted, and utilized indigenous populations to maintain its territorial holdings. The Spanish *encomienda* system included intermarriage between colonists and natives as the foundation of new settlements, and colonial administrators in Madrid considered the creation of mestizo populations an important step in the consolidation of their territorial claims.[7] Although the circumstances of the Spanish Empire and the young United States were very different, Spain's ability to acquire and maintain a vast empire offered important lessons for others encountering the people of the New World. When Jefferson told Indians that "your blood will mix with ours," he was alluding to a Spanish-style melding of populations and a new generation of American children who embodied the best of the Old and New Worlds.[8]

The balanced features and forms of the children in *Penn's Treaty with the Indians* drew upon the conceptions of symmetry and proportion of classical aesthetic ideals. The Indian boy, with his patrician features and robes in the Greek style, seems to have stepped from one of the temples of the Acropolis, while the girl's sage gesture evokes the gravitas of Roman maidens portrayed by Jacques-Louis David and other contemporary European artists taken with classical prototypes. In addition to providing evidence of West's deference to European academic standards, the artistic association of Indians with antique ideals also effected the transformation of the upcoming generation of native peoples that Jefferson saw as the key to enduring social harmony in the United States. The Indian chiefs, with their earrings, feathers, and heavy brows, seem to belong to a different race than their heirs; as they negotiate the terms of the transfer of their land to whites, they are superseded by offspring already characterized as members of a new American order.

Not all whites shared Jefferson's benevolent view of Indian character, much less welcomed the idea of a new generation of mixed-race American children. Benjamin Franklin, one of Pennsylvania's most celebrated residents, dismissed the nation's indigenous peoples as "ignorant savages." Writing about his experiences with Indians in his autobiography, Franklin described a fearsome tribal gathering he had witnessed when he accompanied a group of commissioners planning a treaty with Indians at Carlisle in 1749: "We found they had made a great bonfire in the middle of the square; they were all drunk, men and women, quarrelling and fighting. Their dark color'd bodies, half naked, seen only by the gloomy light of the bonfire, running after and beating one another with firebrands, accompanied by their horrid yellings, form'd a scene most resembling our ideas of hell that could be imagined."[9]

Jefferson's and Franklin's conflicting views of Indian nature are indicative of the broader struggle of white Americans to define the place of Indians in the new republic. Through the 1820s, the official stance of the United States government was that Indians should be assimilated into the white population—and many federal authorities continued to hold this view throughout the century. As frontier settlers streamed farther south and west, however, the pressure to eliminate the logjam of the Indian presence increased. Paradoxically, the Louisiana Purchase in 1803 and the reconnaissance of Lewis and Clark and other early explorers supported the idea of limitless territory that could nurture a diverse American society, but the form of the new order that emerged was not the cohabitative model that Jefferson had championed. By the 1830s, one-third of the white population lived west of the Alleghenies, and many saw Indians' claim to the wilderness as a threat to the newcomers' inalienable right to pursue happiness—including, but not limited to, the rewards of real estate speculation on the frontier.[10] This perception was encouraged by legislation enacted in 1820 that greatly facilitated the settlement of federal lands, including the elimination of credit provisions for homesteaders, a bargain price of $1.25 an acre, and a reduced minimum purchase of eighty acres.

The Indian Removal Act in 1830 was the second part of a one-two punch that began with laws that provided financial incentives for frontier settlement. By mandating that all Indians living east of the Mississippi move west of the Mississippi, the act instantly resolved many of the disputes involving white claims to wilderness land held by Indians. Though all tribes affected by the legislation were supposed to receive fair compensation for their property, many Indian groups, including Creeks, Cherokees, and Seminoles, were forced to leave at gunpoint. Some government leaders openly defined the Indian Removal Act as retaliation for what they perceived as two centuries of Indian aggression; others rationalized the compulsory "migration" as the best way to safeguard Indian health and culture.[11]

The implementation of the Indian Removal Act heightened interest in documenting Indian life. In the 1830s and 1840s, a group of artist-explorers, including George Catlin, Seth Eastman, Alfred Jacob Miller, and John Mix Stanley, traveled extensively among the tribes to make a visual record. They brought back paintings and drawings that were displayed in eastern galleries and reproduced in various media for a national audience. As

FIG. 124   George Catlin, *Chee-Ah-Ka-Tchee* (Iroquois), 1835–1836. Oil on canvas, 29 x 24 in. Smithsonian American Art Museum, Washington, D.C. Gift of Mrs. Joseph Harrison, Jr.

FIG. 125   George Catlin, *Clermont, First Chief of the Tribe* (Osage), 1834. Oil on canvas, 29 x 24 in. Smithsonian American Art Museum, Washington, D.C. Gift of Mrs. Joseph Harrison, Jr.

Indians were ousted from the white community, artists began the symbolic digestion of Indian culture by the society that had enveloped it. Depictions of Indian children were an integral part of this process, which depended as much on the comprehensive visual record as on its dissemination over time (fig. 124). Representing Indian children was a potential problem for artists, however, because they testified to the persistence of peoples who were supposed to be on their way out—both by forced relocation and by their susceptibility to pathogens introduced by their conquerors. For this reason, images of Indian children were often framed by narrative devices that diffused any idea of a resurgent population.

Artists making surveys of Indian life during the first half of the nineteenth century generally abandoned the neoclassical models embodied in the work of Benjamin West and his contemporaries. Instead, emphasis shifted to a quasi-scientific focus on what Indians were at present, emphasizing the exotic features of Indian life and the ways they differed from whites (fig. 125). Artists adopting an ethnographic stance highlighted correctness of detail and a sense of immediacy in contact with Indian subjects. This perspective was aligned with the nineteenth-century American fascination with all things scientific and substantiated the belief that a facility for accurate observation was a special talent of the American people.[12]

A small group of pictures of Indian children emerged out of artists' attempts to create a comprehensive ethnographic survey of the Indian tribes of North America. Within this group of images, pictures of young braves were notably rare. This is somewhat curious, since they were often featured in contemporary literature, with accounts of the routines and rituals of Indian boyhood a regular feature in novels and juvenile magazines of the time (fig. 126).[13] These sources often combined descriptions of youthful innocence with references to the savagery that whites considered an innate Indian trait. In "Good Old Times," a story published in *Our Young Folks* in July 1867, a settler boy strikes up a friendship with an Indian boy named "The Beaver" (fig. 127). After the young pioneer explains to his new friend that he would rather "hoe corn" than fight, The Beaver responds with chilling intensity: "'The Great Spirit has given to the white man a different heart from the Indian's. I love to kill—every Indian does; I love to see blood run; I would like to eat the flesh and drink the blood of the enemies of my tribe.' While he spake the savage gleamed from his whole face; his eyes glared, his nostrils dilated, and his features, seen through the terrors of the war paint, were those of a fiend."[14]

Compared with the temperament of The Beaver and other Indian boys in popular tales, George Catlin's portraits of young Indians were almost tender. Catlin was one of the first artists to devote himself to documenting Indian life in North America and prided himself on the accuracy and scope of his "Indian Gallery." From the beginning, however, his stated mission was at odds with representing the population of Indian children. Writing about his reasons for making pictures of American Indians his life's work, Catlin explained that he had devoted his life "to the production of a literal and graphic delineation of the living manners, customs, and character of an interesting race of people, who are rapidly passing away from the face of the earth."[15]

Catlin's 1832 portrait of the young grandson of the Blackfoot chief Stu-mick-o-sucks, or Buffalo Bull's Back Fat, showed the artist's typical formula for rescuing—at least on paper—a people doomed to extinction (fig. 128). Placing his subject against the neutral background that suited his rapid sketching style, the artist focused his attention on the boy's costume and his facial expression. The young brave carries tiny arrows, a small bow, and a decorated animal skin that identify him as a young hunter. The beaded adornments he wears at his neck and knees, as well as his round face and fat belly—a striking contrast to Catlin's sketches of the very lean adult tribe members—indicate his favored status as the chief's grandson. In the narrative Catlin wrote to accompany the picture, he noted that the little hunter also faced unusual dangers as a consequence of his role as heir apparent. The artist mentioned that the boy's father was dead—perhaps a victim of skirmishes with neighboring tribes—and he had been stolen away twice by rival Crow tribesmen and twice recaptured by his own people "at considerable sacrifice of life." One of his tribe's most valuable assets, the roly-poly brave holds his weapons ready, and Catlin commented that his six-year-old subject "stood forth like a tried warrior." For eastern audiences who read Catlin's popular book published in 1844, *Letters and Notes on the Manners, Customs,*

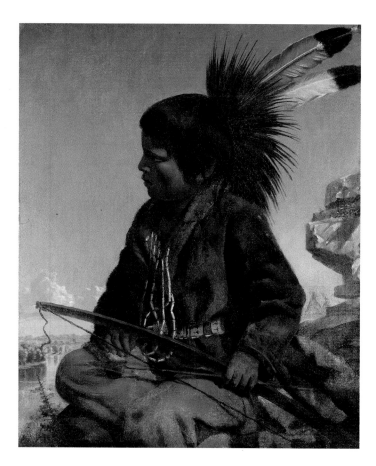

FIG. 126 Thomas Waterman Wood, *Indian Boy at Fort Snelling (Little Crow)*, 1862. Oil on canvas, 30 x 25 in. The Minneapolis Institute of Arts.

FIG. 127 "Good Old Times," from *Our Young Folks*, July 1867. Private collection.

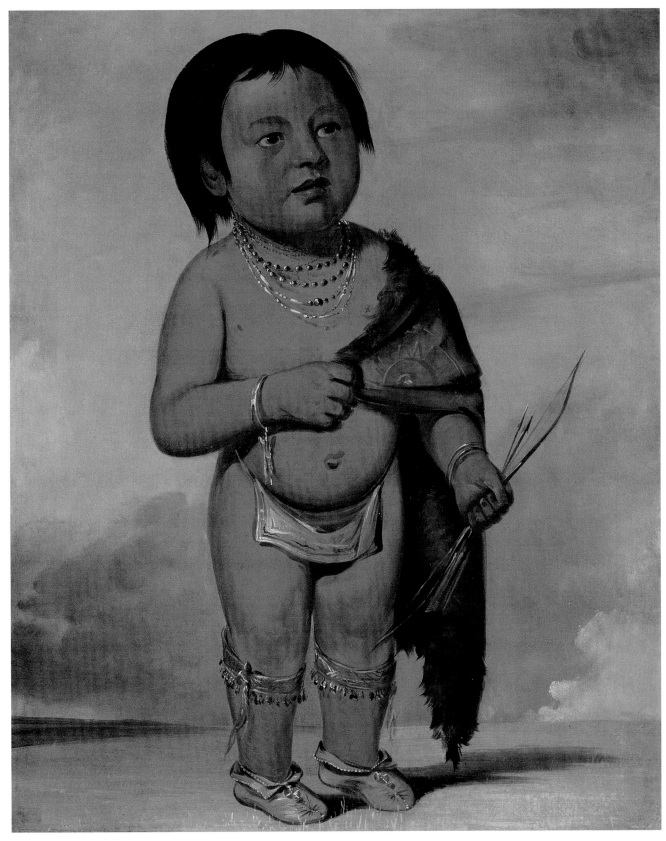

FIG. 128   George Catlin, *Tcha-aes-ka-ding, Grandson of Buffalo Bull's Back Fat*, 1832. Oil on canvas, 29 x 24 in. Smithsonian American Art Museum, Washington, D.C. Gift of Mrs. Joseph Harrison, Jr.

and Conditions of the North American Indians, the threat of a violent ending added a layer of dark meaning to the little brave's story.

In the late 1830s Catlin painted a portrait of a Seminole Indian named Osceola Nick-A-No-Chee, a broad-chested youth approximately nine years of age (fig. 129). The artist depicted Osceola Nick-A-No-Chee poised in midstep, as if tracking in the tropical forest that surrounds him. He is dressed in an elaborate outfit that includes moccasins, leggings, breechcloth, cummerbund, a feathered headdress, and a variety of bracelets and necklaces, and he grips a bow and two arrows tightly in his hand. Despite Catlin's effort to convey a sense of motion, Osceola Nick-A-No-Chee's arrested pose and the artist's careful attention to the details of his costume hint at taxidermy and the diorama. The picture was not, in fact, executed on Seminole lands; it was made when Catlin traveled to Fort Moultrie in South Carolina to see a group of imprisoned Seminoles awaiting transfer to territory west of the Mississippi. The Seminoles of Florida were renowned during the nineteenth century as one of the tribes that resisted at length the United States government's Indian relocation plan. When Catlin took Osceola Nick-A-No-Chee's likeness, government troops were engaged in a drawn-out battle with the tribe, the highly publicized Seminole Wars that lasted from 1835 to 1842. Andrew Jackson, who was elected president in 1828, earned his reputation for military acumen during an early expedition against the recalcitrant tribe in 1818. When the conflict ended in the early 1840s, the United States military had spent twenty million dollars and sustained fifteen hundred casualties—and most of the Seminoles had been wiped out.

In the background of his portrait of Osceola Nick-A-No-Chee, Catlin showed a party of soldiers advancing toward the boy, a feature that complemented his commentary on the Seminoles' plight in *Letters and Notes on the Manners, Customs, and Conditions of the American Indians*. Praising Osceola Nick-A-No-Chee as a "remarkably fine boy," the artist described the Seminoles as "defenseless" participants in an "inglorious war." Catlin also related that, soon after the portrait was finished, the boy was brought to England by a British doctor who took "very great pains" to provide him with an education. Catlin's insistence on recording every bead, feather, and embellishment of the boy's costume takes on a poignant significance in light of the young man's imminent departure from the land of his people.[16]

John Mix Stanley (1814–1870), another artist who specialized in Indian subjects, produced one of the most distinctive paintings of a young Indian brave. *Young Chief Uncas* shows a boy seated on a rocky outcropping in the middle of a wilderness (fig. 130). Like Catlin in his portrait of Osceola Nick-A-No-Chee, Stanley lavished attention on the subject's clothing and decorations, from the strip of turquoise beads on his moccasins and the gleam of the metal studs on his necklace to the vermilion appliqué on the feathers of his headdress. The careful realism of the image was a creative exercise, however, since Stanley based his picture on a character conjured from a storyteller's imagination. Uncas was the Indian hero in one of James Fenimore Cooper's popular Leatherstocking Tales, *The Last of the Mohicans*, published in 1826.[17] Though Cooper's stories of wilderness adven-

FIG. 129   George Catlin, *Osceola Nick-A-No-Chee, a Boy* (Seminole), 1840. Oil on canvas, 52 x 40 in. Smithsonian American Art Museum, Washington, D.C. Gift of Mrs. Joseph Harrison, Jr.

FIG. 130　John Mix Stanley, *Young Chief Uncas*, 1870. Oil on canvas, 24 x 20 in. Autry National Center, Museum of the American West, Los Angeles.

tures were fictional, Americans came to base many of their ideas about Indian life and character on the writer's spirited accounts. Uncas played the role of the noble and doomed savage, the last member of a tribe pushed to extinction by white settlers as well as their own folly. In the novel, Uncas's father, Chingachgook, recognizes that his people have a hand in their own destruction: "The Dutch landed and gave my people the fire-water; they drank until the heavens and earth seemed to meet, and they foolishly thought they had found the Great Spirit. Then they parted with their land. Foot by foot, they were driven back from the shores, until I, that I am a chief and a Sagamore, have never seen the sun shine but through the trees, and have never visited the graves of my fathers."[18]

Stanley's portrayal of Uncas gave visual substance to the lost people of Cooper's story. Holding his tomahawk ready, the boy gazes into the distance, surrounded by symbols of danger. His expression is troubled, and his place on a high overlook where storm clouds brew overhead introduces the idea of surveillance and impending conflict. At the same time, he is not ready for combat or escape. The posture of his body is passive and slouched, contradicting the universal notion, disseminated by travelers' accounts and novels like Cooper's, of Indians' universally upright bearing. In a commentary that accompanied his field sketches of Native Americans, the artist Alfred Jacob Miller remarked on the "straight, erect posture we notice in this people; indeed, we do not recollect, in the whole journey, seeing an Indian with a stoop in his shoulders (we encountered them often enough in civilized life)."[19] Young Uncas's posture, then, embodies quite literally the decline of his culture. Decked out in all his finery, young Uncas is weighed down by a tribal past shaped both by powerful chiefs and by those who gave away their land to newcomers "foot by foot." As he looks out toward the landscape beyond our view, the melancholy Uncas seems to resign himself to an imminent future where he will have neither home nor family.

Although Catlin and Stanley created images of individual young braves, most artists who depicted children showed them as part of larger tribal groups in Indian portfolios that included descriptions of Indian domestic arrangements. Often reproduced as chromolithographs, representations of tribal family life were outnumbered by pictures of scalp dances, buffalo hunts, and intertribal skirmishes; their relatively smaller number in comparison to scenes of violence attests to the priorities of the image makers, as well as those of their patrons and clients (figs. 131–132). Audiences' tastes in Indian subjects at mid-century were influenced by the acceleration of white settlement of Indian lands, making it inconvenient for viewers to confront the human aspect of those being exiled by expansion. Pictures of war parties brandishing clubs and whooping it up around the fire reduced the process to the simplistic equation of savagery versus civilization. Pictures of tribal families, on the other hand, with toddlers lolling in the grass and mothers nursing babies, had the emotional heft to impede Manifest Destiny. Especially for nineteenth-century American women, who were steeped in the gospel of home and family, the question of Christian duty toward indigenous children and families was a thorny one that piqued the conscience. Henry Benjamin Whipple, the first Episcopal bishop of Minnesota, admonished his fellow citi-

FIG. 131   Peter Rindisbacher, *In the Teepee*, no date. Watercolor and pen and ink on paper, 7¹/₈ x 9 in. Gilcrease Museum of Art, Tulsa, Oklahoma.

FIG. 132   Karl Bodmer, *Encampment of the Piekann Indians*, 1840. Aquatint and etching, 17³/₄ x 24³/₈ in. Amon Carter Museum, Fort Worth, Texas.

zens to care for "American pagans whose degradation and helplessness must appeal to every Christian heart. From their past history they have peculiar claims upon the benevolence and protection of a Christian nation."[20] While pictures of Indian children surrounded by extended families prodded viewers' sense of Christian benevolence, such images also argued against the breakdown of tribal units that many considered the key to Indian assimilation into respectable society.

When artist-explorers portrayed Indian children in family groups, they often showed them enmeshed in the cavalcades of tribal migrations and other traveling groups. Pictures of Indian families inside lodges or around campfires had the power to evoke ideas of similarities with white home life, but representations of a nomadic tribal lifestyle maintained a distance with the domestic habits of white viewers. The prominent artists Alfred Jacob Miller and Albert Bierstadt produced numerous pictures of Indian families on the move, with babies carried in papoose cradles and adults and horses transporting blankets, cookware, and other paraphernalia of daily life (figs. 133–134). In 1850, Seth Eastman, an army officer and illustrator stationed at Fort Snelling in Minnesota during the 1840s, made a watercolor field sketch of an Indian family traveling through a treeless landscape. On a horse pulling a travois at the center of the image, an older child holds the reins, while the younger looks out toward the viewer. The children are bracketed by the figures of two adults—presumably their mother and father—and their place in this protected space speaks of the closeness of the family bond (fig. 135).

Eastman's portrayal of the peaceful routine of the migrating Sioux family in *Indian Mode of Travelling* was qualified by his wife's description of the cruel practices that were part of Sioux children's upbringing. While Captain Eastman was producing his portfolio of Indian sketches, Mary Henderson Eastman was busy collecting material for a book on the Sioux tribe planned as an accompaniment to her husband's work. Published in 1849, *Dahkotah or, Life and Legends of the Sioux* brought the author considerable success and she was invited to contribute her stories about tribal life to *The Iris* and other widely circulating journals. Her book on the Sioux included a section that described Sioux children's introduction to the pleasures of winning at war:

> The children of the Sioux are early accustomed to look with indifference upon the sufferings or death of a person they hate. A few years ago a battle was fought quite near Fort Snelling. The next day the Sioux children playing football merrily with the head of a Chippeway. One boy, and a small boy too, had ornamented his head and ears with curls. He had taken a skin peeled off a Chippeway who was killed in the battle, wound it around a stick until it assumed the appearance of a curl, and then tied them over his ears. Another child had a string around his neck with a finger hanging to it as an ornament. The infants, instead of being amused with toys or trinkets, are held up to see the scalp of an enemy, and they learn to hate a Chippeway as soon as to ask for food.[21]

FIG. 133   Alfred Jacob Miller, *Breaking Up Camp at Sunrise*, c. 1845. Oil on canvas, 30 x 44 in. Courtesy of The Anschutz Collection, Denver.

FIG. 134   Albert Bierstadt, *Indians Traveling Near Fort Laramie*, c. 1859. Oil on paper, mounted on paper board, 13³⁄₈ x 19¹⁄₄ in. Museum of Fine Arts, Boston. Bequest of Martha C. Karolik for the M. and M. Karolik Collection of American Paintings, 1815–1865.

FIG. 135   John C. McRae after Seth Eastman, *Indian Mode of Travelling*, c. 1850. Plate 21 in *History of the Indian Tribes of the United States*, by H. R. Schoolcraft, 1851–1857. Private collection.

FIG. 136   Seth Eastman, *Indian Mode of Travelling*, 1867–1869. Oil on canvas, 31 x 44 in. Collection of the United States House of Representatives, Washington, D.C.

FIG. 137 Seth Eastman, *Death Whoop*, 1869. Oil on canvas, 37½ x 28 in. Collection of the United States House of Representatives, Washington, D.C.

FIG. 138 Nathaniel Currier, *Indian Family*, no date. Hand-colored lithograph, 12¾ x 8⅝ in. Graphic Arts Collection, National Museum of American History, Smithsonian Institution, Washington, D.C.

In 1869, Eastman reworked his image of migrating Sioux into a larger format as one of a series of paintings he produced for the United States Capitol building in Washington, D.C. (fig. 136). To add to the historic displays that decorated the rooms of the nation's lawmakers, the artist was invited to execute nine paintings for the House Committee for Indian Affairs. When he finished, the members of the Committee for Indian Affairs were flanked by Eastman's vivid interpretations of tribal life as they worked out new policies. The series included disturbing images of war dances, crowded tribal councils, and one especially graphic portrayal of a Sioux warrior scalping a white victim, titled *Death Whoop* (fig. 137). There is no record of the legislators' opinions of the murals that surrounded them —like so many warriors circling pioneer wagons—but it is conceivable that the images added a note of urgency to the creation of new laws aimed at managing tribal people.

Nathaniel Currier, artist and publisher of prints that decorated American parlors and dining rooms, avoided the graphic realism of *Death Whoop*. Instead, in a lithograph executed

FIG. 139   Charles Deas, *The Voyageurs*, 1845. Oil on canvas 31¹/₂ x 36 in. The Rokeby Collection, Barrytown, New York.

in the 1840s, *Indian Family*, Currier looked back to calmer eighteenth-century sources (fig. 138). In the foreground, an Indian brave and maiden strike athletic poses that embody the Rousseauian ideal of the noble savage. The background is enlivened by a domestic group modeled on the family in Benjamin West's *Penn's Treaty with the Indians*, looking back to the distinguished prototypes associated with the American Revolution and the enlightened virtues it represented. A contrast to Eastman's vision of Indian violence, as well as to accounts of tribal butchery in contemporary newspapers, Currier's *Indian Family* represented an idealized Indian presence calculated to appeal to the American homemaker.

As artists catered to middle-class standards of behavior and morals, they also worked to satisfy their audience's curiosity about those outside the pale of respectable society. The subject of "half-breeds," the children of mixed Indian-white parentage, raised eyebrows among middle-class viewers who were fascinated by Indians' unconventional sexual and religious mores.[22] Spurred by the charged nature of the subject, several artists made detailed portrayals of half-breed families and white-Indian marriages (figs. 139–140). One of these, by George Caleb Bingham, shows a man and a boy in a canoe floating down a placid river at dusk. In 1845, Bingham sent the painting to the American Art-Union for

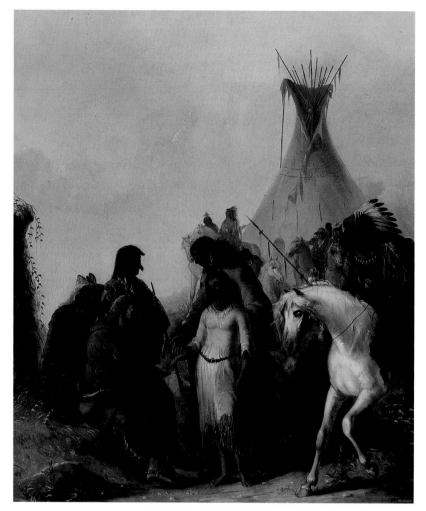

FIG. 140   Alfred Jacob Miller, *The Trapper's Bride*, 1850. Oil in canvas, 30 x 25 in. Joslyn Art Museum, Omaha, Nebraska.

display, titling it *French Trader and Half-Breed Son, Fur Traders* (fig. 141). (The title of the painting was later changed to *Fur Traders Descending the Missouri.*) Rivers leading into the frontier were exotic places where travelers might catch a glimpse of the Indian-white families that usually kept to remote areas where they made their living trapping beavers for pelts. The black-haired half-breed in Bingham's painting is at the center of the canvas, gazing out dreamily at the viewer as he drifts by. His clothing and other belongings speak of the blending of white and Indian cultures: a beaded pouch, a store-bought shirt, leather breeches, and a rifle. Smiling contentedly, the boy seems to luxuriate in his physical well-being and idyllic natural surroundings.

The half-breed's happy face contrasts with the suspicious look of his father, who glares out across the water to take the viewer's measure. His surliness says he is used to the disapproval of strangers, and his lean and weathered face hints at sparse rations and hard winters. Though the father does not convey a sense of paternal warmth, the boy's relaxed

FIG. 141   George Caleb Bingham, *Fur Traders Descending the Missouri (French Trader and Half-Breed Son)*, c. 1845. Oil on canvas, 29 x 36^{1}/$_{2}$ in. The Metropolitan Museum of Art, New York. Morris K. Jessup Fund, 1933. Photograph © 1992 The Metropolitan Museum of Art.

FIG. 142 Alfred Jacob Miller, *Indian Hospitality (Conversing by Signs)*, no date. Pencil with brown, gray, and yellow washes, heightened with white, on paper, 8 1/2 x 11 in. The Dentzel Collection, Los Angeles.

attitude as he leans toward him suggests a close bond. Theirs is a working relationship, with the boy representing the hunting and tracking skills of his tribal family and his father the savoir faire to navigate in white society. Ready for market, the wrapped bundle between them—furs, Indian trinkets, dried meat, herbs, and other trade goods from the hinterland —is a symbol of the intersection of different peoples around the commerce of goods from the wilderness. Representing the point where the frontier ceded to the urban marketplace, *French Trader and Half-Breed Son, Fur Traders* was aimed toward audiences who were consumers at the end of the line. Many who saw the painting when it was displayed in the east wore beaver-skin hats, muffs, and collars that were prized by the well-to-do during the nineteenth century. Bingham's painting served as a reminder of the personal connection between the half-breed at the outer rim of civilization and the distant city dwellers who were his ultimate customers.

In the last decades of the century, Indian children appeared more frequently in paintings exhibited in eastern galleries, and in prints and illustrations seen by a wide audience (fig. 142). The papoose in particular emerged as a central icon of tribal life, one that took its place along with the tomahawk and the feathered headdress as a universal marker of

Indianness. The focus on the papoose and the increased interest in Indian childhood in general was linked to a gradual change in the government's attitude toward Indians after mid-century. In the aftermath of the Indian Removal Act of 1830, some legislators began to express a sense of contrition about the "excesses" of the campaign. They were urged to act by reformers from different arenas of public life—educators, ministers, authors, and state leaders—who called for a more Christian approach to Indian affairs. During his tenure as president in the 1870s, Ulysses S. Grant inaugurated a "Peace Policy" aimed at resolving conflicts with native tribes by establishing a supervised reservation system. For citizens eager for signs of Indians' readiness for change, pictures of Indian children augured the success of the new reform campaigns.

Although the increase in portrayals of Indian children was connected to a widespread desire to improve the nation's Indian policies, it was also linked to the emergence of a tourist industry that marketed excursions to the west. The completion of the transcontinental railroad in 1869 gave elite and middle-class easterners easy access to Indian territory, and pictures of tribal toddlers and papooses complemented strategies aimed at increasing ticket sales. Of course, in showing that the west offered a variety of scenic attractions— and was safe for travel—artists catering to railroad magnates and the tourist trade needed to make fine distinctions between excitement and danger. Eastern city dwellers had heard for decades that Indians were on their last gasp, and they needed to be assured that the colorful traditions of native people were still alive and kicking before boarding a train routed through the desolate stretches of Utah or Nevada. At the same time, paintings, prints, and advertisements needed to assuage fears about scalping, ritual torture, and other fiendish practices that popular "dime novels" described as part of Indians' daily routine.

Travel literature and journal articles about excursions to the west regularly included illustrated accounts of what travelers might see along the transcontinental line. In 1874, *Harper's Weekly*, which billed itself as a "Journal of Civilization," published an article about the papooses of the Shoshone tribe. An accompanying image, titled "Two Bits to See the Pappoose," showed a group of male and female Indians with their babies at one of the stops en route to the Pacific (fig. 143). As the Indians huddle next to a building with a sign that reads Union Pacific Hotel, passengers disembarking from a train crowd around to see them. The construction of the image encouraged readers to note the proximity of sightseeing opportunities to the hotel and the railroad line. As the Indian women turn their babies forward for easy viewing, one of the women extends an open hand toward the new arrivals. A well-dressed passenger, a man in a long coat and bowler hat, leans forward and proffers a bill, the "two bit" gratuity for a peek at the papoose. The text that accompanied the image described the "interesting" encounter: "To all those who have come into contact with Indians on their native plains, the sight of the squaws and pappooses is very interesting. The poor creatures crowd about the railroad stations on the arrival of the trains, and pick up many a penny by showing off their babies to the lady passengers."[23]

As they informed readers about the habits of the Shoshone, the publishers of *Harper's*

FIG. 143   Paul Frenzeny and Jules Tavernier, "Two Bits to See the Pappoose," from *Harper's Weekly*, October 24, 1874. Library of Congress, Prints and Photographs Division, Washington, D.C.

also made a different kind of commentary about native peoples with an image that appeared on the cover of the issue. The front page showed the president of the United States, Ulysses S. Grant, staggering under the weight of "A World of Cares and Responsibilities" (fig. 144). Like a monstrous papoose on his back, his load is made up of a heap of national problems, including a "Financial Crisis," "Corrupt Carpet Baggers," and "Civil Rights." Near the top of the pile are "Indian Troubles," identified as one of the most significant difficulties facing the Grant administration. Though the caption beneath the beleaguered president claimed he would seek a third term, Grant was just the sort of overworked administrator who might be targeted by promoters of tourist excursions to the west—an ideal prospect for a rejuvenating getaway to Indian country.

While the *Harper's* illustration of squaws and their papoose babies revealed that, after the 1860s, many encounters between tourists and Indians were contrived, pictures of the papoose typically relied on visual precedents established by earlier artists representing Indian tribes largely untouched by white society. George Catlin, Seth Eastman, and Alfred Jacob Miller used the papoose as a visual respite from what was often a relentless parade of Indian costumes and rituals. Miller described the contraption in the narrative that accompanied one of his paintings of a mother with an infant (fig. 145). "These cradles are of the most simple construction, but could not be safer or more efficient with any amount

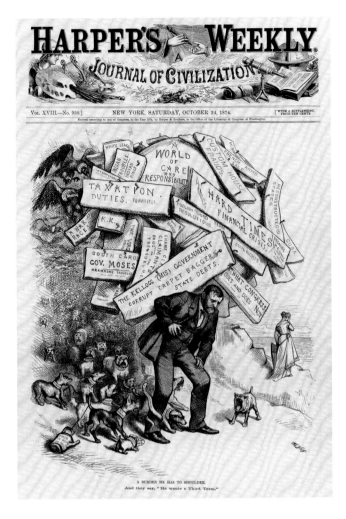

FIG. 144 Thomas Nast, "A Burden He Has to Shoulder," from *Harper's Weekly*, October 24, 1874. Library of Congress, Prints and Photographs Division, Washington, D.C.

FIG. 145 Alfred Jacob Miller, *A Young Indian Woman Fording a Stream*, 1867. Watercolor, gouache, and pen and ink over pencil on paper, 11 13/16 x 9 1/2 in. Library and Archives Canada c-000419, Ottawa, Ontario.

of elaboration," he explained. "Two flaps of buckskin are fastened, one to each side of a board; the child is placed between them and they are laced over it." Miller remarked that the papoose was usually "hung from the limb of a tree or lodge poles, where it may be rocked by the wind, while the mother attends to her domestic duties."[24]

In addition to enlivening the paintings of artists who specialized in frontier subjects, the papoose was also a common topic in juvenile literature aimed at educating white children about the nation's geography and peoples. These sources often included descriptions of readers' young Indian counterparts, as well as guidance on the correct attitude toward them. At mid-century and before, the tone of such literature was often disdainful or, at best, ambivalent. An 1849 book, *Talk About Indians*, used the example of the papoose to instruct students about "good sense." The lesson was set in the format of two children, Walter and Lucy, having an informal conversation with their mother, Mrs. M..

MRS. M. While history has been so minute in picturing the dark shades of Indian character, I'm afraid some of the brightest spots have been nearly overlooked.

WALTER. As you are such a stickler, sis, for names, I will tell you, had you been born an Indian, you would have rejoiced in that of papoose, in stead of the pet one, of baby. Besides you might have had the pleasure of being lashed to a board to make you straight, and kept so for months.

LUCY. Oh Mother, does Walter tell the truth? Do Indians really treat their little ones in such a cruel and silly manner just to make them look, as they think a little prettier?

MRS. M. Yes. Absurd as the practice seems to you my child, and as it really is, it is no more so than one which has been sanctioned by many fair daughters of christian mothers, even in our own happy and beautiful land. May this teach you, my dear child to let good sense, and ready perception of propriety always prevail over any injurious or ridiculous fashion.

As the century progressed, the attitude in children's books toward the papoose grew more congenial (fig. 146). By the time of the Civil War, the papoose had become a symbol of innocence and vulnerability in narratives devoted to the "brightest spots" of tribal life. *Little Folks' First Steps*, a children's picture book from the 1860s, included a picture and a poem describing two papooses hanging from a tree in a forest.

See these Indian Papooses; without any fear,
Their squaw mothers have left them here,
With an Indian dog to guard them all day,
And amuse them a little with his play.

The abundance of lurid tales of white children and families murdered or taken hostage by Indians offset the sweetness of storybook visions of Indian babies swaying in the breeze. One example, an illustration in *An Easy Introduction to the Study of Geography*, in 1848, showed the doomed members of a pioneer family trying to defend themselves against

See these Indian Papooses; without any fear,
Their squaw mothers have left them here,
With an Indian dog to guard them all day,
And amuse them a little with his play,

FIG. 146   "See These Indian Papooses," from *Little Folks' First Steps*, 1860. Private collection.

marauding braves (fig. 147). As white menfolk in the picture blast away with their rifles, a bare-chested warrior in the foreground seizes a mother with an infant. The baby clings to its mother, who looks up in horror as her assailant raises his tomahawk to take her scalp. Though the image of the papoose introduced the gentler side of Indian life, such depictions of Indian cruelty dominated schoolbooks throughout the century.[25]

The papoose signified more than whites' conflicting ideas about Indian nature, however. The popularity of the subject also expressed whites' anxieties about their own culture and prevalent concerns about the well-being of American youth. For nineteenth-century Americans preoccupied with child-rearing issues and the welfare of young republicans, the papoose introduced the possibility that civilized society might somehow be inadequate in dealing with the young. Though the papoose represented an archaic way of life, descriptions of the functionality of the practice of cradling and its reportedly healthful result on the child's lifelong constitution and posture invited uncomfortable comparisons with "civilized" practices. Writing about the children he observed during his travels among Native Americans, George Catlin remarked that tribal lifestyles imbued Indian children with

FIG. 147 "Indian Warfare," from *An Easy Introduction to the Study of Geography*, by S. Augustus Mitchell, 1848. Private collection.

"strong constitutions . . . which, in a measure, may account for the simplicity and fewness of their diseases, which in infancy and childhood are very seldom known to destroy life."[26] Whether it was accurate or not, many Americans who read Catlin's popular account had a keen interest in the subject. Most parents suffered the loss of at least one child in infancy, and many authorities believed the erosion of the family structure and the amenities of modern life had made American children weak and susceptible to disease. In contrast, the papoose represented the close family ties and wholesome outdoor habits of Indian traditions —precisely the elements that many believed were withering in American society.

Grace Carpenter Hudson, an artist working at the turn of the century in Ukiah, California, made the papoose her specialty. She earned a living selling pictures of the Pomo Indians who worked in Lake, Mendocino, and Sonoma counties of California as agricultural laborers or domestic help. Although the artist attained a modest degree of success in her early career, in the mid-1890s one of her numerous pictures of papoose babies vaulted her to national recognition. Her painting titled *Little Mendocino* was selected for one of the coveted display spots in the California Building at the World's Columbian Exposition in Chicago in 1893. It was so popular that it had to be moved to a central location in the building to accommodate the crowds who stopped in front of it (fig. 148). *Little Mendocino* was reproduced by other artists wanting to cash in on its popularity, and unauthorized postcards of the work proliferated. To protect her right to her valuable asset, Hudson had the painting copyrighted, one of the first American works of art to be protected by law.[27]

Carpenter's painting featured a crying infant in a papoose propped up against a redwood tree. The attentive care of the child's mother is evident in the soft blanket wrapped around

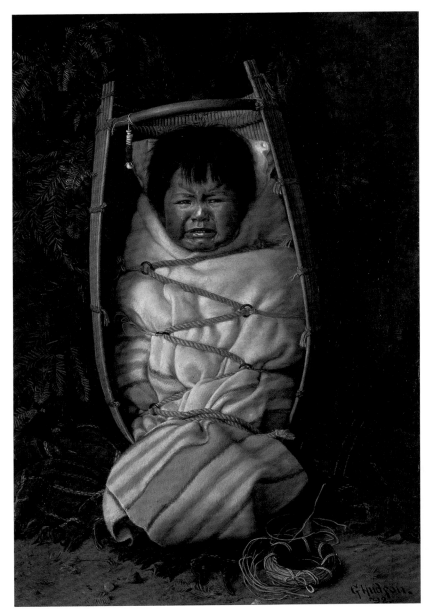

FIG. 148   Grace Carpenter Hudson, *Little Mendocino*, 1892. Oil on canvas, 36 x 26 in.
California Historical Society, San Francisco. Louis Sloss, Jr., Collection.

him and the taut strapping that keeps him safely in his cradle. Despite his well-tended
circumstances, the baby howls miserably, and the artist paid special attention to the glis-
tening tears that stream down his face. A reviewer in a local California newspaper surmised
that the baby was missing its mother, who "has undoubtedly left to gather blackberries or
perchance acorns, or to hunt for a savory mess of young yellow jackets."[28] Hudson herself
gave a less picturesque reason for *Little Mendocino*'s unhappiness when she explained the
working method behind the painting and her numerous other portrayals of papoose
babies crying:

When I want a subject, I first have to find a squaw with a papoose. If the child's face suits me, I enter into negotiations with the mother to do some work for me, usually scrubbing floors or cleaning windows. She leaves the baby strapped up in his basket and braced up against the side of the house, where it will be under her eye. The next maneuver is to get possession of the papoose. I must make it cry so that I may have some reasonable excuse for taking an interest in it. This is where Mascot, our St. Bernard, "does his turn," as the theatrical people say. Here, Mascot, speak. . . . That will usually make an Indian baby cry.[29]

Hudson's account of the effort involved in making Indian babies cry raises the question of why she depicted the subject so often and why it enchanted the audiences at the World's Columbian Exposition. Since the fair was devoted to the nation's past and future—focusing mainly on the achievements of the United States during the preceding century—*Little Mendocino* could have been interpreted as an unpleasant reminder of one of the darkest episodes in the nation's history. In the decades that followed the 1848 Gold Rush, thousands of members of the peaceful hunter-gatherer tribes of California had been slaughtered in a series of attacks by white settlers. Despite the national government's professed commitment to safeguard friendly tribes, it did little to stop the local extermination campaign.[30] The plight of the California Indians became a subject of national attention in the 1880s, when Helen Hunt Jackson, an investigative reporter for *Century Magazine*, published a novel titled *Ramona*. The book, which included descriptions of the wretched circumstances of the Golden State's native people, became a national best-seller and inspired nationwide calls for reforms of Indian policies.

While Hunt's *Ramona* alerted American audiences to the tragic situation of the California Indians, newspapers also kept the nation informed about the corruption and cruelty that often characterized the nation's management of its Indian affairs. During the 1880s the dailies were filled with heartrending stories about Native Americans' determined efforts to reclaim their independence, including the futile attempt of Chief Joseph and his group of Nez Percé Indians to retain their beloved homeland in the Wallowa Valley and the struggle of the Northern Cheyenne to leave a hated reservation in Indian Territory. Damning evidence of the ignoble treatment of a subjugated people, these accounts fixed in the public mind the urgent need for change.[31]

At a time when many Americans were ready to make amends with their Native American brethren, Hudson's *Little Mendocino* suggested that redress would be a straightforward process. The painting was, in fact, the visual counterpart of new legislation confirming the dependent status of Indians, as well as the parental role of the United States government in the management of tribal affairs. The Indian Appropriation Act, passed by Congress in 1871, nullified all treaties that recognized tribes as autonomous entities and made all Indians wards of the state. Following on the heels of this divestiture, recently formed Indian reform organizations stepped in to help oversee the government's new charges.

One of the most influential was the Indian Rights Association, which sought to "secure the civilization of the two hundred and ninety thousand Indians of the United States (inclusive of thirty thousand natives of Alaska), and to prepare the way for their absorption into the common life of our own people."[32]

Indian children were targeted as the centerpiece of assimilation campaigns. Beginning with their removal from parents and the tribal environment, the training of the young included enrollment in special boarding schools. Reformers claimed that education would allow Indian children to skip over the centuries of evolution usually required to reach advanced civilization, with one Indian commissioner explaining, "a good school may thus bridge over for them the dreary chasm of a thousand years of evolution."[33] Reformers usually sought out the youngest Indian children for their programs, since they were considered the easiest to control and most likely to benefit from elementary schooling and instruction in the manual trades. In 1886, an agent working with the Ute tribe described his dream for the children in his care:

> It is food for thought to note the number of handsome, bright-eyed children here, typical little savages, arrayed in blankets, leggings, and gee-strings, their faces hideously painted, growing up in all the barbarism of their parents. A few years more, and they will be men and women, perhaps beyond redemption, for, under the most favorable circumstances, but little can be hoped from them after grown and matured, weeded and steeped in the vices of their fathers. It is rather the little children that must be taken in hand and cared for and nurtured, for from them must be realized the dream, if ever realized, of the philanthropist and of all good people, of that day to come when the Indian, a refined, cultured, educated being will assume the title of an American citizen, with all the rights, privileges, and aspirations of that favored individual.[34]

At the World's Columbian Exposition, *Little Mendocino* beckoned to fairgoers keenly attuned to publicity about the benevolent efforts currently under way on behalf of the nation's Indian children. National newspapers lauded the successes of Indian schools and congratulated readers for shouldering the parental responsibilities they described as the "white man's burden." Piggybacked on the premise of Native American inferiority, *Little Mendocino* reduced a century's worth of transgressions and crimes by politicians, soldiers, Indian agents, ranchers, and railroad builders into one tiny bundle of woe. The small size of the problem boded well for redemption and seemed to promise that the nation's native people would soon be able to share all the rights and privileges of their fellow citizens at the fair.

Chapter 6

THE NEW SCHOLAR

It cannot be doubted that in the United States the instruction of the people powerfully contributes to the support of the democratic republic.

ALEXIS DE TOCQUEVILLE, *Democracy in America*, 1838

In the 1870s Winslow Homer produced a series of paintings, watercolors, and engravings devoted to the subject of children in school. These works showed children inside or near a little red schoolhouse in a variety of situations—sitting in the classroom, gathering at the school entrance in the morning, and playing at recess. It is possible that Homer based his school paintings on a visit he made to Hurley, New York, in the bucolic Hudson Valley region, during the summer of 1871. Often working up his canvases later from drawings made on sketching excursions, Homer may have executed the paintings in his New York studio. Although the setting and figures of the images are markedly similar, in each work the artist chose a few elements for special scrutiny—a student's earnest expression, the rough finish of classroom benches, the outline of figures set against the surrounding landscape —making a visual inventory of the subject that was both repetitive and innovative (fig. 149).

In *School Time*, a painting he made in the early 1870s, Homer offered viewers a close-up view of a small clapboard schoolhouse, using the frontal illumination of a rising morning sun to call attention to the plainness of the structure (fig. 150). Set on flat land without walkways or planted beds, the small building is the embodiment of architectural economy. An expression of the people who built it—hardworking local farmers with little time for aesthetic refinements—the schoolhouse is also emblematic of the unornamented education offered inside. This was not a temple for meditations on abstruse algebraic equations, Greek, or Latin, but a place where America's newest citizens could learn to read and write. In a playful reference to the plain education occurring within—as well as to the independent spirit of young republicans—Homer included on the right of the canvas the figure of a boy holding a paint bucket and daubing the artist's initials on the side of the schoolhouse.

OPPOSITE: Detail of fig. 154.

FIG. 149   Winslow Homer, *Homework*, 1874.
Watercolor on paper, 8 x 5 in. Canajoharie Library
and Art Gallery, Canajoharie, New York.

FIG. 150   Winslow Homer, *School Time*, c. 1874.
Oil on canvas, 12 x 19 in. Collection of Mr. and Mrs.
Paul Mellon, Upperville, Virginia.

FIG. 151   Winslow Homer, "The Noon Recess," wood engraving from *Harper's Weekly*, June 28, 1873. Library of Congress, Prints and Photographs Division, Washington, D.C.

Although Homer's school series did not follow an explicit narrative sequence, another work in the group portrayed a student's punishment, a subject that suggests the denouement of the graffiti artist in *School Time*. The engraving titled "The Noon Recess," published in *Harper's* in 1873, shows a pupil obliged to remain at school after the rest of his classmates have been dismissed (fig. 151). Obviously in a bad temper, the teacher stares sullenly out a side window while her little nemesis buries his face in a book. The tension between the pair is pulled taut by the tantalizing glimpse of the outdoors visible through the window between them. There, in a brilliant afternoon sunlight, schoolchildren smile and frolic next to a stand of trees. The hint of a soft breeze, made visible by the way the muslin curtain lifts just slightly at the bottom, heightens the sense of the delight of the day— and the misery of the subject's confinement. Although the boy's expression is hidden by the book he holds in front of his face, a poem that accompanied the image in *Harper's* directed viewers to read sadness and disappointment there:

> *Yes, hide your little tear-stained face*
> *Behind that well-thumbed book, my boy;*
> *Your troubled thoughts are all intent*
> *Upon the game your mates enjoy,*
> *While you this recess hour must spend*
> *On study bench without a friend.*[1]

FIG. 152   Winslow Homer, *Country School*, 1873. Oil on canvas, 12 1/4 x 18 11/16 in. Addison Gallery of American Art, Phillips Academy, Andover, Massachusetts.

The figure of the boy with his nose in a book had already appeared in one of the earliest and most critically acclaimed paintings in Homer's school series, *Country School*, from 1873 (fig. 152). In this earlier iteration, the boy was cast as a model student diligently reading along with the teacher as she directs a lesson. In place of the cramped darkness of the classroom shown in the engraving, the artist's representation of a reading lesson is set in a brightly illuminated interior that hints at intellectual enlightenment. Like a broad cranium —the physical attribute that phrenologists associated with mental acuity—the room's vaulted ceiling gives a sense of spaciousness that complements the idea of the expansion of young minds. The highly symmetrical geometry of the setting is also significant. Standing at the center of the canvas, the teacher is a fulcrum against which windows, rows of benches, and writing tables are poised on the right and left. These elements segment and balance the classroom, as if symbolically aligning its activities with the carefully calibrated equalities set forth by the American constitution.

Homer presented his view of the country classroom from the vantage point of a student, putting the viewer at eye level with the other pupils in the room. A nudge to memories of school days past, the low perspective enhances the physical size and authority of the teacher and encourages a nostalgic interpretation of the scene. The benches and configuration of the classroom would have been recognizable to audiences as artifacts of an earlier era. By the 1870s, this order had generally been replaced by rows of individual desks facing forward. Always alert to the symbolic meaning of everyday objects in his work, the artist offered the relics of an old-fashioned schoolroom to audiences eager for patriotic messages and reminders of days gone by. In 1871, wedged between the end of the Civil War in 1865 and the centennial of the American Revolution in 1876, Americans were caught in a moment of looking forward and backward in time. *The Country School* conveyed the prevalent mood of hopefulness about the future and regret about an unchangeable past that audiences across the country shared. At the same time, as the nation attempted to consolidate the tenuous unity earned with the blood of the Civil War dead, Homer's painting of a humble public school was a reminder of opportunities that were held to be the birthright of all Americans. By the second half of the century, public schools were perceived and represented as a melding of interests of the individual and the community, a great common denominator that had the power to bring together the far-flung multiplicity of the American body politic. One writer in 1870 asserted that the nation's public schools were the leading force promoting national unity, and were "as vital to our political system as air to the human frame."[2]

When *The Country School* was displayed at the National Academy of Design in New York in 1872, critics responded enthusiastically to its national themes, extolling the painting as a patriotic triumph. An article in the *New York Evening Express* called the work "a picture thoroughly national" and one that revealed "a thorough acquaintance with our life as a people."[3] In 1878, the painting was one of the works representing the art of the United States at the Paris Exposition. If the common school was already thought to exemplify the best aspect of American life, in Homer's hands it was consecrated as a shrine of democratic virtue. Nevertheless, despite *The Country School*'s success with a broad public, its subject had been the source of controversy since the time of the revolution. Heated debates about public education for the nation's children elicited a range of divergent views on the meaning of democracy and the proper balance between individual liberty and communal welfare.

The works in Homer's school series addressed the subject of education at a time when the issue appeared to have been resolved at last, well after most states had put into place a centralized system of public schooling. Interwoven with the artist's celebration of the success of the nation's education system, however, was an acknowledgment of the ongoing struggle between individual autonomy and centralized authority in American society. The works alternated between a focus on the systemization and structure of the school day and children's assertion of their own ideas and personalities—mirroring the oscillation between the interest in communal welfare and reverence for individual autonomy that had brought American public schools into existence in the first place. *The Country School* and other images in the group envisioned these opposing energies in a state of harmony, showing a realm where freedom and order were perfectly balanced within the figures of young citizens going about the everyday business of learning their lessons.

Although public schools were ubiquitous in the United States by the 1870s, many citizens remained unconvinced that the institutions would fulfill their lofty mission of uniting the nation through common education. They were also wary of the new powers government assumed as part of the administration of school districts, including the levying of new taxes, definition of school curricula, and enforcement of school attendance. During the first quarter of the century, children's education had been the exclusive concern of parents and town and church leaders who organized and administered local schools. The quality of these schools was dependent on local involvement and parents' and townspeople's willingness to pay for schoolhouse construction and teacher salaries. In general, children of the elite and middle classes could depend on regular instruction while those in the laboring classes had to make do with schools that were often inconsistent in both quality and duration. By the 1830s, many Americans feared that disparities in education would lead to the solidification of class hierarchies and ultimately disenfranchise artisans, laborers, and others who made their living through manual labor.

A manifesto published by the Philadelphia Working Men's Committee in 1830 warned of the consequences of a system of education in Pennsylvania that favored the well-to-do: "The original element of despotism is a monopoly of talent, which consigns the multitude to comparative ignorance, and secures the balance of knowledge on the side of the rich and the rulers."[4] Responding to the manifesto, an editorial in the *Philadelphia Gazette* voiced the opinion of prosperous residents who claimed that free schooling benefited the idle at the expense of the industrious. "Authority—that is, the state—is to force the more eligibly situated citizens to contribute a part (which may be very considerable) of their means, for the accommodation of the rest," the article declared. "One of the chief excitements to industry . . . is the hope of earning the means of educating their children respectably or liberally; that incentive would be removed, and the scheme of state and equal education be thus a premium for comparative idleness, to be taken out of the pockets of the laborious and conscientious."[5]

The bitter exchange between Philadelphia workers and the city's elite embodied the larger public debate that surrounded the issue of public education in the first half of the century. Defending their ideas about schooling forced citizens to define the meaning of democracy, to clarify their future expectations for the republic, and to back up their conclusions with their pocketbooks. By the 1840s, much of the American public had accepted the idea that common schooling was the best way to produce a body of loyal and productive citizens who would protect the nation's democratic institutions. During this period the United States became the first major Western nation to offer free public education. Common school systems were established in Massachusetts in 1837, for example, in Delaware in 1829, Pennsylvania in 1834, Vermont in 1850, Indiana in 1851, Ohio in 1853, and Iowa in 1858. Massachusetts was the first state to enact compulsory attendance laws in 1852.[6]

Paintings, prints, and other images of children in school guided Americans' urgent and ongoing analysis of the institutions they believed nurtured and sustained the republic. While grownups with differing views on education squared off, pictures of children in

FIG. 153 William Sidney Mount, *The Truant Gamblers*, 1835. Oil on canvas, 24 x 30 in. Collection of The New-York Historical Society.

school and in school-related activities, and textbooks aimed at schoolchildren around the nation, mapped out the landscape of American freedoms and duties. Paintings and lithographs tended to favor celebrations of childhood freedoms, reveling in anarchic classrooms, happy truants, and the joys of recess frolics. These works provided a counterpoint to the themes of regularity, industry, and obedience that dominated illustrations and lessons in school textbooks. The dichotomy that existed between the anti-authoritarian stance created by prominent artists and the emphasis of educational institutions and publishers on order and respect was a symptom of a persistent ambivalence about the methods and administration of common schools. Though education was universally applauded as the foundation of an advanced society, the nation's proudly self-reliant citizens never resigned themselves entirely to the centralization and expansion of government authority that went hand in hand with the organization of public school systems.

The Truant Gamblers, a painting from 1835 by the Long Island artist William Sidney Mount, communicated the still unsettled status of children's education in the early decades of the century (fig. 153). An artist known for his amusing interpretations of country life, Mount avoided explicit reference to the schoolhouse. He referred to its existence obliquely through the title of his painting, which depicted a group of country boys skipping school to engage in a game of pitching pennies. Far from the teacher's watchful eye, the truants delve into the practical applications of arithmetic as they add up the wins and losses of their gambling game, and celebrate the joys of chemistry with nips of applejack from the jug at their feet. Retribution is nigh, however, in the person of the lantern-jawed farmer who advances with a pitchfork perched on his shoulder and a switch in his hand. As the painting reveals the boys' impending punishment, it also invites the viewer into their delightful conspiracy. The truants' gleeful faces dispel any sense of real wickedness, while the great barn that surrounds them envelops their extracurricular mischievousness in an aura of agrarian healthfulness. Despite the boys' scholarly shortcomings, the farm setting confirms that their account will be settled with manly work—and a hickory stick.

The Truant Gamblers asked viewers to identify with the merry miscreants, an attitude that supported lingering suspicions about the connection between education and highfalutin ways. Especially at the beginning of the Jacksonian Era in the 1830s, when the influence of aristocratic revolutionary elites ceded to the new power of common folk, Americans often associated education with the effete habits of the upper crust. "Self-made" citizens wore their lack of cultivation as a patriotic emblem, a symbol of their contempt for Old World pomp and circumstance. Though the newly prosperous were not averse to wearing the latest French fashions, affluence was uncoupled from the founding generation's love of erudition. In 1829, a southerner writing an open letter to a local newspaper summed up the American impatience with book learning when the nation seemed to abound with opportunities that required no training at all: "Who wants Latin and Greek and abstruse mathematics in times like this and a country like this?"[7] With the concept of an American scholar slow to win the approval of a nation of ambitious populists, Americans paid lip service to the benefits of schooling even as they championed "low-brow" heroes in songs, theater, and paintings. Many artists found they could make a respectable living producing pictures of the common folk and portrayals that made fun of those who put on genteel airs. Mount sold *The Truant Gamblers* to Luman Reed, a wealthy New York entrepreneur who may have seen something of his own modest rural beginnings in the artist's depiction of naughty country boys.

Where *The Truant Gamblers* showed what schoolboys did outside the classroom, *The New Scholar*, painted by Francis William Edmonds in 1845, brought viewers inside for a closer look (fig. 154). The picture played up the familiar routines and characters of school life, including a detestable schoolmaster and a green schoolboy. Holding up his hand in feigned concern, the schoolmaster seems to cluck in sympathy with the trepidations of the new arrival. The unwilling "new scholar," open-mouthed with fear, clutches at the skirts of his mother as she pushes him forward with a firm grip on his shoulder. The schoolmaster—wisely prepared for all eventualities—carries a whip in one hand behind his back. Before new theories calling for gentler disciplinary methods in the classroom took hold at mid-century, schoolmasters were often portrayed with whips—the emblem of their absolute authority over children. Some teachers made sure their punishments fit

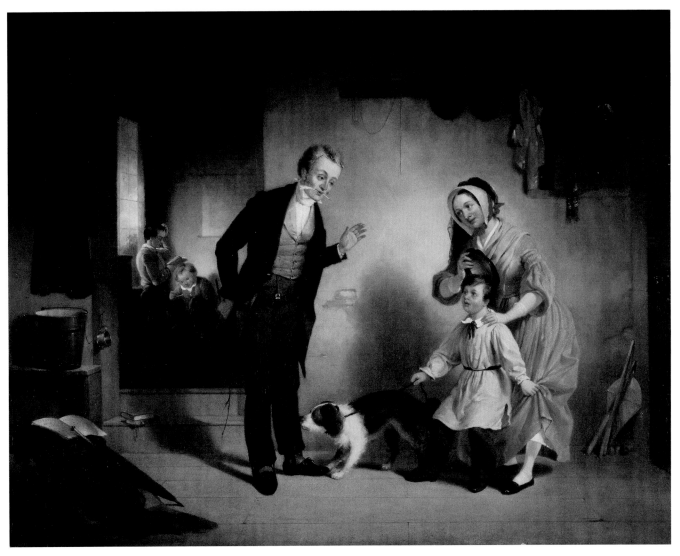

FIG. 154   Francis William Edmonds, *The New Scholar*, 1845. Oil on canvas, 27 x 34 in. Manoogian Collection, Detroit.

the crimes of their pupils by having a range of whip sizes on hand. One student explained that in his classroom the "larger switches were graded, partly by the size of the boys and partly by the gravity of the offense." In addition to a selection of hazel-tree twigs, the largest weapons in the arsenal were made "of oak and would have been better called clubs."[8]

Smelling the deceit of the wily schoolmaster, the loyal family dog raises its lip in a snarl as his young companion is propelled toward a classroom visible on the left of the canvas. Two boys attend to their studies there, framed by a narrow doorway that offers just a glimpse of the hall of learning. A dough-faced pupil sits awkwardly on a chair as he writes on his slate, while the other scratches his head dully and stares at a book. Left to their own devices while the schoolmaster greets the new prospect, the boys give a lackluster introduction to the business of education. A contemporary art critic summed up the anti-intellectual stance of *The New Scholar* when he wrote that the painting appealed "not to the intellect, but to the heart."

The critique of schooling's petty tyrannies inherent in Edmonds's portrayal was also connected to other problems that citizens associated with the classroom experience. In particular, American parents, educators, and physicians were deeply concerned about the physical toll exacted by "book learning." In 1855, an article in *American Medical Monthly* raised the question that was on the minds of many: "Are Our Public Schools Injuring the Bodies of Our Children?" Warning about the debilitating effects of long hours of study, the authors observed that the short days of the winter made it especially difficult for children to get enough exercise after school. "In winter there is no . . . margin for play between the last hour of school and the first of night." The article condemned the practice of giving lengthy homework assignments with a withering assessment of school administrators' competence, declaring that "Our Board of Education and excellent corps of teachers could scarcely adopt a more ingenious device to secure a generation of puny people."

In spite of public anxieties about the puny, the civic leaders responsible for the establishment of the public school system dismissed the threat of stunted growth, calling instead for a redoubling of efforts to provide a basic level of education for America's youth. In 1848, the Massachusetts legislator and educator Horace Mann expressed his passionate conviction that uneducated children were doomed to a life of misery and struggle. Using the sweeping hyperbole typical of his crusade for public schooling, Mann declared that "every state is morally bound" to establish a system of free schools, and failing that it might as well "enact a code of laws legalizing and enforcing infanticide."[9] Common schools were already spread throughout the United States, but Mann and other reformers wanted to centralize control in order to set common standards for instruction and teachers. They also wanted to ensure that elementary education would be free or at minimal cost for all students in order to include the poor and immigrant population—those they considered most in need of the benefits of schooling. In many states in the first half of the century, free education was offered only to families who were willing to testify that they were unable to pay for tuition. Reformers wanted to eliminate the social stigma of the free school to reduce the disparities between the haves and have-nots. They believed that, through common lessons, common speech, and common values communicated in free public schools, a cohesive American community could be stitched together from the threads of the nation's many regional and economic groups.

A painting by Charles Frederick Bosworth, *The New England School*, showed a classroom in 1852, the year that Massachusetts became the first state to pass the compulsory attendance laws that put real teeth into the notion of common education (fig. 155). Though systems of enforcement were inconsistent, the laws represented a new level of government influence over the personal autonomy of Americans. For those who were worried about the encroachment of bureaucratic authority, Bosworth's painting showed the schoolhouse as a cheerfully egalitarian environment. Scholarly activity concentrates in the middle, where a

FIG. 155   Charles Frederick Bosworth, *The New England School*, c. 1852. Oil on wood panel, 16 1/2 x 20 1/2 in. Courtesy of the Massachusetts Historical Society, Boston.

schoolmistress and a group of pupils discuss a lesson in a book. Outside this nucleus of learning, students of different ages spin off in independent orbits. Several young children amuse themselves by tossing hats in the air, while an older boy embraces a willing young schoolmate. In the second tier of the classroom's row of benches, a pair of chums lean comfortably on their elbows as they enjoy a relaxed chat. Alone in the left corner of the canvas, a solitary pupil resists the distractions of the classroom by hiding under the teacher's desk to read his book. A little girl who has discovered him titters behind her hand, cuing viewers to the boy's curious predicament.

The shenanigans of rowdy schoolchildren, a key element in *The New England School*'s narrative, addressed the issue of democratic discipline that was a persistent question throughout the nineteenth century. Teachers complained about the problem of imposing obedience on those who had imbibed with mother's milk the habit of questioning authority. According to administrators' reports, many American schools were in a perpetual state of rebellion. During the 1870s, the British author Frederick Marryat reported seeing signs in a New Jersey schoolhouse that advised students, "No kissing girls in school time" and "No licking the master during holydays."[10] Nevertheless, the adult body politic seemed to be assured rather than alarmed by displays of youthful independence, and artists like Bosworth and Mount shaped their portrayals to reflect common attitudes. Their works were complemented by a variety of widely read novels, including Mark Twain's best-selling *Adventures of Tom Sawyer* and *Huckleberry Finn*, that made popular heroes of boys who were happily ungovernable and especially adept at making fools of their teachers.

While *The New England School* showed American children asserting their place in a republican society, the map prominently featured on the schoolroom wall mirrored the United States' growing desire to assert its own place in the world, particularly in relation to Great Britain and the rest of Europe. Through the antics of its independent-minded scholars, the painting also showed that newly expanded levels of education had not spawned a generation of aristocratic Old World effetes. On the contrary, the New England classroom appeared as a cradle of democracy, with children of varying ages, abilities, and interests bonded together by their interactions and common purpose. In 1908, William A. Mowry, who had been a rural schoolteacher for more than fifty years, explained that equality was the first and most important lesson of the common school: "Here the boys receive their first lessons in democracy. All children of the same neighborhood meet on a common level. To all are accorded the same right, to all are assigned the same tasks, and all are subject to the same discipline."[11]

Instructing pupils about the nation's relationship to other countries, the map in *The New England School* was also a clue about the wide open marketing territory that public education represented. During the second half of the century, American entrepreneurs developed an array of new products to meet the skyrocketing demand for educational materials. Emerging from the expanding consumer networks that were part of the modernizing economy, maps, desks, blackboards, mechanical pens, slates, copy books, alphabet cards, and other school paraphernalia were markers of the expansion of industry, the incorporation of businesses, and the diffusion of new information technologies—developments that also required a highly literate populace to ensure their continued growth.

One new item in the classroom inventory, the printed "rewards of merit" sold to educators by publishing companies, represented more explicitly the connection between capital and classroom (fig. 156). Instructors passed out rewards of merit to hardworking students to encourage good behavior. These tokens reflected the change in attitude toward school discipline that occurred after mid-century, when educational authorities began to look on whipping and other forms of corporal punishment as methods of last resort. In addition to compensating students for the industrious use of time, the similarity between rewards of merit and bank notes prepared recipients for an economy that was increasingly wage-based and accustomed them to managing credits, debits, and shares of stock. One lavishly illustrated reward of merit printed in the 1860s encouraged the idea of the authenticity of the not quite legal tender by including an assortment of images related to finance, progress, and material abundance. On the left of the note, a little girl stands in a garden full of fruits and flowers above a picture of a steaming locomotive, the kind of transport

FIG. 156   Reward of Merit, c. 1860. Lithograph by Charles Schuber, Chicago. Private collection.

used to convey such goods to distant markets. On the right, a boy and a girl read about "knowledge" and "duty" in a large book. At the center of the image, "National Bank of Merit" appears in large letters above the words "4 Shares of Stock to the Holder."

Although *The New England School* paid pointed attention to activities that certainly would not accrue as receivables in rewards of merit, the painting centers on what was often the focal object of classroom routines: the textbook. A student looking at a book scratches his head in a gesture that conveys his lack of understanding, while his teacher offers an explanation. The issue of which texts to use was an important one in the public schoolroom, since administrators wanted to employ only books of broad appeal that would support schools' egalitarian mission. In the early part of the century, American schoolchildren used a motley assortment of books in class—usually whatever their parents had available on bookshelves at home. By mid-century, common-school organizers adopted standardized, mass-produced textbooks to regularize curricula meant to serve a variety of populations. In the west, the frequent migration of families and the scarcity of trained teachers affected the continuity of children's schooling, while in the south, the isolation of plantation-based communities made public school systems difficult to organize and regulate. The northeast established an extensive and well-regulated system of common schools, but it struggled to adapt to the growing number of immigrant children with different languages and customs.

By the second half of the century, American children in all parts of the country were learning to read from the same books and were being instructed with the same lessons on diligence and obedience, liberty and independence, featuring the same illustrations of George Washington and fresh-faced boys and girls in the countryside. These books made frequent mention of the importance of the nation's democratic institutions and the uniqueness of the American character. One of the most common school texts was Noah Webster's

American Spelling Book, which, after the Bible, was the most widely read book in the United States during the nineteenth century. Like many other educational reformers and political leaders of his time, Webster believed that the unity of the young nation depended on Americans learning to speak similarly. American culture during the nineteenth century was primarily an oral one, with sermons, prayers, political speeches, and songs more influential than the written word. Public speaking was considered an essential ingredient of the political process, and schoolchildren were taught to declaim as part of their training in democratic responsibilities.[12]

To counteract the divisive effects of regional differences in speech, Webster argued for an American revolution in the use of words: "As an independent nation, our honor requires us to have a system of our own, in language as well as government. Great Britain, whose children we are, and whose language we speak, should no longer be *our* standard; for the taste of her writers is already corrupted and her language on the decline." To cast off the shackles of British cultural hegemony, Webster challenged Americans to develop their own system of correct and incorrect usage and pronunciation. He promoted common schooling as the means through which speakers of English could be redeemed as speakers of American. In addition to the use of American words, Webster urged parents and teachers to nurture children with patriotic stories and names. "Begin with the infant in his cradle," he advised. "Let the first word he lisps be WASHINGTON."[13]

The readers and primers published by William Holmes McGuffey expanded on the nationalist themes pioneered by Webster, adapting them for optimal utility in the public school context. Rather than original publications, McGuffey's books were gleanings from many different texts, with stories, pictures, and maxims pieced together so they could be used in most American classrooms most of the time. McGuffey's readers combined vocabulary lists and lessons in history, geography, and natural history with nonsectarian commentary on sobriety, discipline, and hard work. Before publication in the readers, selected passages were stripped of overt regional, ethnic, class, or political associations, translating them into a generic language suitable for children across the nation. Standardized and mass produced, McGuffey's textbooks represented the application of the celebrated "American system" of industrial manufactures to education. The uniformity of McGuffey's common school readers seemed to respond to the recommendation of Benjamin Rush, the eminent revolutionary statesman and physician who in 1786 called for the youth of America to be educated so thoroughly in the content and practice of democratic principles that they would be transformed into "republican machines."[14]

A young man depicted in a portrait painted in the 1840s by the Massachusetts artist William Bartoll appears to epitomize quite literally Rush's vision of the republican machine (fig. 157). The fixedness of his gaze and his unmodulated, cylindrical torso and tubular arms borrow from the visual lexicon of factory parts, while the lines of his playsuit echo the stripes of the American flag. The vectors of the striped fabric converge on the book the boy holds on his lap, which is turned outward so the view can easily make out the

FIG. 157   William Bartoll, *Boy with Dog*, c. 1840–1850. Oil on canvas, 30⅛ x 24¹³⁄₁₆ in. From the Collections of The Henry Ford Museum, Dearborn, Michigan.

letters of the alphabet on its pages. The prominence of the primer in the image clues the viewer to the significance of schooling in the boy's upbringing, although, like the letters in his primer that have not yet coalesced into words, he is shown in an early stage of his educational development. Accordingly, Bartoll's portrayal eschews the romantic posturing and painterly nuance typical in contemporary European child portraiture, presenting the subject as an unembellished icon of republican virtue. Still, with the opulent curtain behind the boy that hints at the opening of his life's first act, the artist allows an element of polish to assert itself in his work.

The prominently displayed ABC book connects the boy's tidy and well-mannered appearance to the merits of education—as well as to the strict educational protocols designed to help teachers manage classrooms with fifty students or more. Like the late-nineteenth-century efficiency experts who systematized factory workers' movements to increase their productivity, educators scrutinized every aspect of classroom activities in an effort to develop a body of rules that would expedite the governing of the nation's students. A manual setting forth the correct posture for pupils reading aloud reveals the meticulous attention to detail that child management involved: "While reading, as the eye rises to the top of the page, the right hand is brought to the position, with the forefinger under the leaf, the hand is slid down to the lower corner, and retained there during the reading of the page. . . . This is also the position in which the book is to be held when about to be closed; in doing which the left hand, being carried up to the side, supports the book firmly and unmoved while the right hand turns the part it supports over the left thumb. . . . The thumb will then be drawn out between the leaves and placed on the cover; when the right hand will fall by the side."[15]

In addition to classroom practices aimed at fostering obedience and uniformity, the content of schoolbook lessons revolved around stories of virtuous children whom students were expected to emulate. A lesson in McGuffey's *Second Reader* demonstrates the kind of material that students like the youth in Bartoll's painting were required to memorize and recite aloud in class. "The Truant" related the sad tale of a boy who slept late and, after waking and seeing how late it was, resolved to skip school and go back to sleep again. Even this brief interruption from the nurture of the classroom has grim consequences for the young man, including a deterioration in his physical appearance and social isolation. The lesson ended with a dire admonition that young readers were presumably expected to deliver in the resounding tones practiced during their elocution lessons: "Wretched are the parents of such a son, grief and shame are theirs, his name shall be stamped with the mark of infamy when their poor broken hearts shall molder in the grave." Intended to counteract the insidious persuasions of a warm bed or a beautiful spring morning, McGuffey's weighty indictment made strange bedfellows of death, infamy, and irregular school attendance.

While male students circumventing the disciplines of the classroom appeared frequently in art and popular imagery, girls were usually depicted as the bulwarks of school—and

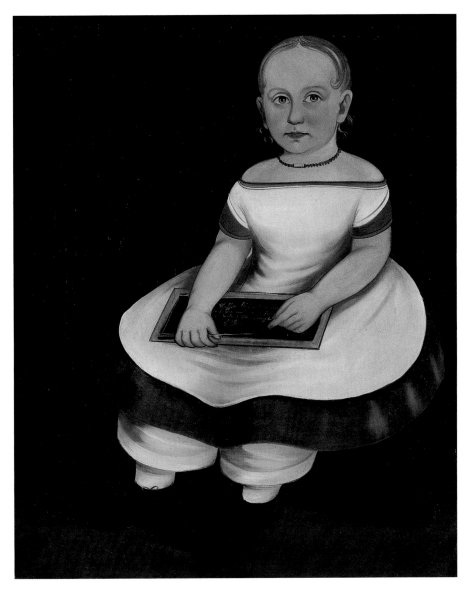

FIG. 158   Prior-Hamblin School, *Little Girl with Slate*, c. 1845. Oil on canvas, 27¹/₈ x 22¹/₁₆ in. National Gallery of Art, Washington, D.C. Gift of Edgar William and Bernice Chrysler Garbisch.

society's—order. A portrait of a young girl by an unidentified artist in the 1840s defined the place of females in the emerging hierarchy of opportunities available through education (fig. 158). On her lap the girl holds a slate on which she has copied a passage from the New Testament: "Suffer Little Children to come unto me for of such is the kingdom of heav[en]." The words, spoken by Jesus when his disciples tried to chase away a group of children who had approached him, refer to the ultimate purpose of schooling for young ladies. When their school years were finished, among the only vocations available to female students were motherhood and teaching, both of which were expected to revolve around the inculcation of moral virtue and study of the Bible. It is noteworthy that the text held by the boy in the portrait by William Bartoll faces outward to engage the viewer, while the writing on the girl's slate turns toward her. A small difference, this variation nevertheless suggests the significant disparity in the education of male and female children. Where boys were continually pressed to look out to the world beyond the classroom and to see their education as a conduit to an array of career opportunities, girls were directed to the interior pursuits of the home, where, as mothers and teachers to future generations of citizens, they would suffer little children to come unto them.

If the little girl holding the slate and the boy with his alphabet primer represent artists' conception of the national student body—and the types around which the body of school-related imagery evolved at mid-century—there were other students who remained largely invisible in depictions of classroom life from the period. Immigrants, Native Americans, and former slaves and freedmen made up a sizable part of the school-age population, but they generally were excluded from artistic depictions until the last decades of the century. While the question of the viability and value of public schooling still hung in the balance, artists may have been reluctant to create pictures of schoolchildren who did not fit national norms, exposing the danger of racial intermingling that their middle-class patrons feared. In the years following the Civil War, public schooling came to be accepted by the public as the best way to assimilate and make useful the nation's disparate peoples. Those who had always been absent from portrayals of American classrooms began to seep into paintings, book illustrations, and other imagery offered to the American public, and, for many viewers, they even acquired special status as emblems of Christian tolerance and national unity. Non-white and immigrant schoolchildren often were pictured in documentary photographs made for organizations charged with the education of marginalized groups. Representing a new medium that belonged primarily to the realm of science during the nineteenth century, these photographs incorporated the promise of remedial systems and technologies into their visual report on atypical American students.

In the 1890s, the published exposés of investigative reporter and urban reformer Jacob Riis juxtaposed images of homeless waifs with pictures of "reformed" children in city schools that appeared as the antidote for poverty and rising levels of immigration. Eastern cities had grappled with the problem of destitute immigrant children since the early part of the century, and urban reform groups debated whether local schooling or "placing out" children with families in the countryside was the best solution. In the 1860s, the Boston School Committee described what it viewed as the principal challenges and goals of educating children who came—or whose parents came—from across the ocean: "Taking children at random from a great city, undisciplined, uninstructed, often with inveterate forwardness and obstinacy, and with the inherited stupidity of centuries of ignorant ancestors; forming them from animals into intellectual beings, and . . . from intellectual into spiritual beings; giving to many their first appreciation of what is wise, what is true, what is lovely and what is pure."[16]

FIG. 159   Jacob Riis, *Saluting the Flag in the Mott Street Industrial School, New York*, c. 1892. Library of Congress, Prints and Photographs Division, Washington, D.C.

Riis's photograph of children saluting the flag at Mott Street Industrial School in New York captured immigrant students as they were learning to discern what was wise and true (fig. 159). The flag salute was one of many patriotic rituals in the choreography of Americanization that was meant to transform pupils who spoke no English and whose customs were derived from "centuries of ignorant ancestors." Riis described the scene for his audience: "Every morning sees the flag carried to the principal's desk and all the little ones, rising at the stroke of the bell, say with one voice, 'We turn to our flag as the sunflower turns to the sun!' One bell, and every brown right fist is raised to the brow, as in military salute: 'We give our heads!' Another stroke, and the grimy little hands are laid on as many hearts. 'And our hearts!' Then with a shout that can be heard around the corner: '—to our country! One country, one language, one flag!'"[17]

The children of immigrants were not the only students to receive special attention in photographs documenting school activities. In the far reaches of the west, where Native American peoples were assigned to reservation lands, photographs made at the many "Indian schools" organized in the second half of the century unveiled the process of cultural assimilation that was well under way (figs. 160–163). Photographic accounts inventoried

FIG. 160   John N. Choate, *Three Students, as They Looked on Arrival at Carlisle, left to right, Mary Perry, John (Chaves) Menaul, and Benjamin Thomas*, July 31, 1880. Cumberland County Historical Society, Carlisle, Pennsylvania.

FIG. 161   John N. Choate, *Three Pueblo Students After a Few Years at Carlisle, left to right, John (Menaul) Chaves, Mary Perry, and Benjamin Thomas*, c. 1884. Cumberland County Historical Society, Carlisle, Pennsylvania.

FIG. 162   Unidentified photographer, *Conversation Lesson Subject—The Chair*, 1880s. Library of Congress, Prints and Photographs Division, Washington, D.C.

FIG. 163   Unidentified photographer, *Indian Girls Ironing School Laundry*, 1880s. Library of Congress, Prints and Photographs Division, Washington, D.C.

every aspect of the educational program and its progress at boarding schools for Native American children—recording pupils in tribal clothing on their arrival at school, the alteration of their dress and hair styles, classroom study, and training in the behaviors common in middle-class households. Photographs of vocational training in the jobs considered suitable for Indian children—as carpenters, shoemakers, farm laborers, and domestics—transmitted the idea that Indian children would not ascend to middle-class status themselves but rather would act as producers and helpmates for those who were already there.

Whereas pictures of Native Americans in school represented a small portion of education-related imagery in the second half of the nineteenth century, depictions of African-American schoolchildren were produced in relatively large numbers and were disseminated widely during and after the Civil War (figs. 164–165). *Harper's Weekly* published several illustrated articles on the education of freedmen that described the students and routines of schools run by northern missionaries and those operated by African-American organizers. The journal made special mention of the importance African-American students placed on learning to read, explaining: "The alphabet is an abolitionist. If you would keep a people enslaved refuse to teach them to read."

In 1877, the year that marked the end of the Reconstruction period in the former Confederate states, Winslow Homer painted *Sunday Morning in Virginia* (fig. 166). Alluding to the education of black children in the South, the painting shows a group of African-American children seated next to a brick hearth in the company of an older

FIG. 164   After A. R. Ward, "Zion School for Colored Children, Charleston, South Carolina," from *Harper's Weekly*, December 15, 1866. Stanford University Libraries and Department of Special Collections.

woman. Younger children listen intently as a teenage girl whose tidy dress and white apron contrast with the ragged clothes of her companions appears to read from the Bible. With an abbreviated notation of color and form, the artist sketched in the walls and fireplace of the reader's humble abode, a visual shorthand for the dilapidated cabin that was inextricably linked to African-American identity in nineteenth-century imagery.

Through the distinct clothing of the reader—clothing that Homer's audiences would have seen as respectable attire—the artist linked the act of reading and education to the upward mobility of African-Americans after the Civil War. In the decade following the war, more than fifty religious and secular organizations rushed to the South to establish elementary schools and colleges, and the reader's clothes identify her as a student of one of the new public schools organized for freed children. In addition to providing instruction in reading and arithmetic, the schools tutored their pupils in moral values, self-discipline, and conventional speech and dress—a curriculum intended to nurture self-reliance and economic independence. By the 1870s, Reconstruction reformers and educators were impatient to see evidence that former slaves were ready to use their education to achieve economic autonomy, and their evaluations focused on literacy statistics and other measurements of the abilities and progress of freed students. As early as 1864, an administrator appointed by President Grant to supervise education for freedmen in the South proclaimed that "the seeds of knowledge have been sown," asserting that government officials had completed their job and the work of self-betterment was now in the hands of the freed people.[18]

FIG. 165 Unidentified artist, "Noon at the Primary School for Freedmen, Vicksburg, Mississippi," from *Harper's Weekly*, June 23, 1866. Stanford University Libraries and Department of Special Collections.

FIG. 166 Winslow Homer, *Sunday Morning in Virginia*, 1877. Oil on canvas, 18 x 24 in. Cincinnati Art Museum. John Emery Fund.

FIG. 167   Krebs Lithographing Company, "Family Record," lithograph, 1880. Library of Congress, Prints and Photographs Division, Washington, D.C.

Sunday Morning in Virginia recognized that the "seeds of knowledge" had been sown, blossoming in the figure of the young girl who reads to younger children. The portrayal left hanging in the balance, however, the question of the ultimate harvest of the efforts that had produced this literate, devout, and properly dressed young woman. Her respectable appearance underscores the evidence of poverty around her, a reminder that the wretched conditions of slavery persisted after freedom had been granted by the Emancipation Proclamation. In spite of the precarious economic status of freed blacks after the war, however, some northern companies positioned themselves to be ready for a new market of African-American consumers. A lithograph published by the Krebs Company in 1880 targeted African-Americans who aspired to the middle class. For people whose lineages had been lost and families dispersed, the Krebs "Family Record" offered black families a way to reassemble what had been taken from them and a method to keep track of future births, deaths, and marriages (fig. 167). The literacy of buyers was implicit in the document,

FIG. 168 "The Freedman's Home," from *The Freedman's Second Reader*, published by the American Tract Society, 1865. Library of Congress, Prints and Photographs Division, Washington, D.C.

which also included vignettes of prosperous African-Americans in pleasing domestic environments. Surrounded by places for the inscription of names of mothers, fathers, siblings, and grandparents, these images portrayed well-to-do parents and children watched over by a portrait of George Washington on the wall, and landowners recreating on acreage they had once worked as slaves.

Both the Krebs "Family Record" and Homer's *Sunday Morning in Virginia* blended together notions of education, family ties, and economic status in their portrayals of black families. These works reformulated the same themes that appeared in textbooks published by northern missionary societies soon after the war. *The Freedman's Second Reader* of 1865 included a lesson on "The Freedman's Home" that focused on the act of reading (fig. 168).

Underneath lists of evocative vocabulary—"wake," "dawn," "clean," "scrub," "school"—an image shows a father reading to his children in a comfortable parlor. The picture and the accompanying text worked to exorcise from pupils' minds the specter of old plantation cabins like the one Homer used as the backdrop for his painting. "See this home!" it commanded. "How neat, how warm, how full of cheer it looks!" Bound up in an ensemble representing domesticity, freedom, and prosperity, the reading that binds the family together is also the key to the prosperity they enjoy, the symbol of the education that allowed them to pull themselves up from slavery.

Unlike the idealized family pictured in the schoolbook for freedmen, the children in *Sunday Morning in Virginia* are still remote from the prosperous life of the American middle class. Nevertheless, the book at the center of the canvas, with its references to knowledge, virtue, and diligent labor, embodies the young people's right to claim the privileges of citizenship that had previously been denied to African-Americans. In a circle around their book, the children of Virginia slaves assemble for a rite of passage to the broader American community—and the freedoms and comforts that communal membership entailed. *Sunday Morning in Virginia* recycled for freedmen the themes of childhood, education, liberty, and opportunity that Homer introduced in his paintings of New England school subjects in the early 1870s. The painting also referred back to a century of portrayals of young Americans in the process of becoming citizens—country boys and girls, city ragamuffins, and Native American babies who foretold a glorious destiny for the nation. Through pictures of children and the lessons of the ABC, new generations of Americans learned to parse the words of unity that had been passed down from the Founding Fathers: *E Pluribus Unum.*

Notes

INTRODUCTION

1. Quoted in Steven Mintz and Susan Kellogg, *Domestic Revolutions: A Social History of American Family Life* (New York: Free Press, 1988), 15.

2. Herman Humphrey, *Domestic Education* (Amherst, Mass.: J. S. and C. Adams, 1840), 21.

3. Catherine M. Sedgwick, *The Boy of Mount Rhigi* (Boston: Crosby and Nichols, 1848), 6.

CHAPTER 1. THE COUNTRY BOY

1. Henry Ward Beecher, "The Advance of a Century," *The New York Tribune* (Extra no. 33, Independence Day Orations, July 4, 1876), 39.

2. Quoted in Richard L. Rapson, "The American Child as Seen by British Travelers," *American Quarterly* 17, no. 3 (Fall 1965): 526–527.

3. In the early part of the nineteenth century, most states restricted the right to vote to adult white males who either owned property or paid taxes in their place of residence.

4. Andrew Jackson, letter to William B. Lewis, August 19, 1841, from "Letters of W. B. Lewis," Andrew Jackson Papers (Library of Congress, Department of Special Collections, Washington, D.C.). Arthur M. Schlesinger, Jr., provides an engaging account of the radical changes that occurred from the 1820s through the 1840s as the Jeffersonian Age ceded to the Jacksonian Era in his book *The Age of Jackson* (Boston: Little, Brown, 1945).

5. Alexis de Tocqueville, *Democracy in America* (1838; rpt., New York: Bantam Classic, 2000), 726.

6. Quoted in David Cassedy and Gail Shrott, *William Sidney Mount: Works in the Collection of the Museums at Stony Brook* (Stony Brook, N.Y.: The Museums at Stony Brook, 1983), 40.

7. William H. McGuffey, *McGuffey's New Fifth Eclectic Reader* (New York: Van Antwerp, Bragg, 1866), 92. Ohio schoolteacher William McGuffey was one of the foremost authors of children's textbooks during the nineteenth century. Between 1836 and 1920 approximately 120 million copies of McGuffey's readers were published. The readers set the standard for educational texts in American public schools during the nineteenth century. Their lessons also created a specific model of virtuous behavior for American boys and girls.

8. William H. McGuffey, *The Eclectic First Reader* (Cincinnati: Truman and Smith, 1836), 24–25.

9. Herman Humphrey, *Domestic Education* (Amherst, Mass.: J. S. and C. Adams, 1840), 18–19.

10. Lydia M. Child, *The Mother's Book* (Boston: Carter and Hendee, 1831), 26.

11. "Looking Out For Number One," *The Nursery* (1878), 108.

12. This description is from an anonymous letter of 1843 addressed to would-be teachers that was published in the *Newburyport Daily Herald*. Quoted in Rebecca Noel, "Culture of Boys' Play in Mid-Nineteenth-Century New England: The Case of James Edward Wright," unpublished paper presented at the Dublin Seminar: The Worlds of Children, 1620–1920 (June 15, 2002), 14.

13. Quoted in Noel, "Culture of Boys' Play," 14.

14. "Physical Health: To the Young People of America," *Our Young Folks*, January 1865, 38–44.

15. In her book on genre painting in America, Patricia Hills discusses Ward's painting as a symbol of rural cooperation. *The Painter's America: Rural and Urban Life, 1810–1910* (New York: Praeger, 1974), 75.

16. Frances Trollope, *Domestic Manners of the Americans* (London, 1832), 110.

17. Because snap the whip was considered too rough for polite young readers, most nineteenth-century children's books providing explanations and instructions for children's recreations did not include a description of the game. One popular book on juvenile pastimes described wrestling as too boisterous for well-mannered children, and presumably snap the whip was relegated to this "forbidden" category.

18. *New York Commercial Advertiser* (December 10, 1872); *New York Herald* (October 13, 1873); *Harper's Weekly* (September 20, 1873).

19. During the course of the nineteenth century, Americans went through a radical transition in timekeeping. Before railroad companies began to use Standard Railway Time in 1883, there was no national system of timekeeping and local communities had distinct methods for coordinating the time of public routines and events. Within a span of approximately fifty years, the nation made the transition from the natural time dictated by day and night, and lunar and seasonal rhythms, to the mechanical time of clocks, watches, regional time zones, and railroad schedules. The subject of time was a central concern during the nineteenth century as Americans adjusted to a new system that transformed the way they perceived and managed their everyday routines. Two important books examining this subject are Ian R. Bartky, *Selling the True Time: Nineteenth-Century Time Keeping in America* (Stanford, Calif.: Stanford University Press, 2000), and Michael O'Malley, *Keeping Watch: A History of American Time* (Washington, D.C.: Smithsonian Institution Press, 1990).

20. As babies and toddlers, American boys often wore skirts and dresses. During the nineteenth century, "breeching" was one of the most important rituals of boyhood. The significance of putting away "long coats" in favor of "manly breeches" (which were usually held up by suspenders) was the subject of a poem by nineteenth-century juvenile book authors Charles and Mary Lamb. The poem also took up the subject of the kind of games considered appropriate for boys:

> *Sashes, frocks, to those that need 'em—*
> *Phillip's limbs have got their freedom—*
> *He can run or he can ride,*
> *And do twenty things beside,*
> *Which his petticoats forbad;*
> *Is he not a happy lad?*
> *Now he's under other banners,*
> *He must leave his former manners;*
> *Bid adieu to female games,*
> *And forget their very names.*
> *Puss in corner, hide and seek*
> *Sports for girls and punies weak!*

Quoted in Monica Kiefer, *American Children Through Their Books* (Philadelphia: University of Pennsylvania Press, 1948), 190.

21. Quoted in Mary Lynn Stevens Heininger et al., *A Century of Childhood, 1820–1920* (Rochester, N.Y.: Margaret Woodbury Strong Museum, 1984), 132.

22. Louis Auchincloss, ed., *The Hone and Strong Diaries of Old Manhattan* (New York: Abbeville, 1989), 176.

23. Quoted in Alan Trachtenberg, ed., *Democratic Vistas, 1860–1880* (New York: George Braziller, 1970), 14.

CHAPTER 2. DAUGHTERS OF LIBERTY

1. Quoted in John Wilmerding, et al., *An American Perspective: American Paintings in the Collection of Jo Ann and Julian Ganz* (Washington, D.C.: National Gallery of Art, 1981), 57.

2. During the colonial period there was no social sanction against women working outside the home. Women worked as printers, sextons, silversmiths, gunsmiths, tavern keepers, shopkeepers, and a variety of other occupations. They also owned and managed mills, plantations, hotels, and shipyards. For a description of how this situation changed during the nineteenth century, see Gerda Lerner, "The Lady and the Mill Girl: Changes in the Status of Women in the Age of Jackson," in *A Heritage of Her Own: Towards a New Social History of American Women*, ed. Nancy Cott and Elizabeth H. Pleck (New York: Simon and Schuster, 1979), 182–196.

3. Catharine Beecher, *A Treatise on Domestic Economy* (Boston: T. H. Webb, 1842), 37. Beecher was the sister of Harriet Beecher Stowe, the author of *Uncle Tom's Cabin*, and the prominent minister Henry Ward Beecher. She was a leading authority on education and moral and religious issues. On Beecher, see Kathryn Kish Sklar, *Catharine Beecher: A Study in American Domesticity* (New Haven: Yale University Press, 1973).

4. Quoted in Susan B. Anthony, Elizabeth Cady Stanton, and Matilda Joslyn Gage, eds., *History of Woman Suffrage* (Boston, 1889), 1:70–71.

5. On ideas and portrayals relating to girlhood during the nineteenth century, see Jane H. Hunter, *How Young Ladies Became Girls: The Victorian Origins of American Girlhood* (New Haven: Yale University Press, 2002).

6. Quoted in Herbert G. Gutman, *Work, Culture, and Society in Industrializing America* (Oxford: Basil Blackwell, 1977), 5.

7. Flowers in paintings were part of a symbolic language in which specific meanings were ascribed to particular flowers. I do not take up this subject because it relates to courtship and other topics outside the scope of this chapter. For a general discussion of floral symbolism in nineteenth-century American culture, see Annette Stott, "Floral Femininity: A Pictorial Definition," *American Art* 6, no. 2 (Spring 1992): 61–78; Judith Walsh, "The Language of Flowers in Nineteenth-Century American Painting," *The Magazine Antiques* (October 1999): 518–527; and Ella M. Foshay, *Reflections of Nature: Flowers in American Art* (New York: Alfred A. Knopf, 1984). A nineteenth-century American book that deals with floral symbolism is Elizabeth Washington Gamble Wirt, *Flora's Dictionary* (Baltimore: Fielding Lucas, 1829).

8. Dennis R. Anderson, *American Flower Painting* (New York: Watson-Guptill, 1980), 10.

9. Quoted in Linda K. Ferber, *Women of the Republic: Intellect and Ideology in Revolutionary America* (New York: W. W. Norton, 1980), 229.

10. Quoted in Ferber, *Women of the Republic*, 222.

11. Martha N. Hagood and Jefferson C. Harrison, *American Art in the Chrysler Museum: Selected Paintings, Sculpture, and Drawings* (Norfolk, Virginia: Chrysler Museum of Art, 2005), no. 12, 36–37.

12. On the popular conception of education for American women during the nineteenth century, see Eleanor Wolf Thompson, *Education for Ladies, 1830–1860: Ideas on Education in Magazines for Women* (Morningside Heights, N.Y.: King's Crown, 1947).

13. Quoted in William H. Gerdts, *Painters of the Humble Truth: Masterpieces of American Still Life, 1801–1939* (Columbia: Philbrook Art Center with University of Missouri Press, 1981), 27.

14. In 1827, the American art critic Daniel Fanshaw defined the hierarchy of art subjects in a review published in the *United States Review and Literary Gazette*. In descending order of importance, Fanshaw outlined ten categories of painting. Historic works and "Poetic Portraits" were featured at the top of the list, which concluded with "common portraits," "animals, cattle pieces," and "still life and dead game." For further discussion of the ranking of painting subjects, see Gerdts, *Painters of the Humble Truth*, 22.

15. On the development of the biological sciences in nineteenth-century America, see Philip J. Pauly, *Biologists and the Promise of American Life* (Princeton: Princeton University Press, 2000), and Elizabeth B. Keeney, *The Botanizers: Amateur Scientists in Nineteenth-Century America* (Chapel Hill: University of North Carolina Press, 1992).

16. Quoted in Keeney, *The Botanizers*, 69.

17. Quoted in Laurel Thatcher Ulrich, *The Age of Homespun: Objects and Stories in the Creation of an American Myth* (New York: Alfred A. Knopf, 2001), 23.

18. Ulrich describes the Daughters of Liberty and the colonial rebellion against British taxes in *The Age of Homespun*, 176–191. The book is also an exhaustively researched examination of the female-centered production of textiles and other objects in pre- and post-revolutionary America.

19. Catharine E. Beecher and Harriet Beecher Stowe, *The American Women's Home: or, Principles of Domestic Science* (New York: J. B. Ford, 1869), 126.

20. Nineteenth-century newspapers frequently reported on the harsh conditions of seamstresses, milliners, and other women employed in the urban garment industry. An account of 1869 described "numbers of 40, 50, and 60 in a shop, at less than $3.50 a week. . . . You can see them in those shops seated in long rows, crowded together in a hot, close atmosphere." On female work in the sewing trades, see Thomas Dublin, *Transforming Women's Work: New England Lives in the Industrial Revolution* (Ithaca: Cornell University Press, 1994), 163–192.

21. Ulrich, *The Age of Homespun*, 21.

22. Some girls working in textile factories later wrote memoirs recalling their years in the mills. See Harriet H. Robinson, *Loom and Spindle, or, Life Among the Early Mill Girls* (New York: T. Y. Crowell, 1898).

23. Louisa May Alcott, *Jack and Jill* (Boston: Little, Brown, 1928 [1880]), 310. Anne Scott MacLeod discusses literary portrayals of girls' transition to adulthood in *American Childhood: Essays on Children's Literature in the Nineteenth and Twentieth Centuries* (Athens: University of Georgia Press, 1994), 3–29.

24. Alcott, *Jack and Jill*, 198.

25. Hallways and hallway tables were an important element in middle-class courtship rituals, since they were the place where prospective suitors announced their intentions by leaving calling cards, which were then either received or ignored. On hall furnishings and the role of domestic hallways in American culture during the second half of the nineteenth century, see Kenneth L. Ames, *Death in the Dining Room and Other Tales of Victorian Culture* (Philadelphia: Temple University Press, 1992), 7–43.

26. On domesticity, housework, and the cult of the home during the nineteenth century, see Harvey Green, *The Light of the Home: An Intimate View of the Lives of Women in Victorian America* (New York: Pantheon, 1983); Mary P. Ryan, *The Empire of the Mother: American Writing About Domesticity, 1830–1860* (New York: Haworth, 1982); and Katherine C. Grier, *Parlor Making and Middle Class Identity, 1850–1930* (Washington, D.C.: Smithsonian Institution Press, 1988).

27. William A. Alcott, *The Young Wife; or Duties of Women in the Marriage Relation* (1837; rpt., New York: Arno, 1972).

28. Elizabeth Johns discusses the ideology of female virtue in America and foreign observers' reaction to the restricted status of American women in *American Genre Painting: The Politics of Everyday Life* (New Haven: Yale University Press, 1991), 140–142.

29. Beecher and Stowe, *The American Women's Home*, 127.

30. On feminism and conflicting ideals of womanhood during the nineteenth century, see Frances B. Cogan, *All-American Girl: The Ideal of Real Womanhood* (Athens: University of Georgia Press, 1989), and Rosalind Rosenberg, *Beyond Separate Spheres: Intellectual Roots of Modern Feminism* (New Haven: Yale University Press, 1982).

CHAPTER 3. CHILDREN OF BONDAGE

1. Quoted in John G. Nicolay and John Hay, eds., *Complete Works of Abraham Lincoln* (New York: Frances D. Tandy, 1905) 3:2.

2. On free blacks in the antebellum period, see Ira Berlin, *Slaves Without Masters: The Free Black in the Ante-bellum South* (New York: Oxford University Press, 1981). For an overview of the history of African-Americans in the United States, see Mary Frances Berry and John W. Blassingame, *Long Memory: The Black Experience in America* (New York: Oxford University Press, 1982).

3. Quoted in David Brion Davis, *Antebellum American Culture: An Interpretive Anthology* (Lexington, Mass.: D. C. Heath), 285.

4. Eugene Forster, et al., "Thomas Jefferson Fathered Slave's Last Child," *Nature* (November 1998), 396. On Jefferson's relationship with the slave Sally Hemings, see Annette Gordon-Reed, *Thomas Jefferson and Sally Hemings: An American Controversy* (Charlottesville: University Press of Virginia, 1997).

5. Andrew A. Lipscomb, ed., *The Writings of Thomas Jefferson* (Washington, D.C.: Thomas Jefferson Memorial Association, 1903), 16:12–13.

6. On portrayals of African-Americans in nineteenth-century American art, see Albert Boime, *The Art of Exclusion: Representing Blacks in the Nineteenth Century* (Washington, D.C.: Smithsonian Institution Press, 1990).

7. Two important studies on the lives of slave children are Wilma King, *Stolen Childhood: Slave Youth in Nineteenth-Century America* (Bloomington: Indiana University Press, 1995), and Marie Jenkins Schwartz, *Born in Bondage: Growing Up Enslaved in the Antebellum South* (Cambridge: Harvard University Press, 2000). On the broader issue of the effects of slavery on African-American children and their families, see Herbert G. Gutman, *The Black Family in Slavery and Freedom, 1750–1925* (New York: Pantheon, 1976).

8. Frederick Douglass, *Narrative of the Life of Frederick Douglass, An American Slave* (1845; rpt., New York: Penguin, 1982), 71–72.

9. Quoted in Sam Dennison, *Scandalize My Name: Black Imagery in American Popular Music* (New York: Garland, 1982), 142.

10. Elizabeth Johns, *American Genre Painting: The Politics of Everyday Life* (New Haven: Yale University Press, 1991), 110, discusses Clonney's *In the Cornfield* and the various meanings of "corn" and "ploughing the corn" in contemporary American speech. "Ploughing the corn" was used as a metaphor for the political maneuverings of election campaigns, and "corn" indicated suspicious campaign rhetoric.

11. During the nineteenth century, many scientists supported maintaining racial "purity" on the grounds that the mixing of races resulted in inferior human stock. Louis Agassiz of Harvard University was a leading opponent of amalgamation and he carried out a variety of research projects to substantiate his ideas about the separate genesis of the black race. For more information on "scientific" racism, see William Stanton, *The Leopard's Spots: Scientific Attitudes Toward Race in America, 1815–1859* (Chicago: University of Chicago Press, 1960), and Reginald Horsman, *Race and Manifest Destiny: The Origins of American Racial Anglo-Saxonism* (Cambridge: Harvard University Press, 1981).

12. For her various portrayals of African-Americans, Spencer drew on her observations of blacks in Ohio. Spencer grew up in the state and spent several years living in Cincinnati, which had a large population of free blacks. A number of abolitionist publications and anti-slavery organizations based their operations in Cincinnati, which was also a meeting point for runaway slaves.

13. *The Child's Anti-Slavery Book* (New York: Carlton and Porter, 1859), 2.

14. Quoted in Peter H. Wood and Karen C. Dalton, *Winslow Homer's Images of Blacks: The Civil War and Reconstruction Years* (Austin: University of Texas Press, 1988), 14.

15. In *The Black Image in the White Mind*, a landmark study of white beliefs about African-Americans during the nineteenth and early twentieth centuries, George Fredrickson discusses Northerners' attitudes

toward black recruits during the Civil War. Though Union supporters acknowledged African-Americans' important contribution to the Northern effort, they also believed the success of black troops depended on the supervision of whites. The New England abolitionist minister Thomas Wentworth Higginson, who commanded the black regiment of the First South Carolina Volunteers, stated that African-American soldiers "will depend more upon their officers than white troops, and be more influenced by their conduct. If their officers are intimidated they will be; and if their officers stand their ground so will they. If they lose their officers the effect will be worse on them than upon white troops, not because they are timid, but because they are less accustomed to entire self-reliance." *The Black Image in the White Mind: The Debate on Afro-American Character and Destiny, 1817–1914* (New York: Harper and Row, 1971), 169–170.

16. Quoted in Dennison, *Scandalize My Name,* 197–198.

17. Elizabeth Kilham, "Tobe's Monument," *Our Young Folks,* February 1872, 80–87.

18. *Hand Shadow Stories* (Boston: Taggard and Thompson, 1863), 15.

19. By the end of the Civil War, Zouave troops had suffered a disproportionate number of casualties. Two of the most famous companies, the Duryee's and Hawkin's regiments, lost half to three-quarters of their men. With their flamboyant outfits and high attrition rates, the Zouaves after the war became symbols of early Northern optimism about the war that was soon dashed by the consuming devastation of the conflict.

20. Robert C. Toll, *Blacking Up: The Minstrel Show in Nineteenth-Century America* (New York: Oxford University Press, 1974), 45. On blackface minstrelsy, see also the brilliant examination of the class and gender conflicts embodied in blackface performances in Eric Lott, *Love and Theft: Blackface Minstrelsy and the American Working Class* (New York: Oxford University Press, 1993).

21. Margaret Eytinge, "Going Halves," *Our Young Folks,* April 1867. 238.

22. On the 1863 portraits of the Louisiana slave children, see Kathleen Collins, "Portraits of Slave Children," *History of Photography* 9 (July–September 1985), 187, 210, and Mary Niall Mitchell, "'Rosebloom and Pure White,' Or So It Seemed," *American Quarterly* 54 (September 2002): 369–410.

23. The Louisiana slave children appeared in the public eye just as a widespread public argument erupted over the issue of interracial marriage, or "miscegenation." The controversy revolved around an anonymous pamphlet titled *Miscegenation* that created a sensation in the North when it was published in 1863. It argued that the mixing of races was a welcome benefit of Republican policies and claimed that mixed races were superior to unmixed strains. It was a hoax perpetrated by two Democratic journalists who wanted to discredit the Republican Party in the election of 1864, but the booklet provoked a vehement response—mostly in opposition to the mixing of races. The Northern press was at the center of the debate, with the *Tribune,* the *Independent,* the *World* and other journals expressing a range of views on the matter. Ultimately, the subject did not appear as a significant issue in the presidential campaign of 1864 because members of both parties agreed that amalgamation was unthinkable. For more information on the *Miscegenation* pamphlet, see Fredrickson, *The Black Image in the White Mind,* 171–174.

24. A native Virginian, Elder abandoned an art career in New York to serve in the Confederate army. After the Civil War, the artist remained in the South and returned to painting, specializing in Southern genre subjects, portraits of the local gentry, and representations of Confederate military victories.

25. The Virginia Breakdown was usually described as a vigorous dance incorporating rapid body movements, but the artist represented it here as a more subdued affair. The restraint of the dancing boy's posture in Elder's painting is consistent with descriptions of the slow-paced "Shuffles" seen in minstrel performances, rather than the more frenetic Breakdown. On African-American dance forms during the nineteenth century, see Lynn Fauley Emery, *Black Dance in the United States from 1619 to 1970* (Palo Alto, Calif.: National Press Books, 1972).

26. On Mount's portrayals of African-Americans, see Karen Adams, "The Black Image in the Paintings of William Sidney Mount," *The American Art Journal* 7, no. 2 (November 1975): 42–59.

27. After emancipation, former slaves tested their freedom by speaking and singing when it suited them. In 1868, four black women singing in their home in Virginia were beaten by a white man who was outraged when he asked them to stop and they refused. As former slaves and former masters adjusted to the new order brought about by emancipation, music and other kinds of soundmaking became an arena for confrontation. On African-American music in the nineteenth century, see Richard Crawford, *America's Musical Life: A History* (New York: W. W. Norton, 2001), 407–428, and Mark M. Smith, *Listening to Nineteenth-Century America* (Chapel Hill: University of North Carolina Press, 2001), 239–260.

28. Douglass, *Narrative of the Life of Frederick Douglass*, 57–58.

29. Quoted in Fredrickson, *The Black Image in the White Mind*, 296.

30. During the decades surrounding the turn of the century, many African-American intellectuals held that blacks were uniquely suited to be artists. In 1913, W. E. B. Du Bois wrote: "The Negro is primarily an artist. The usual way of putting this is to speak disdainfully of his sensuous nature. This means that the only race which has held at bay the life destroying forces of the tropics, has gained therefrom in some slight compensation a sense of beauty, particularly for sound and color, which characterizes the race. The Negro blood which flowed in the veins of many of the mightiest of the Pharaohs accounts for much of Egyptian art, and indeed, Egyptian civilization owes much in its origins to the development of the large strain of Negro blood which manifested itself in every grade of Egyptian society." W. E. B. Du Bois, "The Negro in Literature and Art," *The Annals of the American Academy of Political and Social Science* 49 (September 1913): 233.

CHAPTER 4. RAGAMUFFIN

1. *New York Times*, July 14, 1863.

2. This description of New York's impoverished class borrows from the language that nineteenth-century newspapers used. In his book *Free Soil, Free Labor, Free Men* (New York: Oxford University Press, 1970), historian Eric Foner created a list of the names used by the *New York Times* in July 1877 to describe those who had joined a railroad strike: disaffected elements, roughs, hoodlums, rioters, mob, suspicious-looking individuals, black characters, thieves, blacklegs, communists, rabble, labor-reform agitators, dangerous class of people, gangs, tramps, drunken section-men, law breakers, threatening crowd, bummers, ruffians, loafers, bullies, vagabonds, cowardly mob, band of worthless fellows, incendiaries, enemies of society, reckless crowd, malcontents, wretched people, loud-mouthed orators, rapscallions, brigands, robbers, riffraff, terrible felons, idiots.

3. On foreign immigration to the United States during the nineteenth century, see Roger Daniels, *Coming to America: A History of Immigration and Ethnicity in American Life*, 2nd ed. (New York: Perennial, 2002).

4. Quoted in Alan Trachtenberg, *The Incorporation of America: Society in the Gilded Age* (New York: Hill and Wang), 70.

5. Indigent girls posed a special problem for reformers who managed houses of refuge for impoverished city children. In general, young females were held to a higher moral standard than males and were more closely scrutinized for indications of immorality. By adolescence, girls were less likely than boys to be accepted into juvenile asylums; supervisors selected only those who were "either too young to have acquired habits of fixed depravity, or those whose lives in general have been virtuous." For more on the subject of females in houses of reform, see Joseph M. Hawes, *Children in Urban Society: Juvenile Delinquency in Nineteenth-Century America* (New York: Oxford University Press, 1971).

6. After the death of his young wife in 1850, Blythe became increasingly bitter about what he saw as

the failure of the democratic political process and the corruption of social institutions. He battled alco-holism for much of his adult life and died in 1865 of what was diagnosed as "mania potu" or delirium tremens. For more information on the artist, see Bruce W. Chambers, *The World of David Gilmour Blythe, 1815–1865* (Washington, D.C.: Smithsonian Institution Press, 1980).

7. Charles Mackay, *Life and Liberty in America* (New York, 1859), 122.

8. Henry W. Bellows, "The Influence of the Trading Spirit Upon the Social and Moral Life of America," *The American Review: A Whig Journal of Politics, Literature, Art, and Science* 1 (January 1845): 98.

9. On the influence of phrenology in American art, see Charles Colbert, *A Measure of Perfection: Phrenology and the Fine Arts in America* (Chapel Hill: University of North Carolina Press, 1997).

10. Elijah Devoe, *The Refuge System, or Prison Discipline Applied to Juvenile Delinquents* (New York, 1848), 24.

11. Elizabeth Oakes Smith, *The Newsboy* (New York, 1870), 33.

12. Quoted in Edwin P. Whipple, *The Great Speeches and Orations of Daniel Webster* (Boston: Little, Brown, 1879), 351. One of the first metropolitan newspapers, *The New York Sun*, advertised itself as a paper for the "Common Man."

13. Quoted in Daniel J. Boorstin, *The Americans: The National Experience* (New York: Random House, 1965), 125–126.

14. On the English fancy picture, see Martin Postle, *Angels and Urchins: The Fancy Picture in Eighteenth-Century British Art* (London: Aldridge, 1998).

15. New York Children's Aid Society, *First Annual Report* (New York, 1854), 6.

16. Charles Dickens, *American Notes for General Circulation* (London, 1842), 1:114.

17. For more information on the painting *Christmas Time (The Blodgett Family)*, see Theresa Carbone, "The Genius of the Hour: Eastman Johnson in New York, 1860–1880," in *Eastman Johnson: Painting America*, ed. Theresa Carbone and Patricia Hills (New York: Rizzoli, 1999), 62–63.

18. "Luck and Pluck" was the title of one of Alger's many books describing the life of poor boys in the city.

19. Andrew Carnegie, "The Gospel of Wealth," *North American Review* 148 (June 1889), 653–654.

20. Quoted in Robert H. Bremner, ed., *Children and Youth in America: A Documentary History, Volume 1, 1600–1865* (Cambridge: Harvard University Press, 1970), 400.

21. Quoted in Rosamund Olmstead Humm, *Children in America: A Study of Images and Attitudes* (Atlanta: High Museum of Art, 1979), 27.

22. "A Painter of Street Urchins," *New York Times Magazine* (August 27, 1899), 4.

23. Quoted in Stephen O'Connor, *Orphan Trains: The Story of Charles Loring Brace and the Children He Saved and Failed* (Boston: Houghton Mifflin, 2001), 117.

24. Quoted in Martha J. Hoppin, *Country Paths and City Sidewalks: The Art of J. G. Brown* (Springfield, Mass.: George Walter Vincent Museum of Art, 1989), 24.

25. Hoppin discusses Brown's portrayal of multiethnic groups of street children in *Country Paths and City Sidewalks*, 23–24.

26. Jacob A. Riis, *How the Other Half Lives: Studies Among the Tenements of New York* (1890; rpt., New York: Dover, 1971), 153.

27. On the rise of urban tourism in the United States, see Catherine Cocks, *Doing the Town: The Rise of Urban Tourism in the United States, 1850–1915* (Berkeley: University of California Press, 2001), and Neil Harris, "Urban Tourism and the Commercial City," in *Inventing Times Square: Commerce and Culture at the Crossroads of the World*, ed. William R. Taylor (New York: Russell Sage, 1991), 66–82.

CHAPTER 5. THE PAPOOSE

1. Though the tribes of North America are highly diverse, throughout this chapter I discuss them as if they were one people because this is the way they were generally perceived and represented by whites during the nineteenth century.

2. While most Indian tribes shared a focus on children, they represented a variety of family structures and relationships that included polygamy, polyandry, and serial marriages. Children played different roles within these family systems. For more information on tribal families, see "Native American Families," in *American Families: A Research Guide and Historical Handbook*, ed. Joseph M. Hawes and Elizabeth I. Nybakken (New York: Greenwood, 1991), 291–317; Jay Miller, "Kinship, Family Kindreds, and Community," in *A Companion to American Indian History*, ed. Philip J. Deloria and Neal Salisbury (Malden, Mass.: Blackwell, 2002), 139–153; and the section on Indian childhood in Anthony F. C. Wallace, *The Death and Rebirth of the Seneca* (New York: Alfred A. Knopf, 1969), 34–39.

3. Wallace, *Death and Rebirth of the Seneca*, 35.

4. For more information on eighteenth-century American portrayals of Native Americans, see the chapter "Colonial Images" in Elwood Parry, *The Image of the Indian and the Black Man in American Art, 1590–1900* (New York: George Braziller, 1974), 14–34. For a broad examination of white portrayals of Native Americans, see Robert F. Berhofer, *The White Man's Indian: Images of American Indians from Columbus to the Present* (New York: Alfred A. Knopf, 1978).

5. Quoted in Reginald Horsman, *Race and Manifest Destiny: The Origins of American Racial Anglo-Saxonism* (Cambridge: Harvard University Press, 1981), 107.

6. Quoted in Horsman, *Race and Manifest Destiny*, 108.

7. On the Spanish colonial structure in North America and the *encomienda* system see David J. Weber, *The Spanish Frontier in North America* (New Haven: Yale University Press, 1992), and Lesley B. Simpson, *The Encomienda in New Spain: The Beginning of Spanish Mexico*, 2nd ed. (Berkeley: University of California Press, 1950).

8. Quoted in Horsman, *Race and Manifest Destiny*, 108.

9. Benjamin Franklin, *The Autobiography of Benjamin Franklin and Other Writings*, ed. L. Jesse Lemisch (New York: New American Library, 1961), 136–137.

10. By the 1830s, one-third of the United States population lived west of the Alleghenies.

11. On Indian policy during Jackson's administration, see Ronald Satz, *American Indian Policy in the Jacksonian Era* (Lincoln: University of Nebraska Press, 1975). On the broader issue of the prevalent perception of Indians that lay behind the formulation of Indian policies during the nineteenth century, see Francis Paul Prucha, *The Indian in American Society from the Revolutionary War to the Present* (Berkeley: University of California Press, 1985).

12. The documentary aspect of these artists' works complemented the emerging science of ethnography. During the nineteenth century, Samuel G. Morton, Henry Rowe Schoolcraft, and other ethnologists made Native American tribes the focus of their research, which often included extensive visual documentation. On Native Americans and nineteenth-century ethnology, see Robert E. Bieder, *Science Encounters the Indian, 1820–1880* (Norman: University of Oklahoma Press, 1986).

13. At the turn of the century, one of the most noteworthy books about a young Indian brave was *Indian Boyhood*, an autobiographical account by Charles Eastman, a Sioux also known by the name of Hakadah. Accompanied by illustrations by E. L. Blumenschein, an artist renowned for his portrayals of Indians, Eastman's narrative describes his memories of buffalo hunts, games, and childhood rituals among the Sioux during the 1870s and 1880s. The author snared young readers with his opening question: "What boy would not be an Indian for a while when he thinks of the freest life in the world?" Charles Eastman, *Indian Boyhood* (1902; rpt., New York: Dover, 1971).

14. "Good Old Times," *Our Young Folks*, July 1867, 431.

15. George Catlin, *Letters and Notes on the Manners, Customs, and Conditions of the North American Indians* (1844; rpt., New York: Dover, 1973), 1:3. For more information on George Catlin and his role as a mediator between white society and the Indian world, see Patricia Nelson Limerick, *Legacy of Conquest: The Unbroken Past of the American West* (New York: W. W. Norton, 1986), 181–188. The book's chapter "The Persistence of Natives" also deals with the broader issue of the intersection of Indian and white cultures during the nineteenth century.

16. Catlin wrote about Osceola Nick-A-No-Chee in *Letters and Notes on the Manners, Customs, and Conditions of the North American Indians:* "This remarkably fine boy, by the name of Os-ce-o-la Nick-a-noo-chee, has recently been brought from America to London, by Dr. Welch, an Englishman, who has been for several years residing in Florida. The boy, it seems, was captured by the United States troops, at the age of six years: but how my friend the Doctor got possession of him, and leave to bring him away I never heard. He is acting a very praiseworthy part however, by the paternal fondness he evinces for the child, and fairly proves, by the very great pains he is taking with his education." Catlin, *Letters and Notes on the Manners,* 221.

17. Though the character of Uncas in Cooper's novel was fictional, a Mohegan chief named Uncas lived in the colony of Connecticut in the mid seventeenth century. He was a Mohegan, not a "Mohican," an important difference that is often confusing to historians. The real chief Uncas was not the last of his tribe; Mohegan people still live in New England today. For more information on the subject of the historical Uncas, see Michael Leroy Oberg, *Uncas: First of the Mohegans* (Ithaca: Cornell University Press, 2003).

18. James Fenimore Cooper, *The Last of the Mohicans* (1826; rpt., New York: New American Library, 1962), 37–38.

19. Quoted in Michael Bell, *Braves and Buffalo: Plains Indian Life in 1837* (Toronto: University of Toronto Press, 1973), 88. Posture was an important theme in nineteenth-century American culture, in which an unspoken vocabulary of body positions served as markers of class and social status. On the subject of posture during this period, see "An Erect Posture," *Gleason's* (August 28, 1852), 142, and David Yosifon and Peter N. Stearns, "The Rise and Fall of American Posture," *American Historical Review* 103, no. 4 (October, 1998): 1057–1095.

20. Henry Benjamin Whipple, *Lights and Shadows of a Long Episcopate* (New York: Macmillan, 1899), 52.

21. Mary Henderson Eastman, *Dahkotah or, Life and Legends of the Sioux* (1849; rpt., Afton, Minn.: Afton Historical Society Press, 1995), 23.

22. On the subject of half-breeds and the emergence of an Indian-white population, see William J. Scheik, *The Half-Blood: A Cultural Symbol in Nineteenth-Century American Fiction* (Lexington: University Press of Kentucky, 1979), and Jacqueline Peterson and Jennifer S. H. Brown, eds., *The New Peoples: Being and Becoming Métis in North America* (Lincoln: University of Nebraska Press, 1985).

23. "The Pappoose," *Harper's Weekly* 18 (October 24, 1874): 880.

24. Quoted in Bell, *Braves and Buffalo,* 88.

25. The Indian captivity narrative was one of the most widely read literary genres in the United States during the nineteenth century. These firsthand accounts of murder and survival also helped to inspire numerous representations by eminent artists, including George Caleb Bingham's *Captured by Indians* from 1848 and John Mix Stanley's *Osage Scalp Dance* of 1845. In her essay "Inventing 'The Indian,'" Julie Schimmel examines these two paintings in the broader context of Indian captivity literature. See William H. Truettner, ed., *The West as America: Reinterpreting Images of the Frontier, 1820–1920* (Washington, D.C.: Smithsonian Institution Press, 1991), 149–189.

26. Catlin, *Letters and Notes on the Manners,* 2:228.

27. Karen Holmes, "Grace Carpenter Hudson," *American Art Review* 11, no. 3 (1999): 163.

28. Quoted in Searles R. Boynton, *The Painter Lady: Grace Carpenter Hudson* (Eureka: Interface California Corporation, 1978), 29.

29. Quoted in Boynton, *The Painter Lady,* 29–30.

30. James Rawls gives an account of the extermination campaign waged against the Indians of California in *Indians of California: The Changing Image* (Norman: University of Oklahoma Press, 1984), 171–201.

31. For more information about the widespread abuses that led to calls for reforms of Indian policies, see David Wallace Adams, *Education for Extinction: American Indians and the Boarding School Experience, 1875–1928* (Lawrence: University Press of Kansas, 1995), 7–27. Helen Hunt Jackson also wrote a book about the government's mismanagement of Indian affairs and the corruption of Indian agents and the reservation system: *A Century of Dishonor: A Sketch of the United States Government's Dealings with Some of the Indian Tribes* (1881).

32. Quoted in Adams, *Education for Extinction*, 9.

33. Quoted in Adams, *Education for Extinction*, 19.

34. Quoted in Adams, *Education for Extinction*, 19.

CHAPTER 6. THE NEW SCHOLAR

1. Quoted in Marilyn S. Kushner, et al., *Winslow Homer: Illustrating America* (Brooklyn: Brooklyn Museum of Art and George Braziller, 2000), 100.

2. Quoted in Nicolai Cikovsky, "Winslow Homer's *School Time*: 'A Picture Thoroughly National,'" in *Essays in Honor of Paul Mellon*, ed. John Wilmerding (Washington, D.C.: National Gallery of Art, 1986), 65.

3. Quoted in Nicolai Cikovsky, Jr., and Franklin Kelley, *Winslow Homer* (Washington, D.C: National Gallery of Art, 1995), 88.

4. Quoted in David Brion Davis, ed., *Antebellum American Culture: An Interpretive Anthology* (Lexington, Mass.: D. C. Heath, 1979), 36.

5. Quoted in Robert H. Bremner, *Children and Youth in America: A Documentary History* (Cambridge: Harvard University Press, 1970), 459–460. Throughout the antebellum period, some of the most heated disputes over public schooling took place in Philadelphia. In 1844, controversy over the use of the Bible in public schools erupted into the Philadelphia Bible Riots. Following upon citywide demonstrations and skirmishes between opposing factions, the riots resulted in fourteen dead and many wounded—one of the worst episodes of violence in pre–Civil War America.

6. On the creation of the public school system in the United States, see Carl F. Kaestle, *Pillars of the Republic: Common Schools and American Society* (New York: Hill and Wang, 1983); Lawrence A. Cremin, *American Education: The National Experience, 1783–1876* (New York: Harper and Row, 1980); and Robert L. Church and Michael Sedlak, *Education in the United States: An Interpretive History* (New York: Free Press, 1976).

7. Quoted in Davis, ed., *Antebellum American Culture*, 36.

8. Quoted in Barbara Finkelstein, "Pedagogy as Intrusion: Teaching Values in Popular Primary Schools in the Nineteenth Century," *History of Childhood Quarterly: The Journal of Psychohistory* 2, no. 3 (1975): 357.

9. Quoted in Davis, ed., *Antebellum American Culture*, 42.

10. Quoted in Finkelstein, "Pedagogy as Intrusion," 368.

11. William Augustus Mowry, *Recollections of a New England Educator, 1838–1908* (New York: Silver, Burdett, 1908), 15.

12. On Webster's ideas for an American language, see Jill Lepore, *A Is for American: Letters and Other Characters in the Newly United States* (New York: Alfred A. Knopf, 2002), 15–41.

13. Quoted in Ruth Miller Elson, *Guardians of Tradition: American Schoolbooks of the Nineteenth Century* (Lincoln: University of Nebraska Press, 1964), 203.

14. Quoted in Kaestle, *Pillars of the Republic*, 8.

15. Quoted in Barbara Finkelstein and Kathy Vandell, "The Schooling of American Childhood: The Emergence of Learning Communities, 1820–1920," in *A Century of Childhood, 1820–1920*, by Mary Lynn Stevens Heininger et al. (Rochester, N.Y.: Margaret Woodbury Strong Museum, 1984), 70.

16. Quoted in Michael B. Katz, *The Irony of Early School Reform: Educational Innovation in Mid-Nineteenth-Century Massachusetts* (Cambridge: Harvard University Press), 120.

17. Quoted in Finkelstein and Vandell, "The Schooling of American Childhood," 85.

18. Quoted in Robert C. Morris, *Reading, 'Riting, and Reconstruction: The Education of Freedmen in the South, 1861–1870* (Chicago: University of Chicago Press, 1981), 17.

Bibliography

Abbott, Jacob. *Gentle Measures in the Management and Training of the Young* (New York: Harper and Brothers, 1877).

Adams, David Wallace. *Education for Extinction: American Indians and the Boarding School Experience, 1875–1928* (Lawrence: University Press of Kansas, 1995).

Adams, Karen. "The Black Image in the Paintings of William Sidney Mount." *The American Art Journal* 7, no. 2 (November 1975): 42–59.

Alcott, Louisa May. *Jack and Jill* (1880; rpt., Boston: Little, Brown, 1928).

Alcott, William A. *The Young Wife: or Duties of Women in the Marriage Relation* (1837; rpt., New York: Arno, 1972).

Alger, Horatio. *Ragged Dick: Street Life in New York with the Boot-Blacks* (Boston: Loring, 1868).

Ames, Kenneth L. *Death in the Dining Room and Other Tales of Victorian Culture* (Philadelphia: Temple University Press, 1992).

Anderson, Dennis R. *American Flower Painting* (New York: Watson-Guptill, 1980).

Anderson, James D. *The Education of Blacks in the South, 1860–1935* (Chapel Hill: University of North Carolina Press, 1988).

"An Erect Posture." *Gleason's* (August 28, 1852): 142.

Anthony, Susan B., Elizabeth Cady Stanton, and Matilda Joslyn Gage, eds. *History of Woman Suffrage* (1889).

Appleby, Joyce. *Inheriting the Revolution: The First Generation of Americans* (Cambridge: The Belknap Press of Harvard University Press, 2000).

Armstrong, Janice Gray, ed. *Catching the Tune: Music and William Sidney Mount* (Stony Brook, N.Y.: The Museums at Stony Brook, 1984).

Auchincloss, Louis, ed. *The Hone and Strong Diaries of Old Manhattan* (New York: Abbeville, 1989).

Bannister, Robert C. *Social Darwinism: Science and Myth in Anglo-American Social Thought* (Philadelphia: Temple University Press, 1979).

Banta, Martha. *Imaging American Women: Idea and Ideals in Cultural History* (New York: Columbia University Press, 1987).

Barron, Hal S. "Staying Down on the Farm: Social Processes of Settled Rural Life in the Nineteenth-Century North." In *The Countryside in the Age of Capitalist Transformation: Essays in the Social History of Rural America*, ed. Jonathan Prude and Steven Hahn (Chapel Hill: University of North Carolina Press, 1985), 327–343.

Barth, Gunther. *City People: The Rise of Modern City Culture in Nineteenth-Century America* (New York: Oxford University Press, 1980).

Bartky, Ian R. *Selling the True Time: Nineteenth-Century Time Keeping in America* (Stanford, Calif.: Stanford University Press, 2000).

Baym, Nina. *Woman's Fiction: A Guide to Novels by and About Women in America, 1820–1870* (Ithaca, N.Y.: Cornell University Press, 1978).

Beecher, Catharine E. *A Treatise on Domestic Economy, for the Use of Young Ladies at Home, and at School* (Boston: T. H. Webb, 1842).

Beecher, Catharine E., and Harriet Beecher Stowe. *The American Women's Home: or, Principles of Domestic Science, Being a Guide to the Formation and Maintenance of Economical, Healthful, Beautiful, and Christian Homes* (New York: J. B. Ford, 1869).

Beecher, Henry Ward. "The Adventure of a Century." *The New York Tribune*, extra no. 33, Independence Day Orations (July 4, 1876).

Bell, Michael. *Braves and Buffalo: Plains Indian Life in 1837* (Toronto: University of Toronto Press, 1973).

Bellows, Henry W. "The Influence of the Trading Spirit Upon the Social and Moral Life of America." *The American Review: A Whig Journal of Politics, Literature, Art, and Science* 1 (January 1845): 94–98.

Berhofer, Robert F. *The White Man's Indian: Images of American Indians from Columbus to the Present* (New York: Alfred A. Knopf, 1978).

Berlin, Ira. "American Slavery in History and Memory and the Search for Social Justice." *The Journal of American History* 90, no. 4 (March 2004): 1251–1268.

———. *Slaves Without Masters: The Free Black in*

the Ante-bellum South (New York: Oxford University Press, 1981).

Berry, Mary Frances, and John W. Blassingame. *Long Memory: The Black Experience in America* (New York: Oxford University Press, 1982).

Bieder, Robert E. *Science Encounters the Indian, 1820–1880: The Early Years of American Ethnology* (Norman: University of Oklahoma Press, 1986).

Billman, Carol. "McGuffey's Readers and Alger's Fiction: The Gospel of Virtue According to Popular Children's Literature." *Journal of Popular Culture* 11, no. 3 (Winter 1977): 614–620.

Blassingame, John W., ed. *The Slave Community: Plantation Life in the Antebellum South* (New York: Oxford University Press, 1972).

————. *Slave Testimony: The Centuries of Letters, Speeches, Interviews, and Autobiographies* (Baton Rouge: Louisiana State University Press, 1977).

Blumin, Stuart M. *The Emergence of the Middle Class: Social Experience in the American City, 1760–1900* (New York: Cambridge University Press, 1989).

Boehme, Sarah E., Christian F. Feest, Patricia Condon Johnston. *Seth Eastman. A Portfolio of North American Indians* (Afton, Minn.: Afton Historical Society Press, 1995).

Boime, Albert. *The Art of Exclusion: Representing Blacks in the Nineteenth Century* (Washington, D.C.: Smithsonian Institution Press, 1990).

Boorstin, Daniel J. *The Americans: The National Experience* (New York: Random House, 1965).

Boynton, Searles R. *The Painter Lady: Grace Carpenter Hudson* (Eureka: Interface California Corporation, 1978).

Bradley, M. E. *Douglass Farm, a Juvenile Story* (New York: D. Appleton, 1857).

Bremner, Robert H. *Children and Youth in America: A Documentary History, 1600–1865*, vol. 1 (Cambridge: Harvard University Press, 1970).

Bridges, William E. "Family Patterns and Social Values in America, 1825–1875." *American Quarterly* 17 (Spring 1965): 3–11.

Broderick, Dorothy H. *Image of Blacks in Children's Fiction* (New York: R. R. Bowker, 1973).

Bullock, Henry Allen. *A History of Negro Education in the South: From 1619 to the Present* (Cambridge: Harvard University Press, 1967).

Butts, R. Freeman. *A History of Education in American Culture* (New York: Holt, Rinehart and Winston, 1953).

Calvert, Karen. *Children in the House: The Material Culture of Early Childhood, 1600–1900* (Boston: Northeastern University Press, 1992).

Carbone, Teresa A., and Patricia Hills. "The Genius of the Hour: Eastman Johnson in New York, 1860–1880." In *Eastman Johnson: Painting America* (New York: Rizzoli, 1999): 49–119.

Carnegie, Andrew. "The Gospel of Wealth." *North American Review* 148 (June 1889): 653–654.

Carnes, Mark C., and Clyde Griffen. *Meanings for Manhood: Constructions of Masculinity in Victorian America* (Chicago: University of Chicago Press, 1990).

Carpenter, Charles. *History of American Schoolbooks* (Philadelphia: University of Pennsylvania Press, 1963).

Cassedy, David, and Gail Shrott. *William Sidney Mount: Works in the Collection of the Museums at Stony Brook* (Stony Brook, N.Y.: The Museums at Stony Brook, 1983).

Catlin, George. *Letters and Notes on the Manners, Customs, and Conditions of North American Indians*, 2 vols. (1844; rpt., Mineola, N.Y.: Dover, 1973).

Chambers, B. W. *The World of David Gilmour Blythe, 1815–1865* (Washington, D.C.: Smithsonian Institution Press, 1980).

Chevalier, Michael. *Society, Manners, and Politics in the United States* (New York: Augustus M. Kelley, 1966).

Child, Lydia M. *The Mother's Book* (Boston: Carter and Hendee, 1831).

The Child's Anti-Slavery Book (New York: Carlton and Porter, 1859).

Church, Robert L., and Michael Sealak. *Education in the United States: An Interpretive History* (New York: Free Press, 1976).

Cikovsky, Nicolai. "Winslow Homer's *School Time*: 'A Picture Thoroughly National.'" In *Essays in Honor of Paul Mellon*, ed. John Wilmerding (Washington, D.C.: National Gallery of Art, 1986), 47–69.

Cikovsky, Nicolai, Jr., and Franklin Kelley, *Winslow Homer* (Washington, D.C.: National Gallery of Art, 1995).

Clark, H. Nichols B. *Francis W. Edmonds: American Master in the Dutch Tradition* (Washington, D.C.: Smithsonian Institution Press, 1988).

Clemens, Samuel. *The Adventures of Huckleberry Finn* (New York: Charles L. Wester, 1885).

————. *The Adventures of Tom Sawyer* (Hartford: American, 1876).

Cocks, Catherine. *Doing the Town: The Rise of Urban Tourism in the United States, 1850–1915* (Berkeley: University of California Press, 2001).

Cogan, Frances B. *All-American Girl: The Ideal of Real Womanhood in Mid-Nineteenth-Century*

America (Athens: University of Georgia Press, 1989).

Colbert, Charles. *A Measure of Perfection: Phrenology and the Fine Arts in America* (Chapel Hill: University of North Carolina Press, 1997).

Collins, Kathleen. "Portraits of Slave Children." *History of Photography* 9 (July–September 1985): 187–210.

Comstock, J. L., M.D. *The Young Botanist: Being a Treatise on the Science, prepared for the use of persons just commencing the study of plants*, 2nd ed. (New York: Robinson, Pratt, 1836).

Conrads, Margaret C. *Winslow Homer and the Critics: Forging a National Art in the 1870s* (Princeton: Princeton University Press, 2001).

Cooper, James Fenimore. *The Last of the Mohicans* (1826; rpt., New York: New American Library, 1962).

Cooper, Michael L. *Indian School: Teaching the White Man's Way* (New York: Clarion, 1999).

Cornelius, E. *The Little Osage* (Boston: Sabbath School Society, 1822).

Cowan, Ruth Schwartz. *More Work for Mother: The Ironies of Household Technology from the Open Hearth to the Microwave* (New York: Basic Books, 1983).

————. *A Social History of American Technology* (New York: Oxford University Press, 1997).

Crawford, Richard. *America's Musical Life: A History* (New York: W. W. Norton, 2001).

Cremin, Lawrence A. *American Education: The National Experience, 1783–1876* (New York: Harper and Row, 1980).

Cross, Gary. *Kids Stuff: Toys and the Changing World of American Childhood* (Cambridge: Harvard University Press, 1977).

Cubberley, Ellwood P. *Public Education in the United States: A Study and Interpretation of American Educational History* (New York: Houghton Mifflin, 1919).

Daniels, Roger. *Coming to America: A History of Immigration and Ethnicity in American Life*, 2nd ed. (New York: Perennial, 2002).

Darrah, William C. *Cartes de Visite in Nineteenth-Century Photography* (Gettysburg, Pa.: William C. Darrah, 1981).

Davidson, Cathy N., ed. *Reading in America: Literature and Social History* (Baltimore: Johns Hopkins University Press, 1989).

Davis, David Brion, ed. *Antebellum American Culture: An Interpretive Anthology* (Lexington, Mass.: D. C. Heath, 1979).

Degler, Carl N. *The Age of the Economic Revolution, 1876–1900* (Lebanon, Ind.: Scott, Foresman American History Series, 1967).

Delamont, Sarah, and Lorna Duffin. *The Nineteenth-Century Woman: Her Cultural and Physical World* (New York: Harper and Row, 1978).

Deloria, Philip J., and Neal Salisbury, eds. *A Companion to American Indian History* (Malden, Mass.: Blackwell, 2002).

Demos, John. *Past, Present, and Personal: The Family and the Life Course in American History* (New York: Oxford University Press, 1986).

Dennison, Sam. *Scandalize My Name: Black Imagery in American Popular Music* (New York: Garland, 1982).

Devoe, Elijah. *The Refuge System, or Prison Discipline Applied to Juvenile Delinquents* (New York: J. B. M'Gown, 1848).

Dickens, Charles. *American Notes for General Circulation* (London: Chapman and Hall, 1842).

Douglass, Fredrick. *Narrative of the Life of Frederick Douglass, An American Slave* (1845; rpt., New York: Penguin, 1986).

Dublin, Thomas. *Transforming Women's Work: New England Lives in the Industrial Revolution* (Ithaca: Cornell University Press, 1994).

Du Bois, W. E. B. "The Negro in Literature and Art." *The Annals of the American Academy of Political and Social Science* 49 (September, 1913): 233–239.

————. *The Souls of Black Folk*. In *Three Negro Classics* (New York: Avon Books, 1965), 207–389.

Eastman, Charles. *Indian Boyhood* (1902; rpt., New York: Dover, 1971).

Eastman, Mary Henderson. *Dahkotah, or, Life and Legends of the Sioux* (1849; rpt., Afton, Minn.: Afton Historical Society Press, 1995).

Edwards, Lee M. *Domestic Bliss: Family Life in American Painting 1840–1910* (Yonkers, N.Y.: Hudson River Museum, 1986).

Elson, Ruth Miller. *Guardians of Tradition: American Schoolbooks of the Nineteenth Century* (Lincoln: University of Nebraska Press, 1964).

Emery, Lynn Fauley. *Black Dance in the United States from 1619 to 1970* (Palo Alto, Calif.: National Press Books, 1972).

England, J. Merton. "The Democratic Faith in American Schoolbooks, 1783–1860." *American Quarterly* 15 (1963): 191–199.

Epstein, Barbara Leslie. *The Politics of Domesticity: Women, Evangelism, and Temperance in Nineteenth-Century America* (Middletown, Conn.: Wesleyan University Press, 1981).

Evens, Sara M. *Born for Liberty: A History of Women*

in America (New York: Free Press/Collier Press/Macmillan, 1989).

Ewen, Scott. *Captains of Consciousness: Advertising and the Social Roots of the Consumer Culture* (New York: McGraw-Hill, 1976).

Fass, Paula S., and Mary Ann Mason. *Childhood in America* (New York: New York University Press, 2000).

Ferber, Linda K. *Women of the Republic: Intellect and Ideology in Nineteenth-Century America* (New York: W. W. Norton, 1986).

Finkelstein, Barbara. "Pedagogy as Intrusion: Teaching Values in Popular Primary Schools in Nineteenth-Century America." *History of Childhood Quarterly: The Journal of Psychohistory* 2, no. 3 (1975): 348–378.

Finkelstein, Barbara, and Kathy Vandell. "The Schooling of American Childhood: The Emergence of Learning Communities, 1820–1920." In *A Century of Childhood, 1820–1920*, by Mary Lynn Stevens Heininger et al. (Rochester, N.Y.: Margaret Woodbury Strong Museum, 1984), 65–96.

Foner, Eric. *Free Soil, Free Labor, Free Men* (New York: Oxford University Press, 1970).

Forster, Eugene, et. al. "Thomas Jefferson Fathered Slave's Last Child." *Nature* 396 (November 1998): 27–28.

Foshay, Ella M. *Reflections of Nature: Flowers in American Art* (New York: Alfred A. Knopf, 1984).

Foy, Jessica H., and Thomas J. Schlereth. *American Home Life, 1880–1930: A Social History of Spaces and Services* (Knoxville: University of Tennessee Press, 1992).

Franklin, Benjamin. *The Autobiography of Benjamin Franklin and Other Writings*, ed. L. Jesse Lemisch (New York: New American Library, 1961).

———. *Autobiography and Other Writings* (New York: Illustrated Modern Library, 1944).

Fredrickson, George M. *The Black Image in the White Mind: The Debate on Afro-American Character and Destiny, 1817–1914* (New York: Harper and Row, 1971).

Gerdts, William H. *Painters of the Humble Truth: Masterpieces of American Still Life, 1801–1939* (Columbia: Philbrook Art Center with University of Missouri Press, 1981).

Goldin, Claudia Dale. *Understanding the Gender Gap: An Economic History of American Women* (New York: Oxford University Press, 1990).

"Good Old Times." *Our Young Folks* (July 1867): 424–434.

Gordon-Reed, Annette. *Thomas Jefferson and Sally Hemings: An American Controversy* (Charlottesville: University Press of Virginia, 1990).

Graff, Harvey J. *Conflicting Paths: Growing Up in America* (Cambridge: Harvard University Press, 1987).

Grant, Julia. *Raising Baby by the Book: The Education of American Mothers* (New Haven: Yale University Press, 1998).

Green, Harvey. *The Light of the Home: An Intimate View of the Lives of Women in Victorian America* (New York: Pantheon, 1983).

Grier, Katherine C. *Culture and Comfort: Parlor Making and Middle-Class Identity, 1850–1930* (Washington, D.C.: Smithsonian Institution Press, 1988).

Gutman, Herbert G. *The Black Family in Slavery and Freedom, 1750–1925* (New York: Pantheon, 1976).

———. *Work, Culture, and Society in Industrializing America* (Oxford: Basil Blackwell, 1977).

Hale, Edward E. *A New England Boyhood* (New York: Cassell, 1893).

Hales, Peter B. *Silver Cities: The Photography of American Urbanization, 1830–1915* (Philadelphia: Temple University Press, 1984).

Hall, David. "The Uses of Literacy in New England." In *Printing and Society in Early America*, ed. William Leonard Joyce (Worcester, Mass.: American Antiquarian Society, 1983): 1–47.

Halttunen, Karen. *Confidence Men and Painted Women: A Study of Middle-Class Culture in America, 1830–1870* (New Haven: Yale University Press, 1982).

Handlin, Oscar, and Mary F. Handlin. *Facing Life: Youth and the Family in American History* (Boston: Little, Brown, 1971).

Hand Shadow Stories (Boston: Taggard and Thompson, 1863).

Harland, Marion. *Eve's Daughters; or, Common Sense for Maid, Wife, and Mother* (New York: J. R. Anderson and H. S. Allen, 1882).

Harris, Neil. "Urban Tourism and the Commercial City." In *Inventing Times Square: Commerce and Culture at the Crossroads of the World*, ed. William R. Taylor (New York: Russell Sage, 1991), 66–82.

Hawes, Joseph M. *Children in Urban Society: Juvenile Delinquency in Nineteenth-Century America* (New York: Oxford University Press, 1971).

Hawes, Joseph M., and Elizabeth I. Nybakken, eds. *American Families: A Research Guide and Historical Handbook* (New York: Greenwood, 1991).

Heininger, Mary Lynn Stevens, Karin Calvert,

Barbara Finkelstein, Kathy Vandell, Anne Scott McLeod, and Harvey Green. *A Century of Childhood, 1820–1920* (Rochester, N.Y.: Margaret Woodbury Strong Museum, 1984).

Hemphill, Dallett C. *Bowing to Necessities: A History of Manners in America, 1620–1860* (New York: Oxford University Press, 1999).

Hills, Patricia. *The Genre Painting of Eastman Johnson* (New York: Garland, 1977).

————. *The Painter's America: Rural and Urban Life, 1810–1910* (New York: Praegar, 1974).

Holmes, Karen. "Grace Carpenter Hudson." *American Art Review* 11, no. 3 (1999): 158–167.

Hoppin, Martha J. *Country Paths and City Sidewalks: The Art of J. G. Brown* (Springfield, Mass.: George Walter Vincent Smith Museum of Art, 1989).

————. "The 'Little White Slaves' of New York: Paintings of Child Street Musicians by J. G. Brown." *The American Art Journal* 26, nos. 1 and 2 (1994): 5–43.

Horan, James D. *The McKenney-Hall Portrait Gallery of American Indians* (New York: Crown, 1972).

Horsman, Reginald. *Race and Manifest Destiny: The Origins of American Racial Anglo-Saxonism* (Cambridge: Harvard University Press, 1981).

Hounshell, David A. *From the American System to Mass Production, 1800–1932: The Development of Manufacturing Technology in the United States* (Baltimore: Johns Hopkins University Press, 1984).

Humm, Rosamon Olmsted. *Children in America: A Study of Images and Attitudes* (Atlanta: The High Museum of Art, 1979).

Humphrey, Herman. *Domestic Education* (Amherst, Mass.: J. S. and C. Adams, 1840).

Hunter, Jane H. *How Young Ladies Became Girls: The Victorian Origins of American Girlhood* (New Haven: Yale University Press, 2002).

Jackson, Helen Hunt. *Century of Dishonor: A Sketch of the United States Government's Dealings with Some of the Indian Tribes* (1881).

Jacobs, Harriet A. *Incidents in the Life of a Slave Girl* (1861; rpt., Cambridge: Harvard University Press, 1991).

Johns, Elizabeth. *American Genre Painting: The Politics of Everyday Life* (New Haven: Yale University Press, 1991).

Johnson, Deborah J. *William Sydney Mount: Painter of American Life* (New York: American Federation of Arts, 1998).

Kaestle, Carl F. "Literacy and Diversity: Themes from a Social History of the American Reading Public." *History of Education Quarterly* 28, no. 4 (Winter, 1988).

————. *Pillars of the Republic: Common Schools and American Society* (New York: Hill and Wang, 1983).

Kaplan, Sydney. *Portrayal of the Negro in American Art*. Exhibition catalogue (Brunswick, Maine: Bowdoin College, 1967).

Katz, Michael B. *The Irony of Early School Reform: Educational Innovation in Mid-Nineteenth Century Massachusetts* (Cambridge: Harvard University Press, 1968).

Kaye, Myrna. *There's a Bed in the Piano: The Inside Story of the American Home* (Boston: Little, Brown, 1998).

Keeney, Elizabeth B. *The Botanizers: Amateur Scientists in Nineteenth-Century America* (Chapel Hill: University of North Carolina Press, 1992).

Kett, Joseph F. *Rites of Passage: Adolescence in America, 1790 to the Present* (New York: Basic, 1977).

Kiefer, Monica. *American Children Through Their Books* (Philadelphia: University of Pennsylvania Press, 1848).

Kilham, Elizabeth. "Tobe's Monument." *Our Young Folks* 8 (February 1872): 80–87.

King, William. *Stolen Childhood: Slave Youth in Nineteenth-Century America* (Bloomington: Indiana University Press, 1995).

Kinietz, W. Vernon. *John Mix Stanley and His Indian Paintings* (Michigan: University of Michigan Press, 1942).

Kulikoff, Allan. *The Agrarian Origins of American Capitalism* (Charlottesville: University Press of Virginia, 1992).

Kushner, Marilyn S., Barbara Dayer Gallati, Linda S. Ferber. *Winslow Homer: Illustrating America* (Brooklyn: Brooklyn Museum of Art and George Braziller, 2000).

Larcom, Lucy. *New-England Girlhood Outlined from Memory* (Boston: Houghton Mifflin, 1889).

Lears, T. J. Jackson. *No Place of Grace: Antimodernism and the Transformation of American Culture, 1880–1920* (Chicago: University of Chicago Press, 1994).

Le Beau, Bryan F. *Currier and Ives: America Imagined* (Washington, D.C.: Smithsonian Institution Press, 2001).

Lepore, Jill. *A is for American: Letters and Other Characteristics in the Newly United States* (New York: Alfred A. Knopf, 2002).

Lerner, Gerda. "The Lady and the Mill Girl: Changes in the Status of Women in the Age of Jackson." *Midcontinent American Studies Journal* 10 (Spring 1969): 5–14.

Limerick, Patricia Nelson. *Legacy of Conquest: The*

Unbroken Past of the American West (New York: W. W. Norton, 1986).

Lipscomb, Andrew A., ed. *The Writings of Thomas Jefferson*, vol. 16 (Washington, D.C., Thomas Jefferson Memorial Association, 1903).

Loeper, John. *Going to School in 1876* (New York: Atheneum Books for Young Readers, 1984).

"Looking Out For Number One." *The Nursery* (1878): 108–111.

Lott, Eric. *Love and Theft: Blackface Minstrelsy and the American Working Class* (New York: Oxford University Press, 1993).

Lubin, David M. *Picturing a Nation: Art and Social Change in Nineteenth-Century America* (New Haven: Yale University Press, 1994).

MacCann, Donnarae, and Gloria Woodard. *The Black American in Books for Children: Readings in Racism*, 2nd ed. (Metuchen, N.J.: Scarecrow, 1981).

McDermott, John Francis. *Seth Eastman's Mississippi: A Lost Portfolio Recovered* (Champaign: University of Illinois Press, 1973).

McElroy, Guy C. *Facing History: The Black Image in American Art, 1710–1940* (San Francisco: Bedford Arts, 1990).

McGuffey, William H. *The Eclectic First Reader* (Cincinnati: Truman and Smith, 1836).

———. *McGuffey's New Fifth Eclectic Reader* (New York: Van Antwerp, Bragg, 1866).

Mackey, Charles. *Life and Liberty in America* (New York, 1859).

MacLeod, Anne Scott. *American Childhood: Essays on Children's Literature in the Nineteenth and Twentieth Centuries* (Athens: University of Georgia Press, 1994).

Mallon, Isabel A. "Dressing a Growing Girl." *Ladies Home Journal* (August 1893): 21.

Margo, Robert A. *Race and Schooling in the South, 1880–1950: An American History* (Chicago: University of Chicago Press, 1991).

Mayr, Otto, and Robert C. Post. *Yankee Enterprise: The Rise of the American System of Manufacturers* (Washington, D.C.: Smithsonian Institution Press, 1981).

Miller, David C., ed. *American Iconology: New Approaches to Nineteenth-Century Art and Literature* (New Haven: Yale University Press, 1993).

Mintz, Steven, and Susan Kellogg. *Domestic Revolutions: A Social History of American Family Life* (New York: Free Press, 1988).

Mitchell, Mary Niall. "'Rosebloom and Pure White,' Or So It Seemed." *American Quarterly* 54 (September 2002): 369–410.

Morris, Robert C. *Reading, 'Riting, and Reconstruction: The Education of Freedmen in the South, 1861–1870* (Chicago: University of Chicago Press, 1981).

Mowry, William Augustus. *Recollections of a New England Educator, 1838–1908* (New York: Silver, Burdett, 1908).

Murray, Gail Schmunk. *American Children's Literature and the Construction of Childhood* (New York: Twayne, 1998)

Museum of Fine Arts, Boston. *Art and Commerce: American Prints of the Nineteenth Century* (Charlottesville: University Press of Virginia, 1975).

National Collection of Fine Arts. *Lilly Martin Spencer, 1822–1902: The Joys of Sentiment* (Washington, D.C.: Smithsonian Institution Press, 1973).

Noel, Rebecca. "Culture of Boys' Play in Mid-Nineteenth-Century New England: The Case of James Edward Wright." Unpublished paper presented at the Dublin Seminar: The Worlds of Children, 1620–1920 (June 15, 2002).

North, Douglas C. *The Economic Growth of the United States, 1790–1860* (New York: W. W. Norton, 1966).

Oberg, Michael Leroy. *Uncas: First of the Mohegans* (Ithaca: Cornell University Press, 2003).

O'Brian, Sharon. "Tomboyism and Adolescent Conflict: Three Nineteenth-Century Case Studies." In *Woman's Being, Women's Place: Female Identity and Vocation in American History*, ed. Mark Kelley (Boston: G. K. Hall, 1979), 351–372.

O'Connor, Stephen. *Orphan Trains: The Story of Charles Loring Brace and the Children He Saved and Failed* (Boston: Houghton Mifflin, 2001).

"The Old School House and the New; or, Fifty Years Ago and To-Day." *American Educational Monthly* 8 (October 1871): 473–486.

O'Malley, Michael. *Keeping Watch: A History of American Time* (Washington, D.C.: Smithsonian Institution Press, 1990).

"Our Children's Bodies." *Harper's Monthly Magazine* 67 (November 1883): 899–908.

Paine, Harriet E. *Chats with Girls on Self-Culture* (New York: Dodd, Mead, 1891).

Parry, Elwood. *The Image of the Indian and the Black Man in American Art, 1590–1900* (New York: George Braziller, 1974).

Pauly, Philip J. *Biologists and the Promise of American Life* (Princeton: Princeton University Press, 2000).

Peterson, Jacqueline, and Jennifer S. H. Brown, eds. *The New Peoples: Being and Becoming Métis in North America* (Lincoln: University of Nebraska Press, 1985).

"Physical Health of the Young People of America." *Our Young Folks* 8 (January 1865): 38–44.

Pierson, George Wilson. *Tocqueville and Beaumont in America* (New York: Oxford University Press, 1938).

Postle, Martin. *Angels and Urchins: The Fancy Picture in Eighteenth-Century British Art* (London: Aldridge, 1998).

Prucha, Francis Paul. *The Indians in American Society: From the Revolutionary War to the Present* (Berkeley and Los Angeles: University of California Press, 1985).

Rapson, Richard L. "The American Child as Seen by British Travelers." *American Quarterly* 17, no. 3 (Fall 1965): 521–534.

Rawls, James. *Indians of California: The Changing Image* (Norman: University of Oklahoma Press, 1984).

Riis, Jacob A. *How the Other Half Lives. Studies Among the Tenements of New York* (1890; rpt., New York: Charles Scribner's Sons, 1890).

Robinson, Harriet H. *Loom and Spindle, or, Life Among the Early Mill Girls* (New York: T. Y. Crowell, 1898).

Rosenberg, Rosalind. *Beyond Separate Spheres: Intellectual Roots of Modern Feminism* (New Haven: Yale University Press, 1982).

Ross, Marvin C. *The West of Alfred Jacob Miller* (Norman: University of Oklahoma Press, 1951).

Rotundo, E. Anthony. *American Manhood: Transformations in Masculinity from the Revolution to the Modern Era* (New York: Basic, 1993).

Ryan, Mary P. *Cradle of the Middle Class: The Family in Oneida County, New York, 1790–1865* (Cambridge: Cambridge University Press, 1981).

———. *The Empire of the Mother: American Writing About Domesticity, 1830–1860* (New York: Institute for Research in History and the Haworth Press, 1982).

Sadler, Christine. *Children in the White House* (New York: G. P. Putnam's Sons, 1967).

Samuels, Shirley. *The Culture of Sentiment: Race, Gender, and Sentimentality in Nineteenth-Century America* (New York: Oxford University Press, 1992).

Satz, Ronald. *American Indian Policy in the Jacksonian Era* (Lincoln: University of Nebraska Press, 1975).

Saum, Lewis O. *The Fur Trader and the Indian* (Seattle: University of Washington Press, 1965).

Scheick, William J. *The Half-Blood: A Cultural Symbol in Nineteenth-Century American Fiction* (Lexington: University Press of Kentucky, 1979).

Schlereth, Thomas. *Victorian America: Transformations in Everyday Lives, 1876–1915* (New York: HarperCollins, 1991)

Schlesinger, Arthur M., Jr. *The Age of Jackson* (Boston: Little, Brown, 1945).

Schorsch, Anita. *Images of Childhood: An Illustrated Social History* (New York: Mayflower, 1979).

Schwartz, Marie Jenkins. *Born in Bondage: Growing Up Enslaved in the Antebellum South* (Cambridge: Harvard University Press, 2000).

Scott, Donald M., and Bernard Wishy, eds. *America's Families: A Documentary History* (New York: Harper and Row, 1817).

Sheehan, Bernard W. *Seeds of Extinction: Jeffersonian Philanthropy and the American Indians* (Chapel Hill: University of North Carolina Press, 1973).

Simpson, Marc. *Winslow Homer: Paintings of the Civil War* (San Francisco: Bedford Arts, 1988).

Sklar, Kathryn Kish. *Catharine Beecher: A Study in American Domesticity* (New Haven: Yale University Press, 1973).

Smith, Elizabeth Oakes. *The Newsboy* (New York, 1870).

Smith, Henry Nash. *Popular Culture and Industrialism, 1865–1890* (Garden City, N.Y.: Anchor, 1967).

Smith, Mark M. *Listening to Nineteenth-Century America* (Chapel Hill: University of North Carolina Press, 2001).

Smith-Rosenberg, Carroll. *Disorderly Conduct: Visions of Gender in Victorian America* (New York: Alfred A. Knopf, 1985).

Stanton, William. *The Leopard's Spots: Scientific Attitudes Toward Race in America, 1815–1859* (Chicago: University of Chicago Press, 1960).

Starling, Marion Wilson. *Slave Narrative: Its Place in American History*, 2nd ed. (Washington, D.C.: Howard University Press, 1988).

Stearns, Peter N. "Girl, Boys, and Emotions: Redefinitions and Historical Change." *Journal of American History* 80, no 1 (June 1993): 36–74.

Stott, Annette, "Floral Femininity: A Pictorial Definition." *American Art* 6, no. 2 (Spring 1992): 61–78.

Stuart-Wortley, Emmeline, Lady. *Travels in the United States* (London, 1851).

Sturges, Hollister III. *Angels and Urchins: Images of Children at the Joslyn* (Omaha, Neb.: Joslyn Art Museum, 1980).

Suleiman, Susan Rubin. *The Female Body in Western Culture: Contemporary Perspectives* (Cambridge: Harvard University Press, 1985).

Szasz, Margaret Connell. *Indian Education in the*

American Colonies, 1607–1783 (Albuquerque: University of New Mexico Press, 1988).

Temin, Peter. *Engines of Enterprise: An Economic History of New England* (Cambridge: Harvard University Press, 2000).

Thompson, Eleanor D. *The American Home: Material Culture, Domestic Space, and Family Life* (Hanover, N.H.: University Press of New England, 1998).

Thompson, Eleanor Wolf. *Education for Ladies, 1830–1860: Ideas on Education in Magazines for Women* (New York: King's Crown, 1947).

Tocqueville, Alexis de. *Democracy in America* (1838; rpt., New York: Bantam Classic, 2000).

Toll, Robert C. *Blacking Up: The Minstrel Show in Nineteenth-Century America* (New York: Oxford University Press, 1974).

Trachtenberg, Alan. *The Incorporation of America: Culture and Society in the Gilded Age* (New York: Hill and Wang, 1989).

———. *Reading American Photographs: Images as History, Mathew Brady to Walker Evans* (New York: Hill and Wang, 1989).

Trollope, Frances. *Domestic Manners of the Americans* (London, 1832).

Truettner, William H., ed. *The West as America: Reinterpreting Images of the Frontier, 1820–1920* (Washington, D.C.: Smithsonian Institution Press, 1991).

Tyler, Ron. *Alfred Jacob Miller: Artist on the Oregon Trail* (Fort Worth, Tex.: Amon Carter Museum, 1982).

Ulrich, Laurel Thatcher. *The Age of Homespun: Objects and Stories in the Creation of an American Myth* (New York: Alfred A. Knopf, 2001).

Wallace, Anthony F. *The Death and Rebirth of the Seneca: The History and Culture of the Great Iroquois Nation, Their Destruction and Demoralization, and Their Cultural Revival* (New York: Alfred A. Knopf, 1969).

Walsh, Judith. "The Language of Flowers in Nineteenth-Century American Painting." *The Magazine Antiques* (October 1999): 518–527.

Washburn, Wilcomb. *The American Indian and the United States: A Documentary History*, vol. 2 (New York: Random House, 1973).

Webber, Thomas L. *Deep Like the Rivers: Education in the Slave Quarter Community, 1831–1865* (New York: W. W. Norton, 1978).

Webster, Noah. *The American Spelling Book: Containing the Rudiments of the English Language, for the Use of Schools in the United States* (Philadelphia: Robert H. Shelburne, 1828).

West, Elliott, and Paula Evans. *Small Worlds: Children and Adolescents in America, 1850–1950* (Lawrence: University Press of Kansas, 1992).

Westerhoff, John H., III. *McGuffey and His Readers: Piety, Morality, and Education in Nineteenth-Century America* (Nashville: Abingdon, 1978).

Whipple, Edwin P. *The Great Speeches and Orations of Daniel Webster* (Boston: Little, Brown, 1879).

Wiebe, Robert H. *The Search for Order, 1877–1920* (New York: Hill & Wang, 1967).

———. *Self-Rule: A Cultural History of American Democracy* (Chicago: University of Chicago Press, 1995).

Wilmerding, John, Linda Ayres and Earl A. Powell III. *An American Perspective: American Paintings in the Collection of JoAnn and Julian Ganz* (Washington, D.C.: National Gallery of Art, 1981).

Wilson, Jackie Napolean. *Hidden Witness: African American Images from the Dawn of Photography to the Civil War* (New York: St. Martin's, 1999).

Wishy, Bernard. *The Child and the Republic: The Dawn of Modern American Child Nurture* (Philadelphia: University of Pennsylvania Press, 1968).

Wood, Peter H., and Karen C. C. Dalton. *Winslow Homer's Images of Blacks: The Civil War Reconstruction Years* (Austin: University of Texas Press, 1988).

Yellin, Jean Fagan. *The Intricate Knot: Black Figures in American Literature, 1776–1863* (New York: New York University Press, 1972).

Yosifon, David, and Peter N. Stearns. "The Rise and Fall of American Posture." *American Historical Review* 103, no. 4 (October 1998): 1057–1095.

Exhibition Checklist

Abbot, Jacob. *Gentle Measures in the Management of the Young*, 1877. Illustrated book, 7 x 10 in. Private collection.

Alcott, Louisa May. *Little Women*, Boston: Roberts Brothers, 1869. Illustrated book, 4 1/2 x 6 3/4 in. Private collection.

Alger, Horatio, Jr. *Ragged Dick, or, Street Life in New York with the Boot Blacks*, Boston, 1868. Illustrated book, 6 1/2 x 8 1/2 in. Private collection.

American Sunday School Union, publishers. *Alphabet Picture Stories*, 1868. Illustrated book, 6 x 8 in. Private collection.

The Anti-Slavery Alphabet, Philadelphia, 1846. Illustrated book, 6 1/2 x 8 1/2 in. Private collection.

Appleton, publisher. *Grandma Easy's New Pictorial Bible Alphabet*, c. 1870. Illustrated book, 9 1/8 x 13 1/4 in. Private collection.

Babcock, Wm. R., and McCarter and Co., publishers. *The Southern Primer; or, Child's First Lessons in Spelling and Reading*, 1860. Illustrated book, 5 5/8 x 7 1/4 in. Private collection.

Bannister, Edward Mitchell. *Newspaper Boy*, 1869. Oil on canvas, 30 1/8 x 25 1/8 in. Smithsonian American Art Museum, Washington, D.C.

Bartoll, William. *Boy with Dog*, c. 1840–1850. Oil on canvas, 30 1/8 x 24 13/16 in. From the Collections of The Henry Ford Museum, Dearborn, Michigan.

Blythe, David Gilmour. *Boy Playing Marbles*, n.d. Oil on canvas, 25 x 30 in. Smithsonian American Art Museum, Washington, D.C.

Blythe, David Gilmour. *A Match Seller*, c. 1859. Oil on canvas, 27 x 22 in. North Carolina Museum of Art, Raleigh.

Blythe, David Gilmour. *The News Boys*, c. 1846–1852. Oil on canvas mounted on academy board, 29 3/4 x 25 3/4 in. The Carnegie Museum of Art, Pittsburgh, Pennsylvania. Gift of Haugh and Keenan Galleries, 1856 (56.26).

Blythe, David Gilmour. *Street Urchins*, 1856–1860. Oil on canvas, 27 x 22 in. Butler Institute of American Art, Youngstown, Ohio.

Bosworth, Charles F., Jr. *The New England School*, c. 1852. Oil on wood panel, 16 1/2 x 20 1/2 in. Massachusetts Historical Society, Boston.

Brown, John George. *The Beggars*, 1863. Oil on canvas, 15 1/8 x 12 1/8 in. Wichita Art Museum, Kansas.

Brown, John George. *The Berry Boy*, c. 1875. Oil on canvas, 23 x 15 in. George Walter Vincent Smith Art Museum, Springfield, Massachusetts.

Brown, John George. *Fresh Water Sailor*, 1875. Watercolor and graphite on paper, 17 1/2 x 12 1/8 in. Private collection.

Brown, John George. *Marching Along*, 1863. Oil on canvas, 9 1/8 x 12 1/2 in. Private collection.

Brown, John George. *Resting in the Woods (Girl Under a Tree)*, 1866. Oil on canvas, 18 3/8 x 12 1/8 in. Collection of Jo Ann and Julian Ganz, Jr.

Brown, John George. *A Tough Story*, 1886. Oil on canvas, 25 x 30 in. North Carolina Museum of Art, Raleigh.

Carey, Matthew, publisher. *The American Primer, or, An Easy Introduction to Spelling and Reading*, Philadelphia, 1813. Illustrated book, 5 1/4 x 6 1/2 in. Private collection.

Carlton and Porter, publishers. *The Child's Anti-Slavery Book*, 1859. Illustrated book, 5 1/2 x 7 1/2 in. Private collection.

Catlin, George. *Assiniboin Woman and Child*, 1832. Oil on canvas, 29 x 24 in. Smithsonian American Art Museum, Washington, D.C. Gift of Mrs. Joseph Harrison, Jr.

Catlin, George. *Osceola Nick-A-No-Chee, a Boy*, 1840. Oil on canvas, 52 x 40 in. Smithsonian American Art Museum, Washington, D.C. Gift of Mrs. Joseph Harrison, Jr.

Catlin, George. *Pshan-shaw, Sweet-Scented Grass, Twelve-year-old Daughter of Bloody Hand*, 1832. Oil on canvas, 29 x 24 in. Smithsonian American Art Museum, Washington, D.C. Gift of Mrs. Joseph Harrison, Jr.

Catlin, George. *Tcha-aes-ka-ding, Grandson of Buffalo Bull's Back Fat*, 1832. Oil on canvas, 29 x 24 in. Smithsonian American Art Museum, Washington, D.C. Gift of Mrs. Joseph Harrison, Jr.

Child, Lydia. *The Girl's Own Book*, Boston, 1834. Illustrated book, 5$^{1}/_{2}$ x 9 in. Private collection.

Conkey, publishers. *Uncle Sam's ABC Book*, c. 1900. Illustrated book, 6$^{1}/_{4}$ x 4 in. Private collection.

Cotrell, G. W., publishers. *Etiquette for Little Folks*, 1850s. Illustrated book, 4$^{1}/_{4}$ x 7 in. Private collection.

Cozans, Phil J., publisher. *Little Eva: The Flower of the South*, c. 1855. Illustrated book, 8$^{3}/_{4}$ x 11 in. Private collection.

Currier, Nathaniel. *The Barefoot Boy*, 1873. Lithograph, 12$^{3}/_{10}$ x 8 in. Library of Congress, Prints and Photographs Division, Washington, D.C.

Currier, Nathaniel. *God Bless Our School*, 1870. Lithograph, 9 x 12$^{6}/_{10}$. Library of Congress, Prints and Photographs Division, Washington, D.C.

Currier and Ives, publishers, after Lilly Martin Spencer. *Into Mischief*, c. 1857. Lithograph. Library of Congress, Prints and Photographs Division, Washington, D.C.

Davenport, Sarah. *Workbook*, 1807. 13 x 15 in. Private collection.

Eakins, Thomas. *Elizabeth with a Dog*, 1871. Oil on canvas, 13$^{3}/_{4}$ x 17 in. San Diego Museum of Art, California. Museum purchase and a gift from Mr. and Mrs. Edwin S. Larsen.

Eakins, Thomas. *Study for "Negro Boy Dancing:" The Boy*, 1877. Oil on canvas, 24$^{1}/_{4}$ x 12$^{3}/_{16}$ in. National Gallery of Art, Washington, D.C., Collection of Mr. and Mrs. Paul Mellon (1985.64.15).

Edmonds, Francis William. *The New Scholar*, 1845. Oil on canvas, 27 x 34 in. Manoogian Collection, Detroit, Michigan.

Edouart, Auguste. *Caroline Gardiner Cary, Sarah Gray Cary, and Richard Cary*, 1842. Silhouette, 12 x 15 in. Boston Athenaeum, Massachusetts. Gift of Miss Caroline E. P. Cabot.

Elder, James Adams. *A Virginny Breakdown*, c. 1880. Oil on canvas, 18$^{1}/_{2}$ x 22$^{1}/_{4}$ in. Virginia Museum of Fine Arts, Richmond. The Virginia Art Fund.

Francis, C. S., and Co., publishers. *Rhymes for The Nursery*, 1837. Illustrated book, 5$^{1}/_{4}$ x 7$^{5}/_{8}$ in. Private collection.

"Golly I's So Wicked I Was Never Born," 1850s. Theater ticket, 5 x 2$^{1}/_{4}$ in. Private collection.

Gray, Iron. *The Gospel of Slavery; A Primer of Freedom*, New York, 1864. Illustrated book, 6$^{1}/_{2}$ x 9 in. Private collection.

Guerin, F. W. *Country Boy Fishing* (1), c. 1866. Photograph, 25$^{1}/_{2}$ x 21$^{1}/_{2}$ in. Private collection.

Guerin, F. W. *Country Boy Fishing* (2), c. 1866. Photograph, 25$^{1}/_{2}$ x 21$^{1}/_{2}$ in. Private collection.

Guy, Seymour. *Dressing for the Rehearsal*, c. 1890. Oil on canvas, 34$^{1}/_{8}$ x 27$^{3}/_{8}$ in. Smithsonian American Art Museum, Washington, D.C. Gift of Jennie Anita Guy.

Guy, Seymour. *Girl with Canary (The New Arrival)*, 1860s. Oil on canvas, 12$^{1}/_{4}$ x 9$^{1}/_{4}$ in. Private collection.

Guy, Seymour. *Unconscious of Danger*, 1865. Oil on canvas, 20 x 16 in. Private collection.

Hahn, William. *Learning the Lesson (Children Playing School)*, 1881. Oil on canvas, 34 x 27 in. The Oakland Museum, California. Gift of the Kahn Collection.

Harnett, William. *Attention, Company!* 1878. Oil on canvas, 36 x 28 in. Amon Carter Museum, Fort Worth, Texas (1970.230).

Henry, Edward Lamson. *A Country School*, 1890. Oil on composition board, 12 x 17$^{1}/_{4}$ in. Yale University Art Gallery, New Haven, Connecticut. Mabel Brady Garvan Collection.

Henry, Edward Lamson. *Kept In*, 1888. Oil on canvas. 13$^{1}/_{2}$ x 17$^{7}/_{8}$ in. New York State Historical Association.

Hobbs, G. W., publisher. *Songs and Stories*, Charlestown, 1864. Illustrated book, 6$^{1}/_{4}$ x 8$^{3}/_{4}$ in. Private collection.

Homer, Winslow. *Army Boots*, 1865. Oil on canvas, 14 x 18 in. Hirshhorn Museum and Sculpture Garden, Smithsonian Institution, Washington, D.C.

Homer, Winslow. *Country School*, 1873. Oil on canvas, 12$^{1}/_{4}$ x 18$^{11}/_{16}$ in. Addison Gallery of American Art, Phillips Academy, Andover, Massachusetts. Gift of anonymous donor.

Homer, Winslow. *The Last Days of the Harvest*, 1873. Wood engraving, 8 x 13 in. Cornell Fine Arts Museum at Rollins College, Winter Park, Florida.

Homer, Winslow. *The Noon Recess*, 1873. Wood engraving, 9$^{1}/_{8}$ x 13$^{5}/_{8}$ in. Cornell Fine Arts Museum at Rollins College, Winter Park, Florida.

Homer, Winslow. *Snap the Whip*, 1872. Oil on canvas, 12 x 20 in. The Metropolitan Museum of Art, New York. Gift of Christian A. Zabriskie, 1950 (50.41).

Homer, Winslow. *Snap the Whip*, 1873. Wood engraving, 13$^{3}/_{4}$ x 20$^{3}/_{4}$ in. Private collection.

Homer, Winslow. *Waiting for a Bite*, 1874. Wood engraving, 9 x 13 11/16 in. Cornell Fine Arts Museum at Rollins College, Winter Park, Florida.

Homer, Winslow. *Watching the Crows*, 1868. Wood engraving, 5$^{7}/_{8}$ x 3$^{3}/_{4}$ in. Cornell Fine Arts Museum at Rollins College, Winter Park, Florida.

Homer, Winslow. *The Watermelon Boys*, 1876. Oil on

canvas, 24$^{1}/_{8}$ x 38$^{1}/_{8}$ in. Cooper-Hewitt, National Design Museum, Smithsonian Institution Art Resource, New York. Gift of Charles Savage Homer, Jr. (1917-14-6).

Hudson, Grace Carpenter. *Little Mendocino*, 1892. Oil on canvas, 36 x 26 in. California Historical Society, San Francisco, California.

Hudson, Grace Carpenter. *Quail Baby, or The Interrupted Bath*, 1892. Oil on canvas, 38$^{1}/_{2}$ x 23 in. The Monterey Museum of Art, California.

Hurd & Houghton, publishers. *A Treasury of Pleasure Books for Young People*, 1865. Printed book, 5$^{1}/_{2}$ x 7$^{1}/_{2}$ in. Private collection.

Inman, Henry. *News Boy*, 1841. Oil on canvas, 30$^{1}/_{8}$ x 25$^{3}/_{16}$ in. Addison Gallery of American Art, Phillips Academy, Andover, Massachusetts.

Johnson, Eastman. *Back from the Orchard*, 1876. Oil on board, 19$^{7}/_{8}$ x 11$^{7}/_{8}$ in. Hood Museum of American Art, Dartmouth College, Hanover, New Hampshire. Purchased through the Katharine T. and Merrill G. Beede 1929 Fund; the Mrs. Harvey P. Hood W'18 Fund; a gift from the Estate of Russell Cowles, Class of 1909; and a gift from Jose Guerrero, by exchange.

Johnson, Eastman. *Boyhood of Lincoln*, 1868. Oil on canvas, 46 x 37 in. The University of Michigan Museum of Art, Ann Arbor. Bequest of Henry C. Lewis.

Johnson, Eastman. *The Pets*, 1856. Oil on masonite panel, 25 x 28$^{3}/_{4}$ in. The Corcoran Gallery of Art, Washington, D.C. Gift of William Wilson Corcoran.

Johnson, Eastman. *Hannah Amidst the Vines*, 1859. Oil on canvas, 14 x 12 in. Georgetown University Art Collection, Washington, D.C.

Johnson, Eastman. *Little Girl with Golden Hair (Family Cares)* 1873. Oil on canvas, 15 x 11$^{1}/_{2}$ in. Shelburne Museum, Shelburne, Vermont.

Johnson, Eastman. *The Negro Boy*, 1860. Oil on canvas, 14 x 17$^{1}/_{8}$ in. National Academy of Design Museum, New York.

Johnson, Eastman. *The Party Dress (The Finishing Touch)*, 1872. Oil on composition board, 20 x 16 in. Wadsworth Atheneum, Hartford, Connecticut. Bequest of Mrs. Clara Hinton Gould.

Johnson, Eastman. *Ragamuffin*, c. 1869. Oil on canvas, 11$^{1}/_{2}$ x 6$^{3}/_{8}$ in. Private collection.

Johnson, Eastman. *The Young Sweep*, 1863. Oil on paper board, 12$^{1}/_{4}$ x 9$^{3}/_{8}$ in. Private collection.

Kantner's Illustrated Book of Objects for Children, Pennsylvania, 1877. Illustrated book, 10$^{1}/_{2}$ x 13$^{3}/_{4}$ in. Private collection.

Lambdin, George C. *Girl in a Yellow Dress with Fresh Cut Flowers*, n.d. Oil on canvas, 30 x 25 in. Private collection.

Lambdin, George C. *Two Girls Picking Fruit*, 1867. Oil on canvas, 18$^{1}/_{8}$ x 21$^{3}/_{4}$ in. Private collection.

Leavitt and Allen, publishers. *The Little Folks First Steps on the Ladder of Knowledge*, New York, c. 1850. Illustrated book, 10$^{1}/_{4}$ x 15$^{3}/_{4}$ in. Private collection.

LeClear, Thomas. *Interior with Portraits*, c. 1865. Oil on canvas, 25$^{7}/_{8}$ x 40$^{1}/_{2}$ in. Smithsonian American Art Museum, Washington, D.C. Museum purchase made possible by the Pauline Edwards Bequest.

LeClear, Thomas. *The Truant*, n.d. Oil on canvas, 16 x 12 in. Private collection.

Longley, Elias. *American Ferst Reder*, 1857. Illustrated book, 6$^{1}/_{2}$ x 9 in. Private collection.

Lovechild, Mrs. *Talk About Indians*, Concord, 1849. Illustrated book, 6$^{3}/_{4}$ x 10$^{1}/_{4}$ in. Private collection.

McCarty and Davis. *McCarty's American Primer*, Philadelphia, 1828. Illustrated book. Private collection.

McGuffey, William. *The Eclectic First Reader for Young Children*, Cincinnati, 1836. Illustrated book, 8$^{1}/_{4}$ x 11 in. Private collection.

McGuffey, William. *McGuffey's Newly Revised Eclectic Primer*, Cincinnati, 1848. Illustrated book, 8$^{1}/_{4}$ x 11 in. Private collection.

McGuffey, William. *McGuffey's Pictorial Eclectic First Primer*, 1836. Illustrated book, 8$^{1}/_{4}$ x 11 in. Private collection.

McLoughlin Bros., publishers. *Aunt Mayflower's Alphabet*, 1870s. Illustrated book, 7 x 13$^{1}/_{4}$ in. Private collection.

McLoughlin Bros., publishers. *Dame Wonders' Picture Books; Mary Goodchild*, New York, 1860s. Illustrated book, 4 x 7 in. Private collection.

McLoughlin Bros., publishers. *Dame Wonders' Picture Books; The Table Book.* New York, 1864. Illustrated book, 6$^{3}/_{4}$ x 8 in. Private collection.

McLoughlin Bros., publishers. *Freaks and Frolics of Little Girls*, 1887. Illustrated book, 11$^{1}/_{2}$ x 19 in. Private collection.

McLoughlin Bros., publishers. *Little Child's Home ABC Book*, New York, c. 1880. Illustrated book, 10$^{1}/_{4}$ x 13 in. Private collection.

McLoughlin Bros., publishers. *Miss Rose*, c. 1854. Illustrated pamphlet, 6 x 7 in. Private collection.

McLoughlin Bros., publishers. *Starry Flag ABC Book*, 1899. Illustrated book, 10 x 16 in. Private collection.

McLoughin Bros., publishers. *Yankee Doodle*, 1880s. Illustrated book, 10 x 17$^{1}/_{2}$ in. Private collection.

Magnus, Chas., publishers. *Youth's Diamond Alphabetic Library*, New York, 1880s. Illustrated book, 4 1/4 x 13 1/4 in. Private collection.

Marling, Jacob. *The May Queen (The Crowning of Flora)*, 1816. Oil on canvas, 30 1/8 x 39 1/8 in. The Chrysler Museum of Art, Norfolk, Virginia (80.181.20).

Matteson, Tompkins Harrison. *Caught in the Act*, 1860. Oil on canvas, 22 1/4 x 18 1/4 in. Vassar College Art Gallery, Poughkeepsie, New York. Gift of Matthew Vassar.

Mitchell, S. Augustus. *Mitchell's Primary Geography*, 1851. Illustrated book, 6 1/4 x 10 1/2 in. Private collection.

Morgan and Yeager, publishers. *The History of Little Henry*, c. 1825. Illustrated book, 5 x 7 in. Private collection.

Mount, William Sidney. *Boy Hoeing Corn*, Oil on panel, 15 x 11 5/8 in. Long Island Museum of American Art, History, and Carriages, Stony Brook, New York.

Nelson and Phillips, publishers. *The Mother's Picture Alphabet*, c. 1855. Illustrated book, 13 3/4 x 20 3/4 in. Private collection.

New England Botanic Depot, publishers. *The Illuminated White Pine Alphabet*, 1870s. Illustrated book, 6 1/2 x 9 1/4 in. Private collection.

The Nursery, 1879. Vol. 25. Illustrated journal, 7 1/2 x 11 1/3 in. Private collection.

Parkinson, M. B. *Little Girl Washing*, photograph, 1898. Library of Congress, Prints and Photographs Division, Washington, D.C.

Pering, Cornelia S. *Little Girl with Flowers (Emily Mae)*, 1871. Oil on canvas, 46 1/2 x 37 in. Private collection.

Prang, L., and Co., after J. H. Moser. *The Artist*, c. 1890. Chromolithograph, 20 7/16 x 13 11/16 in. Hallmark Historical Collection, Kansas City, Missouri.

Prang, L., and Co., after J. H. Moser. *Barefoot Boy*, c. 1890. Chromolithograph, 16 x 20 in. Hallmark Historical Collection, Kansas City, Missouri.

Prang, L., and Co., after J. H. Moser. *Boy on a Swing*, c. 1890. Chromolithograph, 3 3/8 x 5 1/6 in. Hallmark Historical Collection, Kansas City, Missouri.

Prang, L., and Co., after J. H. Moser. *Curly Haired Girl*, c. 1890. Chromolithograph, 15 x 15 in. Hallmark Historical Collection, Kansas City, Missouri.

Prang, L., and Co., after J. H. Moser. *Girl with Flowers*, c. 1890. Chromolithograph, 19 x 24 in.

Hallmark Historical Collection, Kansas City, Missouri.

Prang, L., and Co., after J. H. Moser. *The Gourmand (Boy with Watermelon)*, c. 1890. Chromolithograph, 20 7/16 x 13 11/16 in. Hallmark Historical Collection, Kansas City, Missouri.

Prang, L., and Co., after J. H. Moser. *Playing with Dolls*, c. 1890. Chromolithograph, 20 3/8 x 25 13/16 in. Hallmark Historical Collection, Kansas City, Missouri.

Pryor, Paul. *Pocahontas, or The Indian Maiden*, 1873. Illustrated book, 10 x 8 3/4 in. Private collection.

Pyrnelle, Louise-Clark. *Diddie, Dumps, and Tot; or, Plantation Child-Life*, New York, 1882. Illustrated book, 6 x 9 1/4 in. Private collection.

Read, James B. *Portrait of a Boy*, 1856. Oil on canvas, 48 3/4 x 36 in. Minneapolis Institute of Art, Minnesota. Gift of Mr. and Mrs. Patrick Butler.

Riis, Jacob. *The Children of the Poor*, 1892. Illustrated book, 8 x 11 1/2 in. Private collection.

Riis, Jacob. *How the Other Half Lives*, 1890. Illustrated book, 8 x 11 1/2 in. Private collection.

Riis, Jacob. *Street Arabs in Sleeping Quarters (Areaway, of Mulberry Street)*, c. 1890. Photograph, 10 1/2 x 12 1/2 in. Jacob A. Riis Collection of the Museum of the City of New York (90.13.4.126).

Riis, Jacob. *Street Arabs in Sleeping Quarters (a church corner, Mulberry Street)*, 1889. Photograph, 10 1/2 x 12 1/2 in. Jacob A. Riis Collection of the Museum of the City of New York.

Riis, Jacob. *Street Arabs in Their Sleep Quarters*, c. 1890. Photograph, 10 1/2 x 12 1/2 in. Jacob A. Riis Collection of the Museum of the City of New York.

Ryder, Platt Powell. *The Illustrated Newspaper*, 1868. Oil on canvas, 16 7/8 x 13 13/16 in. The Brooklyn Museum, New York. Bequest of Mrs. Caroline H. Polhemus.

Spencer, Lilly Martin. *Choose Between*, c. 1857. Oil on panel, 10 1/4 x 8 1/4 in. Private collection.

Spencer, Lilly Martin. *This Little Pig Went to Market*, 1857. Oil on composition board with arched top, 16 x 12 in. Ohio Historical Society, Columbus.

Stanley, John Mix. *Eleanora C. Ross*, 1844. Oil on canvas, 39 3/4 x 31 1/2 in. Thomas Gilcrease Institute of American History and Art, Tulsa, Oklahoma.

Stanley, John Mix. *Lewis Anderson Ross*, 1844. Oil on canvas, 40 1/2 x 31 5/8 in. Thomas Gilcrease Institute of American History and Art, Tulsa, Oklahoma.

Stanley, John Mix. *Young Chief Uncas*, 1870.

Oil on canvas, 24 x 20 in. Autry National Center, Museum of the American West, Los Angeles, California.

Stowe, Harriet Beecher. *Pictures and Stories from Uncle Tom's Cabin*, 1853. Illustrated book, 8¼ x 6 in. Private collection.

Sully, Thomas. *Juvenile Ambition*, 1825. Oil on canvas, 36 x ¼ x 28¾ in. Hunter Museum of American Art, Chattanooga, Tennessee.

Thompson, Bigelow, and Brown, publishers. *Hand Shadow Stories*, 1863. Illustrated book, 6¾ x 10¼ in. Private collection.

Turner and Fischer, publishers. *My Darling's ABC*, c. 1815. Illustrated book, 3½ x 48¼ in. Private collection.

Twain, Mark. *The Adventures of Huckleberry Finn*, New York, 1884. Illustrated book, 7 x 8¾ in. Private collection.

Twain, Mark. *The Adventures of Tom Sawyer*, New York, 1876. Illustrated book. Private collection.

Unidentified artist. *Mother and Child of Pennsylvania*, c. 1850. Silhouette, paper and brown wash on thin paperboard. The Art Museum, Princeton University, Princeton, New Jersey.

Unidentified photographer. *The Math Lesson*, c. 1853. Quarter-plate daguerreotype. Lost Images Collection of Ron and Sue Humphries.

Unidentified photographer. *Portrait of a Well-Dressed Young Boy*, c. 1857–1858. Sixth-plate ambrotype. The J. Paul Getty Museum, Los Angeles, California.

Unidentified photographer. *Portrait of a Young Boy in Fine Clothes*, c. 1857–1858. Ninth-plate daguerreotype. The J. Paul Getty Museum, Los Angeles, California.

Warner, Charles Dudley. *Being a Boy*, Boston, 1877. Illustrated book, 7¼ x 10½ in. Private collection.

Webster, Noah. *The American Spelling Book*, 1828. Illustrated book, 6½ x 7¾ in. Private collection.

Wood, Samuel, and Sons, publisher. *The Young Child's ABC; or, First Book*, New York, 1806. Illustrated book, 4 x 6¾ in. Private collection.

Index